DATING

VIOLENCE

YOUNG WOMEN

IN DANGER

EDITED BY BARRIE LEVY

THE SEAL PRESS

Book and cover design by Clare Conrad.

Grateful acknowledgement is made for the use of the following copyrighted material:

"A Parent's Story" written by Vicki Crompton, assisted by Ellen Zelda Kessner. © 1990 by Vicki Crompton and Ellen Zelda Kessner, c/o Publishers' Licensing Corporation, P.O. Box 5807, Englewood, N.J. 07631. Used by permission. All rights reserved.

"The Abused Black Woman: Challenging a Legacy of Pain" by Evelyn C. White. Portions of this article appeared in different form in *Chain Chain Change: For Black Women Dealing with Physical and Emotional Abuse*, © 1985 by Evelyn C. White (Seattle: Seal Press, 1985). Reprinted by permission of the publisher.

"Addictive Love and Abuse: A course for Teenage Women" by Ginny NiCarthy. Originally appeared in different form in *The Second Mile: Contemporary Approaches in Counseling Young Women*, edited by Sue Davidson, © 1983 by New Directions for Young Women (Seattle: New Directions for Young Women, 1983). Reprinted by permission of the publisher.

Library of Congress Cataloging-in-Publication Data
Dating violence : young women in danger / edited by Barrie Levy.
     p.   cm.
   Includes bibliographical references and index.
   ISBN 1-878067-03-6
   1. Dating violence--United States. 2. Acquaintance rape--United States. 3. Teenage girls--United States--Violence against.
I. Levy, Barrie.
HQ801.83.D38 1990
362.88--dc20   90-24538
                                            CIP

Printed in the United States of America
First printing, April 1991
10 9 8 7 6 5 4 3 2 1

Foreign Distribution:
In Canada: Raincoast Book Distribution, Vancouver, B.C.
In Great Britain and Europe: Airlift Book Company, London
In Australia: Stilone, N.S.W.

Acknowledgments

I am grateful for the support of many people who have recognized that the violence in the lives of teenagers and young adults is so often overlooked, and who have participated in confronting this by participating in the evolution of this book. I especially want to thank the young women who have shared stories of innocence and strength, pain and success in their violent dating relationships.

Barbara Wilson and Faith Conlon at Seal Press have once again been on the cutting edge in the field of domestic violence by approaching me to edit a book about teenage women. Working with Faith has been a wonderful experience because of the breadth of her knowledge, her editing skill and her collaborative style in guiding me through the publication process.

I want to thank others who gave me invaluable assistance:

Kerry Lobel brainstormed, consulted and reviewed manuscript drafts with me. She and I have talked about confronting teen dating violence for seven years, since we worked together on the Southern California Coalition for Battered Women's Domestic Violence Prevention Project. It was largely due to Kerry's early interest and encouragement that I decided to take on this project.

Ruth Beaglehole facilitated my becoming acquainted with the young women at Business Industry School in Los Angeles. Ruth's wisdom and these young women's stories contributed to the perspectives offered in this book.

Domestic violence and sexual assault experts Valerie Bush, Patti Giggans, Jacqueline Goodchilds, Margaret Klaw and Debbie Lee reviewed articles and offered knowledgeable feedback.

Cathy Johnson did an excellent and thorough job of copyediting.

My great friends, Miriam Black, Patti Giggans, Ellen Ledley and Carol Rabaut, were generous with their time, their thoughtful editing and their encouraging words.

I am especially appreciative of Linda Garnets who was always there in whatever way I needed. She is the best "utility player," pitching in with her many capabilities. We have been mutually supportive this year as we both engaged in writing projects, as we pushed, nurtured, thought, listened and, finally, celebrated.

My daughters, Johanna and Nisa, and their honesty and strength in taking on challenges in all aspects of their lives, have been an inspiration to me. From them I have derived a sensibility about and respect for young women "coming of age" in the eighties and the nineties.

In addition, Johanna assisted me with word-processing, and helped me to "tame" my computer. Our long talks as she worked with me have enriched my perspectives.

I am also grateful to my parents, Faye and Charles Levy, for their contribution to my work: a sense of justice, pacifism, abhorrence and outrage at any kind of violence, commitment to social change, and loving support.

Contents

III. Intervention Strategies

IV. Education and Prevention Projects

Introduction

Barrie Levy

As a prevention specialist in the movement to end violence against women and children, I have spent a great deal of time in classrooms defining rape, sexual abuse and battering as crimes against women, confronting prevailing attitudes towards such abuse, and teaching skills and providing information to enhance prevention and coping. Although I wasn't surprised to find that young people in high schools and middle schools are more sophisticated now than when I was their age in the 1950s—that is to say that they have more exposure to and experience in the world beyond their families—I was surprised to discover two violence-related phenomena among teens. First, their attitudes about hitting one another and about male and female roles in relationships are the same as those that I grew up with: They consider sexual coercion or hitting justifiable under certain circumstances, including in dating relationships. This has been substantiated in research by Goodchilds and Zellman (1984) and by Malamuth (1981). Second, when I talked about violence as something they might encounter when they grew up and had intimate relationships or got married, or about violence they may have witnessed between their parents, some of the young women revealed they currently or had already experienced violence from their adolescent boyfriends. Their stories were as extreme and humiliating as any stories I had heard from adult women who were battered.

As a result of my experiences in the classroom, I realized that adolescents as young as twelve and thirteen years old might be involved in abusive intimate relationships. Although this problem clearly involves both young men and women, I have chosen to focus on the situations of young women, who especially are victimized by relationship violence. We now know that an alarming number of young women are experiencing dating and relationships that include violence and abuse: Research estimates indicate

3

that as many as a third of high school- and college-age youth experience violence in an intimate or dating relationship during their dating years. My concern about the large numbers of victimized young women whose experiences with this kind of violence have been overlooked by experts on youth and on domestic violence led me to compile this book. I feel that the unique aspects of adolescence and adolescent relationships make it important that we focus on this problem as a separate entity—not as a step from childhood violence to marital violence, but as an adolescent phenomenon.

The aim of this book is to give readers an understanding of this phenomenon and to stimulate readers to be creative in reaching out to young women to prevent, identify and assist their extrication and healing from dating violence. For the purposes of reaching out to, understanding and assisting young women in violent relationships, a broad definition of dating violence has been used for this anthology. Abuse in adolescent dating relationships is defined as a pattern of repeated actual or threatened acts that physically, sexually or verbally abuse a member of an unmarried heterosexual or homosexual couple in which one or both partners is between thirteen and twenty years old.

Unique Aspects of Adolescent Abusive Relationships

In distinguishing their individuality in relation to adults, adolescents conform to peer norms. The social demands of adolescence, for example, often "require" that a young woman have a boyfriend. Peer pressure can be intense, and the fear of being different or of violating peer group norms can create rigid conformity or enormous stress.

The norms of adolescent peer groups define what girls do and what boys do. The gender role definitions are often extreme and stereotyped, and young men and women—afraid of being labeled "different"—may not yet have the flexibility to be themselves. For example, fearing the stigma of homosexuality, adolescents may behave in ways that seem exaggerated to prove their heterosexuality. Or, feeling pressure to prove that they are not "too attached" to their families may lead them to behave like exaggerated adult males and females. Definitions of what is normal masculine or feminine behavior often fit stereotyped patterns of dominance and passivity: the women's caretaking role, the women's responsibility for the success of the relationship, her social dependence on the man (and her dread of not being in a relationship), and the man's insistence on having the woman's attention on demand (including sexual attention). Expectations of a "girlfriend" (especially from her boyfriend) may require that the young woman give up activities, talents and other relationships and give priority to her boyfriend and their relationship. Expectations of a "boyfriend" (especially from his peers) may require that he be sexually aggressive, make all of the decisions in the relationship, and be domineering and controlling of her activities and behavior. The sexism inherent in these norms makes adolescent women particularly vulnerable to relationship violence.

Generally inexperienced in relationships, adolescents may have difficulty managing the complexity of feelings, decisions and conflicts that arise. Romanticizing about love and relationships, they often interpret jealousy, possessiveness and abuse as signs of love. Young women are vulnerable to victimization, and their difficulty defining abuse as a problem adds to that vulnerability.

As adolescents struggle for their independence, they may have conflicts with their families and/or become isolated from them to the extent that they may not expect, ask for or get support from them to deal with frightening occurrences in their relationships.

In turn, adults do not always take adolescents seriously. Adults may assume that they are overreacting, acting out, or going through a phase; police may respond to their calls for help by saying, "they are just kids." Parents may expect them to easily break off a dating relationship and go on to date others, minimizing the bonding that takes place in their relationships. School personnel may become impatient with their "drama" and misbehavior and insist that such behavior not be displayed at school, without recognizing the danger of the violence that may be taking place. In fact, adolescents take their relationships seriously and often have "adultlike" experiences in their relationships.

Many adolescents have special circumstances that may make them even more vulnerable to relationship violence. The risk of violence to both adult and adolescent women is higher when they are pregnant (McFarlane, 1989). There is additional risk to pregnant or parenting adolescents because they have fewer resources than adults. The judgments and blaming that they receive from adults and peers may also make them reluctant to use sources of help or may contribute to a sense of helplessness and self-blame when they are abused. The increase in dependency on others (real and/or perceived) associated with pregnancy and mothering of infants increases their vulnerability to domination and control by others. A young woman's pregnant or parenting status is often used by an abusive boyfriend as a reason for abuse.

Young lesbians are also vulnerable to relationship violence. The confusion about norms and roles that characterizes heterosexual adolescent relationships is even more bewildering in teen lesbian relationships. Lack of visible role models or relationships may add to the uncertainty. Adolescents may not be certain about their sexual identity, and conflicts about the acceptability of being a lesbian may be acted out in a relationship. Fear of identifying herself as a lesbian or fear of homophobic responses from parents, peers and others may keep a young woman from telling anyone about her relationship and therefore from seeking help if her relationship is abusive.

Many young women in the United States are immigrants or refugees. The disruption and trauma of immigration—leaving one's home land and traveling to the United States—and the processes of adjustment and acculturation once here increase vulnerability in general, including vulnerability to violence in relationships. Their life after arrival may be one of poverty and extreme stress. If they are here without documentation or without legal residency, they are especially vulnerable to exploitation in a violent relationship, as fear of deportation may make leaving or asking for help seem impossible. If they have fled war-torn or oppressive countries, the trauma of earlier experiences adds to their vulnerability. For example, they may fear calling on law enforcement for help, or fear talking to others because of past fear of informers.

Young women from cultures in which dating and sexuality are restricted and possible sources of shame are vulnerable to relationship violence. Seeking help from the family or outside the family may present conflicts or feelings of shame and helplessness.

Racism and discrimination—if a repeated part of a young woman's experience—can make her more vulnerable to victimization in a relationship. If a young woman feels that her options for succeeding in her education or career are limited by racism, she may count on the relationship to define her future and she may be unable to leave it. If she does seek help, she may expect to be blamed or not responded to seriously. Or she may be unwilling to

discuss her problems outside the family or her culture because of
the protectiveness that comes from understanding the struggles of
her boyfriend in a racist society.

Why a Multidimensional Approach?

This book is structured to give the readers a multidimensional
understanding of young women's experiences in abusive intimate
relationships. What do we know about these relationships? When
we push beyond the secrecy, denial and misunderstanding that
surround them (as we have done in all areas of victimization in relationships and families), we are first struck by how many young
women actually encounter relationship violence. When we look
beyond the stereotypes, we are struck by the diversity of the
women. A social problem emerges that affects so many young
women in such a diversity of communities that it must be viewed
from many perspectives and from many sources of information.
To offer a multidimensional understanding, this book includes a
review of research on dating violence, an analysis of the social
context of dating violence, impressions and observations of people
who work with young women who have experienced abusive intimate relationships, practitioners' recommendations for effective
intervention based on their research and experience, and letters,
stories and interviews with young women about their experiences
as victims or survivors. The information has come from all over
the United States and Canada, from diverse ethnic communities,
from (and about) women with varied class and educational backgrounds, and from lesbian as well as heterosexual women.

The articles chosen represent current views in the authors'
fields and a variety of perspectives on the subject of dating violence. The authors do not necessarily agree with one another, and
some of their views are controversial. However, all of the authors
have valuable perspectives to contribute to the sparse knowledge
about dating violence.

The writings gathered for this book are multidimensional in
another sense: Like other kinds of violence against women, abuse
in adolescent dating relationships must be dealt with at multiple
levels because it is caused by a set of interacting societal/institu-
tional, community, family and personal factors.

Children and teenagers lack power in our society. Young
women have more freedom and control over their environments
than do younger children, but they do not yet have adult status in

terms of their access to resources and their rights to make decisions for themselves. Sexist role expectations keep young women in a childlike state of dependence into adulthood. If they are from an ethnic minority group or are poor, the lack of power and access to resources is compounded.

Community-based approaches to dealing with adolescent dating violence must have the goal of changing the social structures that create a tolerance for victimization of young women as well as goals that make it possible to prevent and intervene with individual cases of violence. The successes of the twenty-year-old movement toward ending both violence against adult women and sexual abuse of children have made it easier to recognize the prevalence of adolescent dating violence. The young women whose stories are in this book are speaking out about a largely hidden problem. This book does not report on successes in making social changes, but on the beginning efforts to identify and confront this problem in many parts of the U.S. and Canada.

Characteristics of Dating Violence

Several themes are emerging from research, practice and young women's stories about dating violence.

Diversity. Dating violence is not unique to one class, community or ethnic group, nor to heterosexual women. To the contrary, it seems to be prevalent in all communities.

Gender. According to research, both men and women can be victims of dating violence. But practitioners are reporting that they are seeing only women as victims, and that young men are hit only when the women fight back. Some practitioners speculate that younger women may be more likely to fight back than adult married women in abusive relationships. There is no consensus among researchers and practitioners regarding the relationship between gender and dating violence.

Invisibility. The research and personal and practitioners' accounts are consistent with one another in identifying the "hidden" nature of dating violence. Young people do not seem to talk about it as a problem or seek help to deal with it. In many cases, this may be because of isolation and/or shame or because the young women are terrified of their abusers and afraid of the violent consequences of talking to others.

Normative confusion. There seems to be a consensus that many young people do not define dating violence as a problem.

Sugarman and Hotaling (1989) identify the evidence of "normative confusion" in their tendency to interpret violence as signifying love. Several authors believe that many teens view aspects of
abuse as "normal" in intimate relationships: "normal" in that
abuse happens so commonly that it is expected or is an accepted
way to express love. "Normal" is what's happening in one's own
relationship and, therefore, is not defined as violence that is prob-
lematic or intolerable. "Normal" may also mean that violence is
not the cause of the problems but a "natural" expression of other
problems, that "if only" solved would resolve the violence.

Patterns of abuse. The patterns of the abuse itself in these relationships are similar to adult battering. The patterns of control
and jealousy enforced by verbal and physical abuse are the same
as those described by adult battered women.

Sexual abuse. Date rape accounts for sixty-seven percent of the
sexual assaults reported by adolescent and college-age women
(Ageton, 1983). Young women between the ages of fourteen and
seventeen represent an estimated thirty-eight percent of those victimized by date rape (Warshaw, 1988). The documentation of this
phenomenon has been significant in confronting the myths that
women are raped only by strangers, that is, by surprise attackers.
However, this new information about date rape has not yet dis-
pelled the disbelief regarding the incidence of *repeated* sexual assault and sexual coercion that takes place in intimate relationships. Public attention has centered on the serious problem of
campus rapes committed by students as a group or individually in
the context of a date or a beginning relationship. These generally
involve one incident that seriously traumatizes the victim. The
sexual abuse described by the young women in this book is different. They describe a form of ongoing sexual slavery, in which they
have been violently forced to have sex or been coerced to by
threats of losing the relationship or by powerful accusations of being unacceptable as women or as lovers (see Barry, 1979). The
bonds of the relationship and the feelings of worthlessness, degradation, humiliation and shame that result from sexual coercion
gradually undermine the victims' ability to escape. Their vulnerability is magnified because they are young and their sense of themselves as sexual beings may be relatively new and fragile.

Substance abuse. This country faces a problem with drug and alcohol abuse that is so pervasive that it is possible that every young
person in United States confronts it in some way. The research,

young women's revelations and practitioners' experiences indicate a connection between substance abuse and relationship violence. It is not a causal connection, but they often coexist. If someone is likely to experience explosive anger or be violent, alcohol and drugs may increase the likelihood, as they reduce inhibitions as well as the ability to make decisions and exercise control over one's behavior. They also reduce the ability to make decisions to protect oneself. Substance abuse can be a means of numbing or emotional escape from overwhelming stress and is often seen as a coping mechanism for people who are being or have been victimized. It seems clear that both substance abuse and violence must be confronted simultaneously. A young person may be better able to stop the violence in a relationship once the substance abuse is confronted, but the factors contributing to the violence must still be addressed directly. The substance abuse is not the cause of the violence. The reverse is also true.

Confronting the Problem

What emerges from the practitioners' and young women's stories is a picture of how difficult it has been to confront the problem of abuse in dating relationships.

Obstacles to intervention. A major obstacle in preventing the violence in an abusive relationship between adolescents—or intervening to stop it—seems to be the hidden nature of the problem, as mentioned earlier. Because of shame, fear, or normative confusion, young people may not seek assistance to deal with or end the violence or the violent relationship. Other equally important obstacles include the tendency of adults (school administrators, judges, counselors, and so forth) to minimize the lethality of the abuse, the intensity of the bonds in adolescent dating relationships, and the lack of legitimacy of adolescent problems in society as a whole. Intervention efforts are often ineffective because of a lack of community response and coordination. Moreover, there is a lack of clear messages in the environments in which youth function (for example, schools) that verbal and physical violence are totally intolerable.

Interfacing problems of youth. There is a tendency to compartmentalize the problems youth have, so that young people who get attention for one problem are not identified as having other equally serious problems. It is clear that there is an interfacing among all problems of youth, such as depression, substance abuse, health problems such as AIDs and other sexually transmitted diseases, learning disabilities, street violence and pregnancy, as well as dating violence.

Need for aggressive outreach by adults. A recurring theme throughout this book is that young people do not easily reach out to adults. Adults must not hold back or wait for them to ask for help. Adults must actively help them define "healthy" relationships and to identify abusive ones. Young people need adults to be supportive, direct and honest, not minimizing, blaming or punitive.

Overview of the Book
Teens and Parents Tell Their Stories

For a picture of the patterns in abusive dating relationships, I have asked young women and adult women to describe their past experiences in their own words. The book begins with their stories as well as two stories from mothers whose daughters have been abused in dating relationships. The stories reveal that, like adult battering relationships, battering relationships between young people are characterized by their lethality, their patterns of domination and control and by their cyclical nature. Abusive dating relationships are not "kids'" problems to be taken lightly: Battering in teen relationships can result in murder. Vicki Crompton tells the story of her daughter's last few months of trying to break up with her boyfriend before being stabbed to death by him. The violence can go on for years, even after the relationship has ended. Salina Stone and her mother had to flee the state to hide from her teenage batterer's violent threats, and now, years after their relationship ended, she continues to have to move frequently to escape his harassment.

Verbal and emotional abuse in the form of hypercritical, demeaning barrages are almost always involved, with or without physical or sexual violence. The abuse is alternated with devotion, love, and, often, passionate sex. The abuser controls his or her partner with jealousy, obsessiveness and suicide threats as well as with physical and verbal violence. Extrication from the relationship can be overwhelmingly difficult for a young woman. Almost all of the personal accounts of battering relationships in this book reflect these patterns.

In my outreach efforts to get young women to tell their stories, I found that a greater response came from young women in pregnant and parenting teen programs than from other settings. It seems that the programs for pregnant and parenting teens provide environments in which young women can and do talk about their relationships and their experiences with abuse. Thus, it has been possible to include the perspectives of young mothers in this book. Although it is true that women are at greater risk for relationship violence when they are pregnant, in talking with high school teachers, college faculty and personnel, and recreation workers, and in surveying research results, I have learned that the majority of dating violence takes place among teens who are not pregnant or parents.

The Context of Dating Violence

To provide a context for the experiences of individual young women, the second section of *Dating Violence* offers an overview of the problem from the perspectives of researchers and social analysts.

Denise Gamache considers dating violence in the context of sexism. Dating functions as a rehearsal of the roles young men and women expect to assume as adults, and dating relationships are influenced by cultural norms that allow some men to believe that violence against their female partners will be tolerated. Gamache identifies the patterns of domination and control in violent dating relationships that reflect sexist social structures. Sexism and racism interact as women of color confront male dominance and abuse in the context of discrimination and unfair treatment encountered in dealing with white social institutions.

Evelyn C. White believes that African-American young women especially are vulnerable to violence in intimate relationships because of the societal expectations that limit their aspirations and their abilities to develop their own identities. They are also affected by the strains and pressures on African-American young men because of drugs, poor health, violence and incarceration. Her remedy for violence in relationships is the social and personal change that makes it possible for African-Americans to believe that they "deserve better," and to define and attain their own dreams and aspirations.

Studies of date rape indicate even greater prevalence than that of dating violence as measured by studies that do not include sexual coercion and assault in their definition. Py Bateman discusses the "justification" of date rape by young men and the difficulty recognizing it by young women based on its congruence with gender role expectations. Expectations that young women are the "gatekeepers" and young men are the "initiators" of sexual intimacy reflect a sexist—and adversarial—view of male-female relationships.

Although more research is needed before we can accurately describe the patterns in violent dating relationships between young people, David B. Sugarman and Gerald T. Hotaling describe several patterns that have emerged from the research that has been conducted with high school and college student populations. The prevalence is clear: Large numbers of young people are affected by relationship violence. If violence occurs once in a dating relationship, it is likely to occur again. Males and females report about equal use of violence, although females are more likely to sustain injuries. Jealousy and uncontrollable anger are perceived by both men and women to be the most pressing cause of violence. In addition, women are twice as likely as men to interpret their own violent behavior as self-defense or retaliation. Men are three times more likely than women to cite intimidation, the intention of striking fear into the other person or forcing the other to do something as their major motive for violence. Young people tend to interpret the violence of their partner as signifying love, thus indicating confusion about what is "normal" in their relationships. Young people rarely seek professional help, although many talk to friends about relationship violence.

Dee L. R. Graham and Edna I. Rawlings have identified the Stockholm (or hostage) Syndrome in the pattern of bonding in violent dating relationships. In contrast to the perspective that young women are in abusive relationships because of their previous experiences, Graham and Rawlings propose that the reasons young women remain in these relationships arise from the relationship itself. They argue that it makes no more sense to explain why women get into or have difficulty escaping from abusive relationships by looking at the women's backgrounds than it does to attempt to explain why American hostages in Lebanon were captured or have had difficulty escaping by analyzing their backgrounds. The backgrounds of the captors or abusers, on the other hand, may be relevant, but Graham and Rawlings's paper focuses on the forces characteristic of the captor-hostage (or abuser-victim) relationship and the survival strategies of the hostage/victim. This perspective is based on extensive research

and is extremely valuable to practitioners and survivors in understanding the cognitive distortions and feelings survivors have as
they extricate themselves and recover from the victimizing
experience—without blaming the victim.

In her article on violence during teen pregnancy, Judith
McFarlane identifies the health risks to pregnant adolescents who
are battered, and to their unborn children. Her findings indicate
that much more research is needed and provide a warning about
the magnitude of the costs of violence, in the present and in the future.

The stories of incarcerated young women reported by Cathleen E. Chadwick and Kenneth M. Greene indicate that factors in
the women's lives that contributed to their criminal behavior may
also have made them vulnerable to dating violence. Those factors
include family backgrounds that discourage self-respect and self-
responsibility, involvement with drugs and alcohol, and the
tendency to assume that violence is the way to express anger.
However, their stories also have the same recurring themes found
in other young women's stories: violence and jealousy as signs of
love, the pressure to be in a relationship, and the unpredictable
circumstances that have led them to be involved with violent
young men.

Intervention Strategies

Dating Violence looks at experiences of young women from different kinds of communities and situations: Asian, white,
Hispanic, African-American; pregnant and parenting; incarcerated; lesbian and heterosexual; and young women and their parents of every class and educational background. Some of the
young women who have been victimized by dating violence grew
up in violent families, others did not. The point is that teen dating
violence is not confined to a particular community or situation: It
takes place in all communities. In this section, practitioners and
organizers describe the patterns they have observed and the intervention strategies they have used in their work with young women
in various settings.

Intervention with and on behalf of young women in abusive
relationships is most effective when using a comprehensive approach. Laura Prato and Regina Braham describe a coordinated
community response that was effective in the case of a young
woman referred to their program. They view the role of domestic

violence programs as key to the coordination of interagency cooperation in such cases.

In telling her story to Bonnie Zimmer, Felicia expresses how profoundly she was affected by the victim-blaming associated with teen pregnancy, as well as the other misfortunes of her childhood. She struggled to feel that her pain was real and that someone would listen. This article emphasizes that Zimmer's nonjudgmental support was key to Felicia's admitting and subsequently confronting her boyfriend's abuse.

Clinical intervention can be valuable in helping young women recover from the effects of an abusive intimate relationship. Johanna Gallers and Kathy J. Lawrence describe Post-Traumatic Stress Disorder (PTSD) reactions to victimization, and the use of a therapy technique called "flooding" to help adolescent date rape survivors to recover. This technique works best to overcome trauma caused by one incident or a set of incidents of violence. However, it can also be effective in conjunction with other therapeutic strategies over a longer period of time for desensitization and recovery from PTSD reactions for young women who have been victimized repeatedly over a period of time and who are no longer in the abusive relationship.

The impact of the clash between cultures is part of the experience of many young women in this country. It is especially evident among young women who were born in countries whose cultures are not Western European. Mieko Yoshihama, Asha L. Parekh and Doris Boyington write about the experiences of young women who are from Asian/Pacific countries. Members of the staff of Project NATEEN describe the impact on young Central American women of leaving their countries of origin and adjusting to their new lives in the United States. They also describe the cultural beliefs that affect these young women as they deal with dating, sexuality, and violence in their relationships.

When I contacted programs that work with gay teens, staff members and teens themselves did not recognize relationship violence as a problem. Gay teens are primarily dealing with coming out and with social stigma, including violence and abuse against them as gays. Yet the reality that abuse does take place in some lesbian relationships emerged as I continued searching for personal stories. Kerry Lobel and I describe our impressions from our work and interviews with young lesbians about the ways they are affected when abuse occurs in a relationship.

Sheila James Kuehl discusses the ways in which existing civil and criminal laws can be used on behalf of young women who have experienced dating violence as well as the changes in the law that are needed to better protect them. Only three states (California, Colorado and Pennsylvania) include dating relationships within the definition of relationships protected by domestic violence laws and allow women under eighteen to seek legal action under these laws. A broader legal definition of domestic violence is needed in other states to provide young women under eighteen the same access to protection as adult women.

Education and Prevention Projects

The consensus among people who work with adolescents and young adults is that stopping dating violence depends on reaching out to them with information that will help them to identify dating violence as a problem, to define it as "not normal." There are prevention program models throughout the United States and Canada that do this. The majority are in high schools and are provided by school staff or by community-based domestic violence programs. These models include (1) classroom education, with curricula that usually cover facts about and definitions of dating violence, relationship skills (for example, conflict management, communication, handling jealousy and anger), and resources for help; (2) speak-outs for youth; (3) saturation of the school environment with policy-setting so that violence is not tolerated, an intervention plan for students and school personnel, and coordination among parents, police and health and mental health agencies; (4) support groups or workshops for high-risk young men and women that focus on nonviolent relationship skills; (5) theater troupe or other dramatic presentations to students by students; and (6) peer leadership/counseling and presentations.

The Dating Violence Intervention Project in Cambridge, Massachusetts, is a model prevention education program that has saturated the environment of a high school, providing classroom education, a peer leadership program, a theatre troupe, support groups, and education and planning with school personnel. Carole Sousa describes the impact of this program: Students confront one another about abusive behavior in the school's halls.

In my article on support groups I define this method of working with young women and its value as an empowering and accessible approach. Several programs that offer support groups for young women in battering relationships in schools and in counseling centers are described as models.

Ginny NiCarthy has conducted "Addictive Love" workshops for young women in Seattle, Washington, and, with Ann Muenchow, has developed an eight-session model for teaching young women about addictive and abusive relationships, the relationships between them and what can be done to prevent or stop them. NiCarthy describes exercises used in the workshops and the responses of participants in the first two workshops conducted.

A teacher-training model for prevention education was adopted by the Minnesota state school system. The Minnesota Coalition for Battered Women developed and evaluated a teacher-training curriculum with the aim of reaching large numbers of students by educating teachers rather than students directly. The Coalition views the teacher as an accessible student resource who, with training and curriculum materials, can be most effective in reaching out to high school youth regarding dating violence. The program and its evaluation outcomes are described by Linda Jones.

Marybeth Roden describes in her article the work of the Rape Treatment Center in Los Angeles, California, conducts high school classroom education presentations on prevention of acquaintance rape that include realities about sexual assault, role playing and discussions regarding sexual coercion in dating situations. With students' active participation, they confront attitudes and expectations and what young men and young women who are intimate, and their friends, can do to support nonabusive and respectful communication about sex.

Carolyn Powell describes her experiences dealing with dating violence on an inner-city high school campus. She approaches the problem directly and indirectly: in the classroom, on the school campus, and in specialized groups she facilitates for teen mothers, students at risk of dropping out of school and students on probation. She finds that dating violence is most effectively dealt with when teachers, counselors, deans, maintenance, security and clerical staff, parents and students work together in an open atmosphere.

Conclusion

Adolescents and young adults are experiencing violence, humiliation and trauma in relationships that is similar to that experienced by adult battered women, but that is also unique because of the circumstances of their young lives. We can use the information we have learned from adult battered women to understand the context, dynamics and reactions to dating violence, and to intervene. But we must also recognize and understand this as a different phenomenon and create new ways of impacting social structures and reaching young men and women to prevent, stop and help adolescents recover from dating violence.

I

**Teens and Parents
Tell Their Stories**

A Parent's Story

Vicki Crompton

Jenny. An ordinary kid, from an ordinary family. Yet an extraordinary event changed our lives completely, and forever.

Mark. He appeared on our doorstep one evening in October 1985. I was tidying up the kitchen when I heard the doorbell ring, so I was the first one to reach the door. There he stood, a tall, blond young man, wearing blue jeans and a black leather jacket. With a charming smile, he asked, "Is Jenny home?" My first reaction was confusion. Who is this boy? Jenny had not mentioned that anyone, particularly a *boy*, was coming over. Then she came bounding down the steps, smiling, thrilled to see him. When I saw how excited Jenny was, I didn't have the heart to say no, to say that I really thought she was too young to have boys calling at the house.

That first evening, I guided them into the living room, where we all sat awkwardly, looking at each other. Jenny was far too shy to make casual conversation, and she was obviously far too taken with him. So my husband, Greg, and I kept the conversation going.

So Mark Smith came into our lives. Although Mark was very polite and answered all my questions about home and school, he was skillful at keeping the real Mark hidden. Later I would review the conversation and realize that I knew nothing about him.

For Jenny, the beginning of her relationship with Mark was a dream come true. Junior high had been an unhappy time in her life, a time when she found herself excluded. Her dream was to find acceptance in high school, to be popular and part of the crowd, and most of all, to find a boyfriend.

21

Her transition from girl to young woman was astounding to watch. Always a pretty child, Jenny, like so many kids, went through an awkward stage. She needed glasses at the age of ten, and with each passing year, the glasses became thicker. She also had braces on her teeth, and she grew taller, skinnier, and awkward. But by age twelve, she really started to change. First came contact lenses, which showed off her blue eyes, and she learned how to style her thick, blond hair. She developed a curvy shape and a sense of style and flair for clothes that was all her own. By the time she met Mark Smith, she was indeed a beautiful girl.

Her childhood attempts at sports were replaced by a love for dance. Through dance, she developed confidence and pride in her body. But her keen intellect was perhaps her most beautiful asset. A voracious reader since early childhood, Jenny continued that love with her studies. She was an honors student without much effort. Her talent for language was so great that by her sophomore year she was studying both French and Spanish. Her dream for her future was to utilize languages in a career, to live in Europe, to see the world.

Her interest in Mark was a bit of a mystery to me. Beyond his obvious good looks, I didn't see what the attraction could possibly be. In contrast to Jenny's love of learning, he was a poor student, uninterested in building for his future. Although my fervent hope was that he would go away to school, far away from Jenny, I was concerned enough about him to inquire about his plans after graduation now that he was in his senior year. I discovered that he had no plans. His parents had not spoken to him about his life after high school. My feeling was that he was just drifting through life. While Jenny was passionately interested in books, dance and her family, Mark's life centered on cars, his motorcycle and "riding around" with his friends. As I observed the differences between them, I knew it was just a matter of time before Jenny would tire of him and wish to be free.

Despite their age difference and lack of common interests, however, Jenny and Mark's relationship appeared to thrive. Apparently they were the talk of the school, the "perfect couple," so much "in love."

He called her daily, sometimes several times a day. They shared a locker at school and walked each other to class. They ate lunch together. He came over to our house about three nights a week. For a child of fourteen, it was pretty overwhelming. My rules were strict, but Jenny did not seem to mind. I think she knew she couldn't have handled a more intense relationship.

Some casual conversation with students employed in my office made me realize that Jenny and Mark might be discussing sex. So I said to Jenny one night in an offhand way, "Jen, if sex ever becomes an issue between the two of you, I hope you will talk to me about it first." The very next night she came to me! Without ever making eye contact, she told me she wanted to have sex with Mark and asked me to take her to a doctor for birth control pills. Horrified, I struggled to maintain my composure. I managed to stammer that I wanted to talk to some professionals first, to please wait for me to get her some help. I called every agency in the book, looking for someone who was skilled at talking to teenagers about the disadvantages of early sex. Finally I connected her with a teen from my office who felt comfortable talking about her own experiences. Jenny came home from that meeting and announced that not only was she not ready to become intimate, but that she also was going to break off her relationship with Mark completely. "I just want to be free, Mom," she told me. "I really envy my friends who don't have boyfriends." And so began the final phase of their courtship.

Mark ignored Jenny's attempts to break up. He still shared the locker, still walked her to class, still called. When she insisted that he stop, that she wanted to break up, he became more insistent, more possessive. The phone calls increased, the unannounced visits to the house more frequent. He would not move out of her locker. Because he made it so difficult, Jenny simply gave up and agreed to go back. When I questioned her, she said that she really cared for him and wasn't sure she wanted to end it. This on-again, off-again routine continued for the next several months, into the summer, until Jenny made the final break.

As Jenny increased her attempts to pull away, Mark intensified his actions to keep her locked in. He seemed to always know her plans. At first she would unwittingly tell him where she was going. Then, as she attempted to keep this information from him, he would turn to her girlfriends and find out about her activities from them. He was so skillful that, on one occasion, he showed up at a family reunion on her dad's side of the family, having been invited by Jenny's cousin with whom he had struck up a friendship. Her trips to the mall were marred by Mark's sudden appearance. Her weekly dance lessons were punctuated by his arrival, cunningly timed just a few minutes before I arrived to pick her up. The boys who expressed an interest in her were quickly squelched by a visit from Mark, who curtly told them, "She's my girl; leave her alone."

As Jenny grew more distant, he became more desperate. I realize now that he must have sat in the dark and watched our house at night. One night we decided on the spur of the moment to walk up the block for an ice cream cone. Outside our door, I noticed movement behind parked cars. Greg investigated and discovered Mark and his friend crouching behind the cars, watching our house. Another night, at midnight, I heard noises at Jenny's second-floor window. She and I looked out to see Mark standing below, throwing rocks at her window, yelling "Jenny, Jenny."

By August 1986, Jenny had had enough. Triumphantly, she called me at work one day and announced that she "had done it, really broken it off with Mark." She sounded happy, excited, relieved to be free. School would be starting in a few weeks, and Mark would not be there (he had graduated the previous spring). I never saw Mark Smith again. I thought he had gone away. The phone calls stopped. There were no more visits.

From Jenny's perspective, however, he never did go away. He just became more deceitful. She discovered that he was entering the school grounds and breaking into her locker, the same locker they had shared the year before. He would go through her things and read the notes her friends had written. She began to suspect that he was entering our home when we were gone; she told her friends that things in her room were often not as she had left them. Mark's picture, which she had put away in a drawer, kept reappearing on top of her TV. He left her threatening notes that hinted she "would not make it to homecoming" and desperate lines that said "I wish you would die." She told her friends about these things and even laughed the day of the homecoming parade, saying, "Well, I'm still in one piece." She never told me.

Friday, September 26, 1986, I woke Jenny to get her into the shower before I left for work. I hugged her and kissed her before leaving, as I always did. That morning I said "I love you, Jen," something I didn't always do. And she replied, "I love you too, Mom." We spoke briefly about the homecoming game that evening, and she asked if I could drive her to the dance or if she should ride with her friends. Then I rushed out the door. My day was uneventful. I was bored and had many things to do at home. I thought about asking my boss if I could leave work early, but I resisted the urge. I left work at my usual time and drove home thinking about the busy night ahead.

When I drove onto my street, the first thing I saw were groups of neighbors standing in their yards, looking toward my house. Then I saw the ambulance, the police cars, the fire truck. I saw police officers running out of my house. I started shaking so violently that I could barely park my car. I ran out, shouting, "What is happening here?" I was stopped from entering my home and told that my daughter had been stabbed, but that "the paramedics are working on her." I watched as they carried her out on a stretcher and took her away in an ambulance. I hung onto a white and shaken Greg as he described walking into the house and finding Jenny "lying in a pool of blood." I sat in the hospital emergency room and heard them tell me that my daughter was deceased. Dead? Not Jenny. I just talked to her this morning. She is only fifteen. How can she be dead?

The days became a blur. Mark was arrested. He was tried and convicted of first-degree murder. At his trial, I learned the truth of my daughter's last months. I learned of the pressure he had put on her and his threats. I learned of the deception he forced her to participate in. I heard fourteen-year-old children describe their attempts to handle a situation adults could not handle. I saw the fear and guilt of her friends as they grappled with the thought that they could have saved her if only they had told someone what was going on. I learned that Mark had abused Jenny, slapping her and roughing her up frequently. I heard the kids say that it happens all the time at school, boyfriends hitting girlfriends, so they didn't think anything of it. I listened to a recreation of the last moments of her life: how she got off the school bus and entered our home alone to find Mark waiting for her, and how he stabbed her over sixty times with a seven-inch butcher knife, leaving her on the living room floor to be found by Greg, who came in from work carrying our one-year-old son. I heard the account of Mark's evening: how he had attended the homecoming football game with a date and how he laughed and ate and appeared very unconcerned that Jenny was dead.

Something rose up in me. Perhaps it started when I returned to work after her funeral. I realized that people expected me to carry on as if nothing had happened. They acknowledged my grief, but refused to mention the way my daughter died! I haunted the library, looking for books on the subject of teen dating violence. I remembered hearing a story, almost twenty years ago, of a young man shooting his girlfriend. Then I read of the Jennifer Levin murder in New York City. Can it be that this is happening all over, and no one is saying anything about it? Why hadn't other mothers spoken out, tried to warn me or warn Jenny of the danger?

My involvement began slowly. I read what I could find on the subject and talked to a lot of teens. My first speech was to a church youth group, a small gathering of teens who were laughing and kidding and poking each other. As I stood at the back of the room before I was introduced, I was terrified, thinking I would never hold their attention. I started out my talk by playing a portion of the song, "The Greatest Love of All." The words are about learning how to love oneself, finding self respect. As the song had recently been popular, the kids started swaying to the music and mouthing the words. Then I turned off the player and said, "I chose that song to play for you today because of the message of the words. I also chose that song to play six months ago at the funeral of my daughter, Jenny." Total silence! For the duration of my talk, not a soul moved. As I looked at the audience I could pick out who in that crowd was being abused by her boyfriend. I saw the looks that passed between friends. I saw the downcast eyes as I described Mark's behavior. Three years and hundreds of speechs later, I still see those things. I can pick out the ones whose lives I am describing.

On Jenny's sixteenth birthday, in an attempt to find some comfort in our grief, Greg and I attended a Parents of Murdered Children Conference. There I met two hundred parents who suffered as we did. In a group of parents who had lost a child to a boyfriend or spouse, I met Ellen Kessner, a writer who had also lost a child by murder. She asked me if she could write Jenny's story for publication. The *Redbook* article that followed (March 1988) educated thousands of parents nationwide. Suddenly teen dating violence became a household word. I was invited to appear on many TV shows. In our community, schools began including the subject in their curriculum.

Jenny is gone, a reality I must live with every day. Sometimes the grief is so overpowering that it seems I cannot survive it. But Jenny has touched so many. Her story has alerted parents and teens to the dangers of abusive relationships. She has saved many lives. And so I am able to say that she did not die in vain, that there was some purpose to her short life. It brings comfort, and it helps me go on. I'll never forget Jen. I miss her so much. I'll always love her.

The author would like to thank Ellen Zelda Kessner for her assistance in writing this story.

They Said I Was
"Young and Immature"

Salina Stone

My mother and father were divorced when I was two years old.
When I was eight, my stepdad began to abuse me in every form of
the word. My dad committed suicide a couple of years later. His
mother and sister blamed me because he had called me to say
good-bye before he did it.

When I was thirteen, I met a guy named Jack, who was about
a year older than me. He was funny, carefree and full of life. He
seemed to be a free spirit, as I wanted to be.

We spent all our time together, which is wonderful when getting to know someone, but it became obsessive: I was either with
him or talking to him on the phone. At one point, I even had to be
on the phone with him when I went to sleep so that he knew I was
at home at night. I was allowed to talk to only two people at
school—both were girls, and he had his friends watch me to make
sure I was obedient.

Then Jack started playing games with my mind. We used to
lie in a field and talk every day after school. One day he got an evil
glare in his eyes and said, "Tell me you love me, Salina." I was
scared and said, "Stop it, Jack." He said, "I'm not Jack. I'm
Lucifer. Tell me you love me and that you want to make love to
me!" I pleaded for him to stop, but he kept it up and told me that
he would hurt Jack and wouldn't let him come back if I didn't say
it. I couldn't say it, so I laid on the ground, curled in a ball, crying
from fear.

The first time Jack was physically violent was on the day he
came to school to walk me home. He had been kicked out of school
and wasn't allowed on the grounds, so the minute he walked in

the building they took him to the office and called the police. When he came out, I immediately asked him what had happened and if he was all right. He wouldn't answer me, or even look at me. He grabbed me by the wrists and dragged me outside and into the woods behind the school. He set me on a log and wrapped a dog's choke chain around my neck. He told me he was going to kill me and started choking me with the chain. He had the same look in his eyes that he did when he played Lucifer. Everything seemed so unreal, and I was so scared, that I just sat there and would have let him kill me. Suddenly, he stopped, giggled and said, "Come on, let's go get something to eat." It was so weird and extreme that I thought maybe I just took it wrong or read too much into it.

A few months later, he raped me for the first time. He would beat me, then rape me. It was supposed to be a loving gesture to make up for when he beat me. That was when I started trying to break up with him. But he would come back crying, "I love you. I'll never hurt you again." I loved him. Compared to the other men in my life, he was wonderful. At least *sometimes* he was really good to me. When I'd see him cry, I'd remember the softness and gentleness he could show, and how much I loved him. It would give me hope that we could work it out. He would buy me things like antique beads, long-stemmed roses or a beautiful jewelry box to make up for my pain. I'd leave him and go back, leave and go back. When those things didn't work, he started threatening to kidnap my dog and hurt my friends. So I'd have to go back to him, and then I'd leave and go back. It even got to the point where he threatened to commit suicide.

On my sixteenth birthday, my mom had a surprise party for me. It was outside so everyone could play volleyball and relax in the sun. Jack made me sit inside with him in the basement and watch TV. When the time came for the ice cream and cake, he allowed me to go out. But before I could have any, I had to kneel on the cement next to his chair and feed him. The moment we were done, he grabbed me by the back of my hair and pulled it to let me know it was time to go back in. At that point, no one could bear to see him be so rough with me, so my friends faded off into the sunset. He was all I had left, so I stayed with him.

The summer before my senior year, he got me a job at a restaurant where he worked. That way he could keep an eye on me. The first day, one of the cooks was asking about me, not knowing that I even knew Jack. Jack came in, threw me up against the wall and told me not to talk to the other workers. I wasn't even allowed to talk to them if it had to do with my job. Luckily I worked a few nights that he didn't, and I learned what it was like to have healthy friendships. That helped me to find a bit of self-confidence. At that time, Jack and I weren't "officially" going out together, but he still "owned" me.

One day after work, he jumped in the backseat of my car and was trying to get me to climb back there and kiss him. I kept telling him to get out. He got angry that I wouldn't obey him and slammed my seat forward, smashing my face into the steering wheel. He was screaming at me about how terrible I treated him and what a fucking bitch I was. That's why he didn't want to go out with me. I said, "Fine. I'm a bitch. So leave me alone." He got out of the car, and I left. I went to the drive-through window at the bank to cash a check and he followed me in his car. He got out and started telling me what a cunt I was and how nobody would ever love me. I was really embarrassed. Everyone was watching through the bank window. When they sent my money out, he took it and my driver's license. We argued, and he called me names. I grabbed my driver's license as he started to crack it, and I turned to run. He grabbed me by my hair and slammed my head into the top of his car. A bunch of my hair ripped out. I fell back against the car. Everything was blurry. He shook me, saying, "Why do you make me hurt you?" I kept trying to kick him in the shin to run away, but it didn't work. It just made him angrier. He slammed my hand in the car door so I couldn't go anywhere. I kicked him hard enough to make him let go. I turned around and got two steps away before he grabbed the back of my hair and slammed me into the pavement. I don't remember how I got away. All I remember is the people standing in the bank watching. They didn't help me.

My senior year of high school I tried desperately to get away from him. My mother gave me a lot of support, which made it easier. Jack flipped out and started threatening to kill himself; he actually started starving himself. He wrote me love songs, sent flowers. He slept in his car outside my house. When I went to catch the school bus, he insisted on driving me to school himself. I knew that if I didn't get in willingly, I'd be forced, and then I didn't know if I'd make it to school or not.

One morning I got in the car and sat so that I was right up

against the passenger's door, as far away from him as I could get. He started telling me that he was going to charge me for the rides. For the first time in my life I stood up to him and said, "No. I don't want to see you. And I don't ask for these rides!" We argued, and he made fun of me, calling me "Miss Independent" and a slut. We got to the school, and I started to get out of the car. I told him, "No, Jack, I don't need you anymore." He pulled me back in the car and took off. He was going to drop me off in the middle of nowhere. He didn't stop for lights or stop signs. I had to jump out of the car while it was still moving.

I started walking quickly back to the school. I got to the edge of the school grounds, and he came walking toward me. He started calling me names. I kept telling him to leave me alone, looking down. When I didn't react to him, he grabbed me by my wrists and dragged me to his car. By this time, everyone was walking by on their way to school. Buses and teachers were driving up. My last hope was to yell for help. I knew it would make him furious, but it was that or get raped or stranded. I started calling, "Help me!" He started slapping me. I kept screaming for help. He grabbed me from behind and put his hands over my nose and mouth. I couldn't breathe. I thought I was going to die. I felt so relieved, calm. It was finally over! I felt a wrenching sadness as I passed out, and the last thing I saw was about twenty or twenty-five of my classmates standing within a few yards of me, watching. As I closed my eyes to die, I heard a voice. I thought they were laughing at me. However, it really was my friend who came running over to help me. If it hadn't been for her, I might be dead. He kept smothering me after I passed out.

When I came to, Jack was threatening my friend. Someone finally went up to the school and got a monitor, who tried to get Jack to leave. My friend got me to the school—and said that if I didn't press charges, she would.

I signed the statement, handed it to the cop and asked if Jack would be arrested. He said no, the city attorney would decide whether or not there was a case. I was terrified. He said, "Well, you are both young and immature." I admit that I was young and immature, but did that mean I didn't have the right to be taken seriously? Did that give him the right to beat me? The report sat on the city attorney's desk until Jack tried to grab me again at the school bus stop. A court date was set.

Jack called me at work and at home and said he wasn't dumb

enough to hurt me when the cops were involved, so he was going to hurt my friends. His father called and threatened my mom. We had to leave the state and hide.

Jack went to court. The man who almost killed me got charged with disturbing the peace. He was "advised" to stay away from me and was put on probation for one year. He continued to harrass me.

It has been a few years since then. Jack continues to find and harrass me. I move almost every other month. Once I came home to find my dog outside practically frozen. I had to have him put to sleep. I kept trying to get an Order for Protection, but I didn't qualify. You have to have lived with the man, been married or had his child. At one point, I was ready to go off the edge. I wanted to kill him. Instead I went to court and lied. I said I had lived with him. I got the Order. It meant nothing. He threw his copy away. He lets me know that he knows where I am and if he wanted to do something to hurt me he could.

When I was in high school, I was a loner. Sometimes I'd wear the same pair of jeans all week. When I was beaten and raped every morning before school, I had a hard time taking care of myself. It's hard enough just to survive. The people at school made fun of the way I looked and acted. Now I speak in schools and share my story, hoping for change. I challenge everyone to look inside people. Look at *why* they are loners, overweight, not taking care of themselves. Reach out. We all have struggles, and everyone deserves respect.

Belonging

Debbie Mattson

I was in junior high during the mid-sixties. Until turning twelve, I had identified myself as a tomboy, interested in boys as companions for searching the creek for critters, playing backyard football and climbing trees. My most constant friends were actually my younger brother's friends. Occasionally I'd have a brief friendship with a girl. But mostly I remember being fairly lonely. During the summer between elementary school and junior high, I went through puberty. All my relationships changed; I was no longer interested in the activities of my brother and his friends, and I developed a circle of girlfriends. We consulted each other on what clothes to wear, how to act, how to look, just everything. We tried to be as much like each other as possible and, at the same time, mimic the behavior and attitudes of older schoolmates. During the first few weeks of junior high, I was surprised to hear that a boy was interested in me. We were soon going steady, and he was the first boy I kissed. The relationship ended a few months later when he told one of my girlfriends he wanted to break up with me. He and I never talked so I never learned why things changed, only felt the rejection. I remember it as a very sweet first relationship and typical of a junior high romance.

I was still twelve years old when I became involved with my second boyfriend, Mike. He was twelve, too, and much more physically mature than the other seventh-grade boys. It started out fun, more fun in that this time I had more experience and confidence in relating to a boy as a girlfriend. This relationship lasted for two years. During those years I was hit constantly and isolated from my friends. His father treated me as a sex object, getting right up in my face with his drunken, smelly breath, and invariably, his hands would slip onto my breast. I felt I deserved this treatment. I believed that men knew that I had become sexually involved; thus I had somehow given them permission to touch me as they pleased and had no authority to deny them.

During the time that Mike and I went together, my identity belonged to him. I was given a lot of support from my peers for being Mike's girlfriend. Another boy, John, became interested in me. He and Mike talked it over and decided that Mike could keep me. I was pleased with the decision. One Friday night, Mike and a couple of his friends spray-painted in large letters on every available surface in town "Mike loves Debbie," "Mike T. + Debbie M." and variations of the same theme. I felt pleased by the public declaration of ownership.

I don't remember being hit anywhere other than my upper arms and thighs. Most of the time I thought what he was doing was okay. A lot of the time it wasn't done in anger; he was just being playful. But my arms and legs were always bruised. Occasionally people would tell me it was wrong, that he shouldn't be hitting me and that it was distressing to them to see it happen. I listened well enough to remember what they said today, over twenty-five years later. Yet at the time, it didn't make enough of an impression on me that I thought the hitting should stop. At times he hit me in anger, but I definitely felt I deserved to be hit and never told anyone about those beatings for fear they would then know I was truly a terrible person, terrible enough that I'd make someone hit me over and over again. I'd wince and cry but not leave the situation, as my greatest fear was losing Mike as a boyfriend. My worth as a person was dependent on that relationship. Sometimes we would be kissing, and all of a sudden he'd pull away with an angry expression on his face and slam his fist into whatever was beside my head. He'd explain to me he had just seen that flirtatious look on my face that he hated.

We'd been going together a little over a year when Mike explained to me that he needed more from me sexually and if I wouldn't give it to him he'd have to break up with me and get it elsewhere. This was at the end of eighth grade. Nothing could be worse than losing Mike, so I agreed. And as time wore on I agreed to more and more. I had no sex education other than being told that I should save my virginity for my husband. I had no idea as to what was "normal" sexual activity and worried that I was abnormal and doing something to be ashamed of. Again, I feared that someone would find out about me being a terrible person. That summer the only person I saw, besides my family, was Mike.

In the fall I began ninth grade. I think the transition from eighth to ninth grade was significant. The academics were different enough that I developed some more interests, more than just Mike. We didn't have any classes in common, and he was absent from school a lot that fall. I began to make new friends and wanted to spend time with them. It seemed as if Mike and I had less and less in common. Our relationship had become exclusively sexual; we did nothing else. I lost interest, and by mid-December I broke up with him. It was merely that, no insight or support from friends or family, merely a loss of interest in being identified as Mike's girlfriend. The effects of the relationship, however, didn't go away as easily. I was scared of getting involved with a boyfriend again. During the remaining years of high school, I rarely dated and did not again have a serious relationship. Mike and I had no association with each other. I avoided him because I was still afraid of him. Still feeling the shame, I never talked with anybody about the abusive nature of this relationship until a few years ago. Even as I write this, I am filled with doubt: I hear myself saying, "You're making this up" and "It's not such a big deal; abuse is a lot worse than this," words I would never say to anyone else. I still worry about people reading this who knew me back then, including my family. In many ways I still feel the false safety of isolation and silence.

I think of myself as having had a fairly ordinary childhood. My father went to work, my mother stayed home with the children until we were all in school, we went to church every Sunday and on family outings, we lived in a middle-class suburb and I was taught to value education and be ambitious. I do believe, though, the reason I stayed in an abusive relationship as a young teenager is that I was taught that girls were inferior to boys. I certainly felt that opportunities were much more limited for girls in comparison to those for boys. And I did feel at a loss about where I belonged because my "tomboy" behavior was constantly being disapproved of by peers, teachers, parents and other adults. I believe that is why it was so important to me to belong to Mike, even at a high cost to myself.

That's All I Can Hope For

Lucille

My daughter was eighteen when she first started seeing her current boyfriend. She is twenty-two now, and he is twenty-four. At first she was fine, but after several months, I found out he was battering her. He would call her on the phone. If she wasn't there when he called, when he'd see her on the street, he'd jump on her. She would come home with bruises, and I would confront her about it, but she would lie to me. It took about four months for me to find out what was really going on.

I think the more I talk to her about this guy, the deeper she gets involved with him. She's trying to rebel against me. I'm really upset. I'm wondering where I failed. The thing that hurts me is that even though I disapprove of him because of the abuse, the only reason she's not seeing him now is because he's in jail. I'm so angry. I have forbidden her to see him, and he's not allowed in my house. She and I hit this wall every time we mention his name.

One time I tried to get her to press charges, but she wouldn't. I don't know where she sees him. The pattern is that he embarrasses her in front of her friends. She said he gets jealous if she's talking to another guy that she knows, someone she grew up with, someone she went to high school with. He gets upset and gets verbally abusive.

She's working and going to college. But she says she can't keep up with her classes. This is her last year of junior college. I asked her about work, and she says she can't keep up with work and school, too. She doesn't see this as a problem. Do you know why she has dropped out of her classes and is staying at home? So she can be at home for all of his phone calls. He calls mornings and nights. He has her in his control but she doesn't see him as controlling her. She is working just to pay her phone bill. I told her there's no way I would work and spend all my money on the phone bill. She got really upset with me about that.

She doesn't say she's afraid not to be home when he calls, but she's definitely there every time he does: 7:00 a.m., 3:00 p.m. and then again in the evening. If she goes out to do something, she does it between those times. She went to the market with me the other day, and she began rushing me through the checkout line. I asked, "What's your hurry?" She said, "I have to get home to get Eddie's call." I rushed with her and didn't say anything. As soon as we walked in the door, the phone rang. I wondered what would happen if she wasn't there. Would he abuse her, ask her where she was, or what? We'll have to wait until he comes back. This relationship could wear out long distance. That's what I'm hoping for.

She's the child I had the most hope for, the one who went to college. She had self-esteem. She got herself to school and has a job. She had the inspiration to have a better life after seeing her sister with a baby. She started pushing herself, and she found out she could do it. This is the year she can transfer to the university. But she's only taking one class, so she's lost that chance. She didn't go to any of the interviews they had set up for her with the universities. She restricts herself because of her boyfriend.

I was battered in my first marriage. She should still remember because she was old enough to understand. She was five when I left her father. She does remember it, because she won't even speak to her father on the street. I tried to show her that the relationship I was in is like hers. But she says Eddie and her father are two different people. I hoped she'd learn from my experience, because I got out of it. She doesn't connect them at all.

It hurts a lot to sit back and watch, and there's nothing I can do about it because she's not listening to anything I'm saying. I'm afraid if I pressure her too much, when he comes back out here, she might try to leave with him. Even when she's hurt by him, she doesn't get angry with him.

She only talks to her friends. Even when she gets hurt by him, she will not talk to me. I find out about it from her friend. I saw this friend, and she had a black eye. I asked her, "What happened to you?" She said, "He hit me, but it was an accident." It's always an accident. I guess she doesn't want to discuss it.

I'm kind of afraid because this friend moved in with her boyfriend last week, and I'm afraid my daughter will do the same thing. If she does, I'll see even less of her, maybe once a month, if that often. I hope that if she moves out with him, that she'll see how he really is and come back home. That's all I can hope for. I hope she sees it soon enough before she gets hurt.

I have one more step I'm going to try. This weekend I'm going to take her shopping. She likes to go shopping. Then when we're shopping, I'll try to talk to her about him. Or maybe when we go shopping, I won't mention Eddie's name. I'll talk to her about school and her plans for her education.

I tried to get her to get counseling. She said she doesn't need counseling. She sees me as her enemy, trying to get her away from him, trying to control her life. She still talks to her sister, but she also gets angry at her. At this point, I think counseling would also help me and her stepfather. It is impossible for parents. She's rebellious. Anything I or her stepfather say to her, she's not going to listen. I have learned not to talk to her about Eddie. I haven't told her not to talk to him on the phone. I hope she'll see it for herself.

I don't know how to reach out to these girls. They're not looking at it the way we are. They're thinking that this is the guy that loves me. They block it out. There's a lot of denial. They don't feel like they're being battered. At this point, I don't think anyone can reach my daughter. She has isolated herself. She doesn't associate with anyone else at school or home. She just goes to school or work and comes home. I don't know what it would take to open up her eyes. I know it's not me. That is the hardest for me. I can't help; I feel so helpless.

She can tell me about her friend's relationship. She can tell me, "How can she stay with that guy? He gave her a black eye!" I feel like saying, "Open your eyes, you're going through the same thing." But I don't. I say to myself that maybe she'll wake up one day. How can she see her friend's situation, but she can't see her own? I have heard her tell her friend, "If I were you, I'd leave him alone." I don't understand it. I feel that she thinks that she's not being battered because she's not getting hit as much. With her, it's the verbal abuse. Either way, it's being battered.

When it happened to me, nothing changed until I told myself, this is it, I'm leaving. I was so afraid; I'd hear his key in the door, and I'd start shaking and trembling. I had left two or three times.

I tried to figure out which was worst, my father or him. I'd go to my parents' house for a time, but then I'd go back home. Then within a week, it would start again. Then I was in the hospital with a black eye, and I said to myself, this is it, and I left for the last time. Now I know that it was a battering relationship. I couldn't talk on the phone. Every time I went to my mother's house, he had to take me and pick me up. There was a lot of controlling. He also had a hold on me because of my kids. He'd tell me to go ahead and leave, but not with my kids.

After I left him, he'd come over to my apartment, kick the door in and terrify me and the kids. He didn't come around to visit them, just to jump on me. It happened for another six or seven years after I left him.

It makes me more scared for my daughter. I'm terrified. I know how bad it can really be. Everything in my daughter's life is changing because of this. I keep thinking that because of what she had been through with her father, that she'd know.

That's hard. She's seen the outcome. She saw the control her father had over me. She's in denial now, not seeing it with her boyfriend. Maybe she'll wake up and see. That's all I can hope for.

"Dating" Is a Heterosexual Concept

Elizabeth

I had heard announcements requesting contributions to a book on dating violence, and although I had come to the awareness that my relationship with Cheryl had been abusive, I didn't register "violence in dating relationships" as having anything to do with me. It wasn't until two friends who know my story asked me about making a contribution that I realized the description "dating violence" applied to my relationship with Cheryl as much as it applied to any heterosexual couple.

Cheryl and I met playing softball in junior high and continued to play on the same teams throughout high school. Things clicked between us and we began spending a lot of time together. We became close and flirted a lot, but nothing sexual happened for about a year. She was a year younger than I, beautiful, sexy and popular. Although she did little things that made me uncomfortable, I tried not to think about them. She criticized me a lot— how I acted, what I wore, how I looked and what I ate. She would make fun of me and make fun of my friends.

Cheryl and I became sexually involved when we were away at a national softball tournament; I was fifteen going on sixteen. We both got drunk, and things just seemed to happen naturally. I woke up the next morning with a sick feeling in my stomach and felt like jumping off the fire escape. It wasn't about being a lesbian; although I hadn't quite come to terms with that, it felt natural. But I felt sick about getting myself into something I couldn't get out of, something I knew wasn't good for me. I was mixed up; I think I wanted to be taken care of by someone. Although I hated how controlling she was, I mistook that for caring—someone who was really interested in me. In addition, I wanted a relationship with a woman, and this was the only possibility I knew of. Although I had "gone steady" with guys in the past, this was my first sexual relationship. I became more and more confused, but I thought this was the way relationships were supposed to be. I thought this was normal.

We spent all of our time together. I would sneak out of my house during the night, ride my bike over to her house and sneak in her bedroom window. We'd spend the night together, then I'd get home in time to get ready for school in the morning. There were also times when she rode over to my house and we snuck into the back room so we could be together. Cheryl didn't define herself as a lesbian, and she often put me down because I did. I tried to change her, to win her. I enjoyed the challenge, but I also ended up feeling extremely inadequate because I was a lesbian. I wasn't a man, and I wasn't good enough as a woman. She would criticize me and insist that I wear makeup and go out with guys. Then when I did date a guy, she became enraged. She didn't want me to see anyone but her. She was also jealous of my friends. She would call me at my friends' houses asking me why I was there and telling me she needed to see me. My friends thought this was strange. They told me they didn't like her and couldn't understand why I put up with her. I couldn't tell them it was because I was in love with her and we were lovers. Somehow I thought that being in a relationship made it all right. I didn't see it as abusive, and I thought that if they knew we were in love they would understand.

She was much smaller than I was, so she couldn't beat me up. I could stop her if I had to. But she punched me, put me down, threatened suicide and forced me to have sex with her. We both drank a lot and did a lot of drugs. Things became more abusive, and I became more and more confused.

Cheryl's parents encouraged our friendship. But when I was seventeen, her father found a letter she had written to me. He also went through her stuff and found letters I had written to her. In response to finding out we were lovers, he beat her up and forbid her to see me. She left home and moved into my house for about four months. My family didn't really like having her there. In fact, neither did I. She told me what to do, ordered me to bring her things and exploded with tirades of verbal abuse. She watched and criticized everything I did.

When I decided that I wanted to break up with her, she threatened to kill herself. One time she even attempted to cut her wrists. I felt responsible, so I backed down. Other times when I talked about breaking up, she stood out in the middle of the street and yelled at me, threatened to bring me "out," took my things or locked me out of my own house.

My mother and my brothers treated the abusive stuff as normal. They didn't seem to react. Of course, they didn't see all of it. Throughout our relationship, my family and my friends couldn't figure out why I let her push me around and control me.

When I was almost eighteen, we tried breaking up and said we'd see other people. She'd spend time with her boyfriend, they'd have sex, then she would come over to my house, say she wasn't satisfied and force me to have sex with her. I would say no, but she'd push me. I was afraid to make a big thing of it because I was afraid of what she would do. Once, as a way to get my attention, she told me she was pregnant. I found out later that she had lied.

I did fight back once, and I still feel extremely guilty about it. She wouldn't leave me alone. I told her to cut it out, to leave, but she wouldn't. I couldn't take it anymore. I grabbed her, shook her and pushed her head into the tiles of the tub. I lost it, and I hurt her. I felt I wanted to kill her for all that she had done to me.

I felt crazy. It was so hard to be clear. The situation got crazier with time. Toward the end, she got more and more abusive. There was more screaming and yelling, more verbal abuse and several suicide threats. It affected everything—throughout high school I was drinking, abusing drugs and getting bad grades.

When I was eighteen, I went to a local college and tried to change. I knew I was smart and could do something with my life. When I finally decided to make the break, it was the hardest thing I ever did. I developed a twitch, and I couldn't concentrate in school. We fought. She stole some of my stuff, and I went to her house with a friend of mine to get it back. She was calmer than usual because my friend was there, but as we left she slugged me in the back. Even after that, I had to make an effort to stay away from her. I got sick, and for four months I thought I'd die. Finally, I stopped drinking so much and focused my energy on school.

Two years later, at twenty, I went away to college. We pretended to be friends and still did things together. Although she still humiliated me at times, I began to feel better about myself. I dated guys and struggled with my identity. Finally, I realized that I was trying to be someone I wasn't, to be the way *she* wanted me to be. I still get caught every now and then, asking myself if am I good enough or if she has changed. And sometimes I wish I could be validated by her, that she would admit how abusive she was and that she would say I am good enough.

It wasn't until five years later that I became aware of how abusive the relationship was. I didn't know what to think when we were together. I am almost twenty-eight now, and it is still confusing. If I could shake her and hurt her, maybe I was abusive, too. I also realize that I had no idea what a lesbian relationship could be like. I had virtually no lesbian friends and no role models. I expected that as a lesbian I would get married and have affairs on the side.

When I went away to college, I got involved in gay and feminist organizations. I have come to a place where I am proud of being a lesbian, and I feel good about myself. My relationship with Cheryl also had a significant impact on later involvements. After several short-term relationships and an unhealthy long-term relationship, I am finally in a healthy, equal and nonabusive relationship with a wonderful woman.

What would have helped? The first things that come to mind are models for healthy lesbian relationships and more contact with other lesbians. I also needed some way of identifying the relationship as abusive. If someone had given a talk at my high school about dating violence from a heterosexual perspective, I wouldn't have thought it had anything to do with me. If the talk had included same-sex relationships, I may have seen my relationship with Cheryl more clearly and perhaps talked with her about it. I also wonder if my mother had confronted me and asked what was going on or suggested that the relationship was abusive, whether I would have listened to her. Given how rebellious I was and how much I minimized the abuse, I doubt that I would have heard her at first. However, I do think that I would have thought about it.

Secrecy about being a lesbian made such a difference. I wasn't isolated. I was on teams, involved in sports. Although I had a lot of friends, the relationship was isolated. I needed allies, people I could relate to. I needed adults not to minimize and not to blame. I think teachers, parents and people who work with youth must be gay/lesbian-affirming, not just open to listening. As a gay/lesbian adolescent, it is so hard to reach out. It is critical that adults reach out.

If Only...

Jan K. Jenson

From my hospital bed, surrounded by vases of beautiful flowers, I studied the reflection of the pathetic creature framed in my mirror. It was more than the blackened eye, the swollen mouth and the tense facial lines. Lifelessly, the dull, sad eyes stared back at me. What has happened to me, I asked myself, as I choked back the sobs. It hurt too much to cry. It hurt to move. My broken leg had just been set in a heavy plaster cast. My doctor had informed me that I would have to walk with crutches for the next six months. How could I take care of my baby and my two young children? What was I going to do?

Tears scalded my eyelids as scenes from last night's attack flashed before my eyes. David had been so angry. I still wasn't quite sure why. It had started at the dinner table. Everything was wrong, according to him. He was sick of spaghetti (normally his favorite meal). Dinner was fifteen minutes late. The baby shouldn't be crying. I had committed the unforgivable sin of buying another head of lettuce when I already had one in the refrigerator. The more I apologized and tried to diffuse the situation, the more violent he became. The inevitable beating culminated with an excruciating surge of pain as my leg snapped when he slammed me down onto the floor.

In the background, I had been aware of the piercing wail of the baby crying out in fear. I could see the terror in the faces of my two toddlers huddled together in the hallway crying silently. What was this doing to my poor, innocent children?

What had happened to the self-confident, intelligent and dynamic high school girl I had been five short years ago? The one with all the dreams and goals, lots of friends and a bright future ahead. What had David done to me? Or, rather, what had I, in the name of love, allowed this man to do to me? It was time to take a good hard look at this stranger in my mirror. Yes, I was David's doormat. Beaten down into fearful submission, my spirit had been crushed. My self-esteem was shot.

The flowers... yes, the flowers... I couldn't escape the irony of it all. Bouquets of fresh flowers delivered to the hospital throughout the day... from David. Little love notes accompanied each delivery. "All my love forever," he signed them. Notes of apology, promises that he would never hurt me again as long as he lived, that he needed me and could never live without me. All this from the man who had just broken my leg. He had cried real tears and begged for my forgiveness. It was the usual "after-the-beating" routine. But this time, something more than my leg had snapped. This time, I found the courage to tell the doctor the truth about what was happening to me. Maybe it was the haunting memory of the faces of my terrified children hiding in the hallway that gave me the strength to face the truth. There would be no more lies about my falling down the stairs or off a ladder.

The lights of the city glowed in the darkness outside my window. Alone in the dark, I wondered what was happening behind the closed doors of all those homes. I wondered if there was anyone else like me out there. But this is *not* me, a small voice cried out from within. Five years ago, when I was sixteen years old there was another me, the real me. Were there other high school girls out there who were madly in love the way I was, blinded from seeing the dark side of their partners until it was too late? If only I could go back in time.

But that was the hard part. Remembering the good times, remembering the way it was when David and I first met and fell in love. We were so in love that we were inseparable. Nothing else seemed to matter except being together. Looking back, I was actually in love with "love" itself, caught up in the glamorous myths of love as portrayed in the movies and the songs that blared from my radio. I believed in living together happily ever after. I believed that if you really loved someone, you couldn't live without him. And even when things didn't always go as smoothly as they should have, I held on to my conviction that by loving someone enough, you could change him.

David came from a violent home: His father beat his mother

regularly, and sometimes David as well. But David promised me that he would never lay a hand on me, especially after seeing what his mother went through. Poor David. I felt so sorry for him. Just knowing what he'd gone through brought out my maternal instincts: I wanted to care for him and make up for his abusive childhood. If only I could love him enough and be a good-enough wife to him someday, I knew I could make him happier. If David didn't love me the way I wanted him to or if he wasn't happy, it had to be my fault. There must be something wrong with me.

As time went on, David reinforced my ideas. If he was moody, depressed or irritable, it was my fault. As a matter of fact, nothing was ever David's fault. When he got into trouble at school, it was because the teachers were picking on him. He frequently got into fights with the other guys, sometimes physical fights. I remember seeing him shove people out of his way and up against the lockers as he walked down the hallways at school. I didn't like that, but David convinced me it was their fault. They had asked for it by the way they treated him! And, of course, if his parents weren't the way they were, he'd have no problems at all.

At least David never hit me, not until later. He "loved" me so much, however, that he'd get extremely upset over the little things I did or didn't do. Stupid little things, he called them. Looking back, belittling me was his way of boosting his own low self-esteem. I had to play the inferior role in our relationship. I figured that would change someday when David was secure enough in my love.

I was sure that he loved me. He often showed it through displays of extreme jealousy and possessiveness. I couldn't talk to another boy. In fact, David wanted me all to himself, to the point that he resented my girlfriends and my family. All we needed was each other, he said. He did a lot of subtle things to discourage me from spending time with anyone else. And if he chose to go out with his friends or not bother to call me, I was still to sit home alone and wait by the phone for his call. If I wasn't there, I was interrogated about where I was, who I talked to, even what I wore. The hassle wasn't worth it. I became more and more isolated, more dependent on David as my sole source of support. Actually, I was a little frightened of David's temper if I didn't do what he wanted me to do. The confusing part was that his expectations frequently changed. I never knew exactly what he wanted from one day to the next. It seemed that I could do nothing to please him. The more I failed to please him, the more I felt like a failure myself.

I felt it was up to me to make this relationship work. You see, we had become sexually involved by this time. To me, that meant commitment. I had to protect my image of myself as a "nice girl." Our sexual intimacy seemed to create a strong bond of ownership. I was now "his" to control and to use as he wished. My boundaries began to disintegrate as I relinquished my self-identity to become a part of David.

We began to fight a lot. That is, David fought. He was often very angry for little or no reason at all. I'd try to calm him down. He'd smash his fist into a wall or destroy something. That also frightened me. Sometimes he'd swear at me or call me names. That hurt a lot. I'd cry. Then he'd cry and hold me close, begging me to forgive him. He promised not to act that way again. I was the only one who could help him change, he always said. He needed me so much, and he was so afraid of losing me. That was why he acted the way he did. So I forgave him... and tried to forget.

We played the "if only..." game. *If only* we could get married and be together all the time, we'd be happy and wouldn't fight. *If only* his dad wasn't so abusive, David wouldn't be so angry. *If only* I was more loving and caring, he wouldn't feel so bad. The game went on and on. The cycle of abuse had begun, although we were both too entrenched in denial to see the reality of it all. I needed to deny what was happening to protect my shaky self-esteem. He needed to deny his actions to avoid taking responsibility for changing his behavior.

The honeymoon stage following a fight was always spectacular and provided the reinforcement and caring I needed to continue the cycle. After one particularly nasty explosion, David surprised me with a beautiful diamond engagement ring. If only we could get married, he wouldn't be so jealous and accusing. I'd be his wife, so he wouldn't have to worry about other guys. We had such big plans and dreams for our future together. With a love as strong as ours, it simply had to work.

We were marrried, expecting to live happily ever after and to have a family as soon as possible. That was all I'd ever really wanted—to be a good wife and mother, and I intended to work hard to make our dreams come true.

Little by little, one by one, all my hopes and dreams were

crushed by the harsh reality of living with an abusive partner who had no desire to change. Little by little, the emotional abuse escalated into threats, which escalated into minor forms of physical abuse. It had been such a gradual process that I'd been almost unaware of what was happening, wanting so much to believe that things would get better. By the time that his increasing violence began resulting in bruises and injuries to me, I'd already been beaten down psychologically to the point of feeling powerless to do anything about it. I actually blamed myself for doing things that caused him to "lose his temper." Maybe I deserved to be abused. After all, by this time my self-esteem had been shattered. I didn't feel like a worthwhile, valuable or lovable person. I'd find myself actually comforting him, wiping away his tears, after he'd slapped and shoved me around! He felt so bad about what he'd done. If only he hadn't been abused as a child! He became the victim and he used that role to justify his inappropriate behavior.

Sometimes, lying awake at night after having been beaten, I thought about leaving. But I felt trapped. He said he would kill me if I tried to leave, and I really believed he would make his threat good. I had no job or money of my own. And I did have three young children to care for and, somehow, provide a loving, happy home for.

One by one, the lights in the city outside my hospital room were turned off for the night until all that was left were the street lights illuminating the freshly fallen snow. It was so quiet, so peaceful. Lost in my thoughts, I almost didn't notice two figures huddled together in the park across the street. They were holding hands, their heads close together. A young couple, I observed, obviously in love. Beneath the street light, they clung together, as the light snow swirled around them. I felt a tug at my own heart as I watched them now playfully throwing snow at each other, stopping every so often for a hug or kiss. Yes, that's the way it should be. For us, it was never meant to be. Maybe, hopefully, for them it would be different.

How Could You Do This to Me?

Consuela

Consuela was interviewed by Barrie Levy in May 1990. She was born in Mexico nineteen years ago, and has been living in the United States since she was three years old. She and her twenty-year-old boyfriend, Carlos, have a three-year-old son. Consuela is studying for her General Equivalency Degree (GED) in Los Angeles. (The names have been changed to protect confidentiality.)

Levy: In what ways has your boyfriend, Carlos, been abusive?

Consuela: I've been with Carlos since I was thirteen but he didn't start beating me until I became pregnant. He used to choke me, do awful things. These things make me hate him. I can't think of them now. He used to make me feel that no one else would want me because I had a baby. I felt I better stay with him. I was scared to go on with my life. He scared me. Sometimes we would drive to the store, and all of a sudden he would take off with me in the car and drive to a parking place. Then he'd hit me because of something wrong I said. I was afraid of everything I said, afraid to say the wrong thing.

Carlos used to get so jealous. I even dropped out of school for almost a year because he wouldn't let me go. He was jealous about me meeting other guys.

He'd yell at me in front of his friends and think he was something big. That's what happens a lot of times. His friends see him, and they think, "Oh, look at that, he has her; she's pretty and he has her like that; I want to have my girlfriend like that, too."

Levy: Why do you think Carlos battered you?

Consuela: He was full of hate. His mom didn't give him any love. His mom only talked to her kids about getting money, being successful. His mom didn't like me. He used to beat me right in front of her, and she didn't do nothing. She must have thought I deserved it. That's why I don't like her at all.

I can give you an example. We both worked on a farm, a family business. We were living in a little house, no rent, no bills, nothing. We used to take care of the place. We lived there for two years. When the season was finished, Carlos drove to the town to work until the season started again. Then his mom went up there and talked him into leaving me and the baby. I had to borrow money to get back to my family in L.A.

Levy: Did you ever tell anyone that Carlos beat you?

Consuela: My mother and my sister knew. There was one time when Carlos beat me pretty bad. I had bruises on my face and everywhere. It didn't even look like me at all. My whole face was purple. Usually he gave me a black eye or something, or scratches, and I had scars. This was the worst ever. I couldn't stand it, so I called the police and pressed charges. My sister helped me go through with it. He didn't hit me anymore after that. He went to court and to jail. They only gave him three months.

Levy: Do you think his going to jail made things better for you and Carlos?

Consuela: He came out of jail, and we talked things out. I asked him how he could do those things to me. He said he wouldn't any more. Then we got back together. He was in jail from November 'til January. We started seeing each other again and moved back together in August, nine months ago. He hasn't hit me. We talk about it, even now. He tells me that he's sorry. I wouldn't put up with that anymore. No way. I guess I was younger. Now I'm not scared so much. It made a difference to have the police and courts stop him.

Levy: How have your family and friends reacted to your relationship with Carlos?

Consuela: My family doesn't like him at all, especially my sister. She went to court with me. They just won't forget what he did.

Some friends are not supportive. They say it's my fault. I heard a lot of that because I wouldn't leave him.

Levy: Do you have any advice for other girls in this situation?

Consuela: How you handle it depends on yourself. Maybe you don't leave him because you're scared of the guy or of the guy's friends. Maybe you have no way out, no money, nowhere else to go, no child care. I am afraid to end up homeless. That's why I want my GED. I want to get a job and get off welfare.

I have to learn different things so I won't get stuck. You never know. He might hit me again. If he does it again, I know I won't put up with it; I'm not going to stay again.

Now I'm thinking about my future. We'll see what happens. We'll see the way he treats me. See if he works, gets a job. If he doesn't, I've got to think about my son. What will I do if he doesn't support my son?

The main thing is to go to school. Get training. Be strong, talk to a friend or other people who have been abused.

He Only Wants to Help Me

This letter was written anonymously, with a note from its author that she has not shared much of this with anyone before.

I was twelve when our family moved to a new area. This meant that I had to go to a new school. In retrospect, I know I fell in with the wrong crowd, but at the time, it seemed cool to smoke cigarettes and, later, to take drugs and to drink. I felt that to fit in with these friends I would have to do all of the things they were doing. Then I met this guy, Andy. He was so cute; all my friends loved him and all of us would have given anything to be with him. He was eighteen, hazel-eyed, all muscle with long blond hair. He was what seemed to be at the time perfect. I was blond, green-eyed and 130 pounds. I competed in gymnastics—until I quit because he wanted to spend more time with me.

At first things were great. The first six months or so, I thought things could not be better. But slowly he started becoming extremely jealous and began pushing or grabbing me harder than normal. I thought nothing of it. I figured I did wear too much makeup, or maybe my skirt was too high cut, or maybe I really was a "stupid, fucking bitch." Maybe I did look like a whore or maybe I shouldn't have gone out for dinner with a girlfriend. He used any excuse to pick a fight with me and try (I feel now) to isolate me totally from my friends. I was being constantly put down, but since I loved him I figured why would he lie to me. He loves me. He only wants to help me.

After a while, the abuse became more frequent and increasingly violent, both in and out of the bedroom. After two years, I weighed over 250 pounds. I never left my house. My education had been suffering. I had one girlfriend with whom I spoke, and that was it.

At this point, my parents still adored him and after almost three years of being together, everyone thought things were great, even me. That year, my parents let me live in the basement apartment of our house, and I started sneaking him in. I did his laundry and made him his meals. Basically, we were living together. My parents were two stories above us, and they never heard a thing. He used to threaten to wake up my parents if I screamed or didn't stop crying. It's very hard to believe I actually was scared to wake up my parents. I get so mad at myself sometimes.

Here are some examples of the things he used to do to me. On one occasion he invited some girl he picked up in a bar over and let her sleep with him in my bed while he made me sleep on the floor of the tool room. He said he would "fucking kill me" if I embarrassed him.

Another night I had two old friends from school, John and Gabe, over to watch movies. It was about midnight, and I went up to the kitchen to make sandwiches. Andy came flying in, in a total rage, and threw all of the sandwich makings all over the floor. Then he came at me. By this time John and Gabe had come up, and they watched him slap me on the side of my head, kick me in the stomach and eventually throw me off our deck, about a three-foot drop. He was screaming at me the entire time, "You fat, fucking, ugly bitch. How could you sleep with my fucking friends, you are a disgusting fucking whore."

When he hit me, usually he did it with the palm of his hand right under my ear. This way, I lost my balance and fell. Eventually I even lost some of my hearing. It was very rare that Andy ever left a bruise or cut on my face, where everyone could see it. It was also rare that he would do something like this with other people around.

Another time I woke up at the hospital on the other side of town. I had apparently arrived there in a cab. I was bruised and had a concussion. To this day, Andy says he knows nothing about it. Who really knows? I know I was with him before, but like everything else, it must have been my imagination.

Two years later, when I was seventeen, Andy moved into a house a friend of his was renovating, and I spent most of my time there. This is about the time I first encountered the police. On one occasion, he pushed me through a window. Luckily my hand and arm blocked my face and were the only things that were cut badly. I called the police, and Andy, while holding me down, called them back and told them it was a joke and that there was no reason to come. "My wife and I were just fighting." I couldn't believe they didn't come. I thought for sure this time Andy would kill me. Sometimes I wonder why he never did, but I used to always wish he would. Suicide was already a daily thought. I used to sit and stare at my father's sleeping pills for hours or even sit with a knife pointed at my stomach. I never had the guts to do it.

It was around this time that I attended an alternative school, and in one of my classes we had to do a big assignment. Wife assault was one of the subject choices, so I decided why not? Also around this time, Andy slapped me across the face so hard that I had a black and blue handprint on the side of my face and my eye was swollen shut. A teacher called Children's Aid, thinking I was a victim of child abuse. That is when the shit hit the fan. I told everyone I had just fallen, but my parents knew, and Andy was never allowed in my house again.

As part of my school assignment on wife assault, a woman from a women's shelter came to my class to speak and we became friends. I must mention that on numerous occasions I had tried to break up with Andy, but after a few days he would cry and tell me he loved me and (that famous phrase) "I promise it won't happen again." It always did.

I now slept upstairs, and Andy was not allowed in the house, but I still continued to see him anyway. A year later, after I had called the police more than a dozen times, an incident occurred that made me make another attempt at calling them. My parents and sister were away, and my friend Vivian was staying at my house. Andy and I had broken up for good this time, but he was now following me around. He sat in his car outside my house for hours at a time just watching for me. It was three o'clock in the morning this time, and he was drunk. He stood outside my bedroom window screaming, "I love you, please give me another chance." When I didn't respond, he started to scream, "You fucking bitch, I'm gonna kill you." Then he began banging on my windows and trying to get into the house. Viv and I were in my bedroom, and we called the police. After waiting for thirty minutes, we called again. Then after another fifteen minutes, we decided to check out the house. So we ran to the kitchen and went from room to room with knives. He wasn't there. About half an hour later, just as we were about to get to sleep, the doorbell rang. It was the police. I was furious. Andy could have come in, raped us, murdered us, taken a shower, cleaned up, made himself something to eat, done his laundry and left with time to spare. As far as I am concerned, the only thing policemen are good for is parking and speeding tickets.

I thought Andy was never going to stop making my life miserable. He slashed my tires, kicked in my headlights and continued to follow me for over a year.

Andy was and still is an alcoholic. I want to stress that it didn't matter if he was drinking or not. His father beats on his mother, and his mother was and is a drunk. I had my go with drugs and booze, but I think because Andy was so bad it turned me off, so I stopped. It's very sad that many people think that the booze or drugs cause the abuse, when they really don't. There is something wrong with the man that abuses. The drinking amplified Andy's mood whatever it was. To cross the line and become abusive was his choice subconsciously. There was no excuse.

I never talked about the sexual abuse with anyone before. Andy humiliated me frequently and made me very self-conscious. I will give you a few examples. After he was violent with me, on many occasions while I was lying on the floor, sofa or bed crying, he would stand over me, call me names, spit, masturbate and ejaculate all over me. Other times he would tie me up. There was little or no foreplay—nothing that ever felt good to me, and all I ever did was lie there. I hated it, but usually I had no choice. On some occasions after we had broken up and decided to get back together he wasn't cruel during sex, but he still didn't let me do anything. In fact the only thing he ever "let" me do was give him a blow job. Sometimes I thought I would die. He literally put his hands behind my head and pushed my head down so far that, a few times, I even threw up. It was gross, and I almost get sick even thinking about it. Not once did sex even feel remotely good.

Finally I met this guy named Steve. He is six-foot-four and 250 pounds and had a very bad reputation as far as fighting, partying and even jail was concerned. Andy was and is still very terrified of him, and when we started seeing each other, Steve asked him to leave me alone. Andy did. Sometimes I think the only reason I started seeing Steve was the protection he could give me and a sense of security I had long since forgotten. By this time, I was very nervous all of the time. I flinched at every movement, and when Steve and I would argue, I would "flip out." By this I mean that when he would show any anger I would just start to scream, get down on my knees in a little ball and cry uncontrollably. He was scared by it, but he would just sit beside me, and when I would finally let him, he would hold me and let me cry. Later on I became more relaxed, and I wasn't afraid to say what I wanted to anyone anymore. Never once did he put me down or even come close to hitting me.

It took a very long time before I actually felt totally comfortable in bed with Steve. He was so patient with me: he gave me all of the time I needed. When we made love, it was better than I had ever imagined.

Steve was good for me at the time, but after he helped me get my life together, it seemed he fell apart. He partied way too much for me, and after a year and a half I moved to another city to go to school and rebuild my life—this time all by myself.

These days things are great for me. I love Steve for all he did for me even though it's better we're apart. I think we will just be great friends. I am and plan to continue working hard at school. I also hope I will never let any man ever do that to me again.

My Advice

Meybel

Meybel is nineteen years old and has attended Business Industry School in Los Angeles for two and a half years. She has a three-year-old son who attends the day care program at the high school. She was born in El Salvador and moved to Los Angeles when she was twelve. Meybel lives on her own. She is no longer involved with her son's father. Meybel was in a battering relationship for two years with her girlfriend, who was also nineteen. One week before this interview, her girlfriend was killed in a car accident.

We started out talking on the phone; then she'd come over. We were really close. We did things together. Romantic things. Things I always wanted to do, like go to the beach at night. Everything I wanted, she gave to me. We'd go out, and she'd buy me things. I did the same for her. We were so close. We got married. We lived together for two years.

But things changed. I was changing. Instead of wearing baggy clothes, I wanted to dress different, like wear short skirts. She picked my clothes. She didn't like anyone to look at me. She would go off, get mad. She didn't want me to have any guys for friends. Before I knew her, I used to have a lot of male friends. She pushed me away from girls *and* guys, because she knew that I was gay, so she didn't like me to talk to anyone. I used to tell her that I liked her and I wasn't going to go with anyone else.

When we started having problems, I got like her. I got jealous. If she looked at someone, I'd jump all over her: "What the hell are you looking at?" I hated that. It was a game, a bad one. She wanted to be in control of me. I wanted to be in control of her.

58

When I wanted to be in control, she didn't like it, and she got violent.

You know, she used to hit me. I used to have to call school to say I couldn't come because I had bruises so bad. No one ever hit me before, not my mom, not anyone. I didn't know how it felt to be hit.

Usually people say that Latino people, especially men, like to be in control. I don't see a difference. I think everybody likes to be in control. My advice to other girls is to tell the person who is hitting you or controlling you to stop it. Tell them, "If you don't like something I do, tell me. Let me be myself." If you start hitting back or hurting back, it gets worse. Don't let yourself get into that. If that person needs to go away, let her or him.

I want to tell teachers and social workers to listen. Pay attention; not only listen but also help people like me. You can talk to teachers or social workers and they will listen, but they don't know the things you go through or how you can't walk away from the person who is battering you. They must see how to help for real. Talking doesn't work. I kept going through the same thing. Then she used to get upset when I told people about our problems. When I talked to others, it got worse, and they didn't even help. They shouldn't say to end the relationship, to just leave her. They have to consider that you have feelings, that you care for the person. You want someone to help with the problems, because these problems can be solved.

Recovery From Violence

Margaret Anderson

I have difficulty telling this story, not because my history is too painful, but because I simply can't remember much of what happened. I've found it very hard to accept that, as a recovering alcoholic, there are large chunks of time that I don't remember or can't remember clearly. I drank constantly during the four-year duration of my battering relationship. The alcohol has wiped out many of my memories.

To write this story, then, I had to research myself like a term paper. I returned to my old journals—those that I rarely reread—that dealt with my relationship with Mike. Reading the words of a seventeen-, eighteen-, nineteen- and twenty-year-old me that I hardly remember, I discovered that over the years I have filled in the memory gaps with nostalgia and with imagination. I forced myself to scrub away the whitewashing that I've done to compensate for such a sad, confused history so that I can speak honestly. This is the story of my struggle to love myself.

I am sure now that if I had stopped drinking while I was seeing Mike, our relationship would have ended. Alcohol was one of the strongest bonds between us; it was the substance which allowed me time and again to ignore my survival instincts and to return to the same problems, the same arguments and the same cycle of violence.

The Beginning

I received straight A's my senior year of high school and had just been accepted to college. I began to venture outside the narrow parameters of total dedication to achievement that I had constructed for myself during high school. I had just started to drink, years after most of my classmates. I had only experimented halfheartedly with dating.

Mike was dark and brooding. He rode a motorcycle and played the guitar. He possessed an intoxicating sense of the romantic, and he flirted masterfully. He was just what I wanted— the complete opposite of my world of good behavior.

During the first months of our relationship, Mike and I shared lots of whimsy and a passion for words. I had spent most of my life devouring books, and he would stay up for hours tinkering with the rhyme of a song lyric. We found common ground in our love of mythology. We took walks in the rain, we flew kites, we went swimming at midnight. Although my journal logs this phase as a short one, followed by violence, I feel lucky to have preserved these initial happy memories.

Sex between us intoxicated me. I had just begun to discover and to explore my sexual self, and Mike and I were both caught up in ourselves as sexual beings. I almost always had sex after I had been drinking. I didn't experience sober sexual intimacy until three years after Mike was out of my life. We used sex as a last resort. Near the end of our relationship, we could barely carry on a civil conversation about the simplest things. Sex became our only way to communicate with each other. Mike was my first, and for many years, my only source of intimate information about myself. I could not associate the person who hit me and called me names with the person who made love to me. I used sex to convince myself that the relationship worked and that I could feel good about being with Mike.

Nine months into our relationship, Mike started being violent. I initially thought that I had pushed him too hard, started an argument at the wrong time, that his rages were something about him that I could change with enough patience and attention. Like most violent relationships, ours followed a pattern. One small disagreement would lead to another; our communications would misfire. Resentment would build to a crescendo, which always ended with us drunk, screaming at each other, and Mike's violence. Then the storm would clear, and we would make up passionately and be blissfully happy for days or weeks until the next storm started to build.

In some ways, this was familiar. I grew up in a landscape of verbal and physical violence. I never doubted that my parents loved me fiercely, and I often felt their support, yet simple stresses exploded into uncontrollable anger in my family. In anger, my father became irrational, violent and dangerous. Anger grabbed my mother like a seizure, and my brother and I learned to wait quietly for her rages to pass.

When I was three years old, my father hit my mother for the last time. I remember him clearly, standing over her shouting. Just as clearly, I remember how long she was gone as she walked, in midwinter, to the police station. She filed charges against my father because she refused to bring her children up in a home with a battered mother. This is my earliest memory, and while our family did not escape other forms of my father's violence, my mother made sure that my brother and I never perceived physical violence as a "normal" or acceptable atmosphere for a family. We saw it rather as something unique to our family and completely uncontrollable.

The Violence

Mike's anger controlled him, and if he mixed anger with alcohol, he almost always resorted to violence. I spent the evening of my grandmother's funeral pleading with him not to destroy our lawn furniture; an argument over what he wore to the funeral had set him off. After another argument, Mike smashed his hands through our front screen door, shaving off most of the skin on his hands. My mother made him repair the door and told him that he was no longer welcome in our house.

One week later, Mike and I each went out with friends and ended up at the same bar. He was so drunk that he barely recognized me, but he remembered that he was angry that we hadn't gone out together that night. He kissed my friend; I dumped a beer over his head and went home. At two o'clock in the morning he appeared in my bedroom, ripped a poster off my wall and hit me five times. As I tried to get him out of the house with my brother's help, he hit my brother. I was shutting the front door on him when he put both hands through the plate glass panel in the door and shattered it. A six-inch piece of glass cut my neck, but by the time we realized how much I was bleeding, Mike had wandered into the street and was trying to avoid being hit by a car.

I took my mother's car and drove Mike to his house. When I crossed the threshold, covered with blood, his mother said to me, "What did you expect? You stood him up tonight." What she meant was not so much that I deserved to be battered, but that Mike could not control his behavior and therefore could not be held responsible for it. It was up to me to shoulder the responsibility, since it had to be shouldered by someone.

In my journal the next day, I wrote:

> *I almost don't feel like really writing now, but I think I need a record of this to keep around—to check up on and to keep me scared. . . . I only moved to defend myself when he went for Steve [my brother]. Even though the glass could have hit me in the eye or his blows could have been harder and landed in a more dangerous place . . . I never really believed that he could hit me. . . . What am I supposed to think of myself? . . . I keep asking myself why people who claim they care about me would treat me like this. . . . He told me that all I ever meant to him was a good lay. . . . I feel cheap and I feel dirty. . . . I'm not angry, I just have this feeling of betrayal and disgust with both of us. . . . It's because I loved him so much that I gave up myself. . . .*

Mike and I were still together two and a half years later. I didn't look back on that journal entry very often because it told the truth. Later, I fielded Mike's drunken, abusive phone calls to my dormitory. I pulled him out of drunken fights with his fraternity brothers. He hit me or called me names more frequently, so that I finally *did* get angry and started hitting back in a rage.

As our relationship grew older and more dangerous, we fought more frequently. We screamed at each other regularly, and Mike was not afraid to call me names in front of other people. After the fights, he would cry, buy me flowers, be twice as attentive, turn into a gentle lover. Then the cycle would start all over again.

Identifying the Abuse

Several violent episodes passed before I began to see violence as a pattern in our relationship, before I began to understand what was happening to me. Before I saw the pattern, I usually blamed myself for the disastrous outcomes of our fights and was often convinced that Mike was the victim instead of me. (After the broken-glass episode, Mike and his mother both asked repeatedly that my mother drop the charges against him for destruction of property, but neither would speak of the violence that led to those charges.)

I am convinced now that keeping a journal played a pivotal role in helping me to identify our relationship as abusive. My journal was the only place that I recorded my own voice without

first editing it to fit others' expectations. My journal tracks my un-
easiness with our relationship beginning a few months after Mike
and I started dating. There, I repeated my own voice until,
months later, I began to hear and remember what I was saying.
Ashamed to talk about the violence with my friends and afraid to
talk about it with my parents, I used my journal as a place to process my feelings. In my journal, I repeated "I don't deserve this,"
until one day I believed it.

Extracting Myself

I spent a long time weaning myself from Mike. I depended
upon him; I had leaned on him during the hard transition from
adolescence to adulthood. For a long time, I chose to remember
the good times that we had shared and the honeymoon periods after the violence. I created a mythology for myself that attributed
Mike's rages to his troubled family history. I convinced myself
that I could help Mike change, that we had strong bonds between
us, that his violence was so sporadic that it posed no real danger
to me.

I kept taking chances with Mike, chances that he would never
seriously injure me, chances that he would put aside his rages. I
lied to friends and parents about the frequency of our contact because I was ashamed that I couldn't manage without him. I used
Mike like a drug: I kept seeing him, hoping that the time spent
with him would make me feel good again. Like any other drug,
though, the good that Mike did became less frequent, and the bad
days began to stack up.

I took tiny steps away from him. I started studying feminist
literature in college. I collected friends who didn't see Mike as a
prince, but as a jerk who telephoned drunk at four o'clock in the
morning to mutter abusive gibberish at me. Every day that I
made my own decisions, every time that I could get through a
week or a month without a call or letter from him, I put a little
more distance between us.

During this time, my journal acted as my only real outlet for
anger. I only allowed myself to get mad when I wrote in my journal; fear of my own emotions and a desire to appear "normal"
kept me from sharing most of my anger with my friends and family. I feared anger; when I was growing up, getting mad was the
special territory of adults. Children who got angry were better off
quiet. Adults who got angry raged around us until their feelings

dissipated. I had no models for a healthy way of dealing with anger.

My journal allowed me space to catalog the brutality of our relationship, making it impossible for me to dismiss the violent episodes as isolated incidents. Without the journal, I would have kept on taking a drink every time I had the urge to get out of the relationship.

Distance helped, too. Nine months of the year, I attended a women's college one thousand miles away from Mike. We kept up frequent phone and letter contact, but the heady physical effects of our sex life could not touch me during the school year. Had we seen more of each other during semesters, my risk of serious injury would have increased greatly.

Away from our abusive fights, I was able to build my self-reliance in small ways. I learned to have fun without Mike, to make decisions that affected only me and to structure a life that did not necessitate seeing him every day. Slowly, depending upon myself built my self-confidence. Armed with stronger self-confidence, I could define myself on my own terms, rather than seeing myself as Mike's girlfriend.

Feminists or not, most of the women I encountered in college had clear ideas about what they wanted in life and were forging plans to meet their goals on their own. Feminist studies became part of the atmosphere on campus, and I began to develop a sense of the political. Feminism gave me the tools that I needed to analyze my relationship with Mike and the strength to leave the relationship behind. When I read feminist literature, I no longer felt so isolated and I found models for freeing myself. Feminism also taught me that survival means getting angry, means placing the blame on the person who does the violence, means saying no.

Finally, Mike's own behavior helped me to break away from him. Although he started dating someone else toward the end of our relationship, I still found it difficult to stay away from him. We slept together for a long time into his new relationship, and this sexual dimension did not end until I finally could tell him that I'd had enough.

At some point, I had to lie one too many times to cover up Mike's behavior. He became more and more volatile. He smashed his fist through his new girlfriend's wall. I had believed until that point that I was the only woman who could really "drive" him to violence.

Two years ago I stopped drinking and began a recovery program for alcoholism. Recovery helped me to put the final pieces in place, to explain how I had stayed in such an abusive relationship. Recovery also helped me to recognize abusive patterns in my own behavior and how to deal with anger before it swept me away.

I can look back on my relationship not with shame but with pride. I am proud of my own courage, which enabled me to grow strong. I am proud that I had the strength to say no to an abusive relationship. I can look back at my younger self and see in her the beginnings of a fighter, someone who would insist that she deserved something better than violence. That woman became someone who loves herself enough to settle for nothing less than happiness and self-respect.

II

The Context of Dating Violence

Domination and Control: The Social Context of Dating Violence

Denise Gamache

The first time it happened, I was about fourteen and my boyfriend was sixteen. He saw me hug my brother in the hall at school, but he didn't know it was my brother 'cause we'd just started dating. He drug me out of school, behind a store and just beat me up—literally. He said if anyone asked me what happened, to tell 'em I got into a fight with someone; not to dare tell anyone he hit me.　　　　　　　　　　　　　　　　　*—Eleventh-grade girl*

An important outcome of the feminist movement in the early 1970s was the identification of battering, or domestic violence, as a significant social problem in America. In order to develop strategies that would effectively intervene and prevent further violence, researchers and activists sought to determine the causes of wife battering. Sociologists cited several cultural factors that they believed contributed to the occurrence and social tolerance of violence against wives: the historical tradition of patriarchal rule over wives and children, a legal tradition of "wife chastisement" laws, which acknowledged a permissible level of physical abuse, and the high value placed on privacy combined with rejection of outside interference in family matters (Dobash and Dobash, 1978). Researchers who surveyed violence in U.S. families concluded that the level was so great and the approval of violence against family members was so widespread, they were justified in calling the marriage license a hitting license (Gelles and Straus, 1988).

These early studies noted that unmarried couples experienced a rate of physical violence equivalent to married couples, raising questions about the onset and extent of violence in courtship and dating relationships among adults. This research led to investigations of the dating experiences of adolescents. Since 1981, several studies have been conducted with college and high school populations to determine the level and causes of violence in these intimate heterosexual relationships. Recent research has also documented the occurrence of violence in relationships of young gay men and lesbians (Waterman, Dawson and Bologna, 1989). This research provides useful information regarding the ways in which abusive dating relationships resemble and differ from violent marriages. Information about dating violence has also been gathered by activists in the battered women's shelter movement. Since their inception in the early 1970s, battered women's shelters and programs have served adult victims regardless of marital status. Most of these programs have also received requests for aid from juvenile victims, which led them to examine and respond to the phenomenon of battering in very young dating couples. A few organizations around the country initiated specific efforts to reach young people, usually through presentations in local high schools and colleges. The perspective on dating violence presented in this article was developed through interviews with teachers, school counselors and youth workers involved in a violence prevention project, a survey of the available literature, and interviews with adolescents and adults, many of whom were victims of dating violence and whose comments are included in the text.

The Social Causes of Dating Violence

After a while, when it starts getting worse, you get scared to leave him. I'd tell my boyfriend I didn't want to go out with him anymore, and it would get worse. He'd start slapping me and say 'I'm not gonna quit till you tell me you're not leaving.'   —*Eleventh-grade girl*

Violence in relationships is reinforced by cultural beliefs that facilitate its occurrence. Individuals and groups use violence to establish or maintain systems of power and control over others. Violence is easier to justify and more socially tolerated when directed at "appropriate" victims, that is, those viewed by the culture as deserving of this treatment. In general, power relationships are organized into hierarchical patterns in which some individuals have greater power than others due to their ascribed status, which brings greater access to resources and the ability to define and control the rules of the hierarchy. These patterns are so pervasive that it appears normal and natural for some people to dominate and for others to be subordinate. Any challenge to those in power is viewed as a threat to the natural order, with violence likely to be used in its defense. The rigidity of these systems also may leave subordinate groups with few perceived or actual alternatives to violence when attempting to alter the power imbalance. Historically and in the present, systems of oppression based on hierarchies of race, religion, class, sexual preference or ethnicity tolerate and engender violence against individuals assigned the subordinate status. Violence in dating relationships and marriages is reinforced by cultural norms that support the need for a hierarchy of power in human relationships. The ideals of equality and nonviolence remain in conflict with persistent beliefs that domination is normal. Individuals who strongly adhere to this belief are most likely to see violence as acceptable behavior and use it to maintain their position and control over others. Same-sex relationships can also become violent if one of the partners seeks to dominate the other.

In intimate relationships between men and women, the use of violence by males is particularly reinforced by sexism, the ideology of male supremacy and superiority. Patriarchy, the institutionalization of male dominance over women in both the public and private spheres, has been the most widespread cultural expression of hierarchy based on sex. Indeed, some historians argue that the subjugation of women by men in the ancient world served as the model for the development of later forms of oppression (Lerner, 1986). The patriarchal family, still the basic unit in most cultures today, continues to express and generate rules and values affirming the primacy of the male's interests in relation to his female partner or children. Research on moral development supports the theory that male aggression is linked to their socialization toward a hierarchical ordering of human relationships that views interdependency as threatening (Gilligan, 1982). Moreover, shifts toward egalitarian relations between the sexes in family life have not altered basic male dominance in the public realm. Similarly, public policies that have enlarged women's rights have not always changed the nature of male-female relations within the family (Lerner, 1986).

Influenced by these cultural norms, batterers articulate strong beliefs that they have the right to control or punish their partners for what they perceive as hostile or harmful behavior.

These cultural norms have also resulted in policies and practices within our religious, judicial, legal and social institutions that keep women trapped in abusive relationships and, at worst, support the batterer's use of violence. For example, some clergy still preach that wives should be subservient to husbands, even abusive ones; judges fail to enforce their own court orders against batterers who continue to harass their victims; men of color who batter are arrested more often than white, middle-class men; divorced women with children cannot find affordable day care and women generally work at lower paid jobs than men. These cultural facilitators (exacerbated by racism and women's lack of economic power) allow battering to continue against a specific victim and explain in part the disproportionate number of women as victims. This cultural context explains how some men come to believe that violence against their female partners will be supported or at least tolerated (Pence, 1987).

In addition, the use of violence typically reaps consequences that are defined and experienced as rewarding by the abuser. Repeated emotional and physical violence tends to ensure that victims will do anything to please the abuser and avoid further violence. Being in control increases one's self-esteem and allows the exaction of revenge for real or imagined wrongs (Gelles and Straus, 1988).

The interaction between sexism and racism and the unique historic experiences of oppression of different communities of women of color may lead them to confront male dominance and abuse differently (Schechter, 1982; Smith and Stewart, 1983). In addition to responses aimed at avoiding further violence, women of color may adopt a protective response toward their male partners. This reflects socialization to "stick by" their men to ensure the survival of family and community in the face of the discrimination and unfair treatment often encountered in dealings with white social institutions (Schechter, 1982; White, 1985).

Given the existing social context, most batterers experience few immediate negative consequences that might motivate them to change their behavior. In order to end battering, researchers and activists alike argue for changes in the structural and cultural arrangements in society that perpetuate it (Dobash and Dobash, 1979; Pence, 1987).

Violence in adolescent dating relationships appears to stem from these same social causes—a logical conclusion as dating functions to allow rehearsal of the roles teens expect to assume in adult relationships. Research studies of both high school and college students found that abuse is more likely in serious rather than casual dating situations (Henton, Cate, Koval, Lloyd and Christopher, 1983; Jones, 1987; Laner and Thompson, 1982). The violence often is initiated when the couple involved perceives that they have entered into an exclusive, marriage-like relationship. This shift in status seems to elicit expectations tied to gender, including the male's right to control his partner and the female's obligation to yield to his wishes. As the following description of violent dating relationships demonstrates, adolescent batterers express similar beliefs in their right to control female partners and employ tactics similar to adult batterers to maintain this position.

The Dynamics of Violent Dating Relationships

Research studies have found that approximately one out of ten high school students had experienced physical violence in dating relationships. Among college students, the figure rises to twenty-two percent, equivalent to the rate for adults (Cate, et al., 1982; Henton, et al., 1983; Makepeace, 1981; Roscoe and Callahan, 1985). A study comparing the responses of high school students with college students concluded that the phenomenon of dating violence in both groups is very similar (Roscoe and Callahan, 1985).

While both young men and women report having inflicted and received physical abuse, the experience and consequences are not equal. Females are more likely to be the victims of severe forms of physical violence and sexual violence (Lane and Gwartney-Gibbs, 1985; Roscoe and Callahan, 1985). While neither a boy or girl in early adolescence may possess the physical ability to dominate the other, the high school years mark the beginning of physical and social power advantages for most males. A slap or punch delivered by an adolescent male has greater physical and emotional effect on his female partner than the reverse. For example, boys report feeling fear much less frequently than girls when asked about their reactions to violent incidents (Jones, 1987). Although some girls may continue to use violence, they usually learn that this response is increasingly unsuccessful. Simultaneously, female socialization reinforces subordination to males, especially in intimate relationships. Additionally, the still common practice of girls primarily dating older boys heightens these power inequities. Acts of emotional or physical violence by either partner in a dating relationship should not be excused or tolerated. However, to understand and prevent systematic dating violence it is important to acknowledge that males are more often in a position to maintain control and therefore more likely to perpetuate battering.

The incidence of battering in gay and lesbian teen relationships suggests the vulnerability of socially isolated couples to the pervasive dynamics of domination and control in intimate relationships in our society.

Because marriage affords an abuser greater proximity and economic control of his victim, it is harder to imagine how battering can occur in dating situations and why a victim feels trapped in the relationship. Specific factors in adolescent and female development contribute to the young victim's vulnerability to entrapment. Pressure to conform to peer group norms and pressure from the sexual intensity of adolescence contribute to an emphasis on having a dating partner. Adolescent rigidity in conforming to female gender role expectations includes the expectation that her status depends on her attachment to a male, and on his status. Teenage women are vulnerable because of the double standard of sexual morality for women and the resulting fear of a "bad reputation" among peers. Female socialization also leads young women to assume responsibility for solving problems in the relationship. Young women usually have not had dating and sexual experience on which to base decisions or to trust themselves to take actions on their own behalf in a relationship. Teens tend to confuse control and jealousy with love. Teens also tend to reject assistance from adult authorities and rely only on peers.

In addition, the following experiences described by young women illustrate the actions taken by abusers to establish their control in the relationship.

Physical Abuse

He didn't threaten me; he just did it. He didn't even warn me he was going to hit me. It was so weird, this look that he got. It was either this real glare, or else it was this real empty blank, like he had nothing inside him. I knew he was feeling this resentment against me and that things were gonna happen.

—College freshman

Teenage victims describe the same range of violent experiences that their adult counterparts do: from slaps and shoves to beatings and attacks with weapons. Clearly, adults have been slow to recognize the seriousness of the violence and to intervene to end it. Each year, an alarming number of young women are murdered by their boyfriends. According to the latest Federal Bureau of Investigation statistics, twenty percent of female homicide victims are between fifteen and twenty-four (Kessner, 1988). Typically, after these tragedies occur, investigation into the nature of the dating relationships reveals patterns of control and physical abuse.

Violence is a powerful means of enforcing compliance, and in many cases, incidents of overt violence may be relatively infrequent as the desired control over the victim can be achieved through other coercive acts.

Emotional Abuse

Lots of times he told me I deserved it. Most of the time he said that I deserved to be treated that way because I was such a whore, such a bitch and stuff. So he almost gloated. It made him feel really powerful. I started feeling real inadequate. My grades went down dramatically. I missed class a lot, because I felt sick—stomach stuff, real nervous stuff. I always felt like a nervous wreck. It was probably a deep depression, but I started feeling sleepy all the time, all I wanted to do was stay in bed. It just seemed like everything just kept going down, down, down.   —College freshman

The insults and mind games that play a major part in battering seem intended to destroy the victim's independence and self-esteem so that she will comply with demands and feel she has no other options besides this relationship. Frequently the girl is told, "No one else will ever want you." The message is "even though you are worthless, because I love you I'll put up with you if you just do what I say." The degradation, humiliation and disrespect attack the girl's feelings of self-worth. This is especially powerful coming from a person she loves and on whom she feels dependent.

It is very confusing for the victim to be told she is worthless by the same person expressing great love for her. The freshman quoted here spoke of her struggle to retain her self-confidence in the face of these attacks. She is a bright, articulate young woman and verbally responded to his insults by asserting that she didn't believe him, that he was just being mean because he was angry.

Yet even for her, the continuous negative messages eventually resulted in depression and immobility.

Coercion and Threats

A student in our college told me that her boyfriend would come into her classes and take her out. He would say to the teacher that he was her probation officer. This was embarrassing for her, but she knew if she said he wasn't, she would pay horribly. It got to the point that he knew her schedule every day, all day.   —*College adviser*

Adolescent abusers use a variety of threats to enforce their demands. Direct threats are made against the victim or her family. An abuser's suicide threats are very frightening to a victim, particularly when he has the means readily available or has made attempts in the past. Abusers may coerce compliance by threatening to expose embarrassing secrets, often regarding the girl's sexual behavior, to her family or to schoolmates.

An abuser may also force his girlfriend to steal money from her parents or give him money she's earned. Some girls have been urged or coerced by boyfriends to engage in illegal acts, such as shoplifting and drug dealing, in order to get money for him or to support them both. Threats to report her illegal activity add to the abusers' ability to control their girlfriends.

The following incident was related by a high school counselor in a small midwestern city. One of the senior boys, a popular athlete, had dated several girls. The counselor was approached by one of the girls for help in dealing with a sexual experience that had occurred on her date with the boy. In the counselor's view, the girl had been raped, although she was having trouble labeling the incident as such. In addition, the boy had contacted the girls he had dated and asked each to participate in making a pornographic video for which he would pay them. In her attempts to hold the boy accountable for his behavior, the counselor found it very difficult to organize the girls' responses because of their shame about the rapes, for which they blamed themselves and because the boy had spread gossip about their sexual behavior. Although this attempt was thwarted, abusers who succeed in manipulating their girlfriends into illegal or embarrassing acts can use their knowledge of these activities for further blackmail and coercion.

Intimidation

He'd say, "If you don't talk to me, I'll come up there and bust up your house."

—Eleventh-grade girl

One thing he did all the time. We'd be lying in bed and he'd just decide to kick me out of the house and make me leave, no matter what time it was— three a.m., whatever—and so I'd have to get out.　　*—College freshman*

Like adult abusers, teenage boys engage in a variety of acts designed to frighten their victims. They may use their greater size to make frightening gestures, smash things, display weapons or objects or drive crazily. Intimidation serves as a reminder to the victim that the abuser has the power to enforce his will should she refuse to comply. Particularly in public situations when overt violence would be observed by others, abusers use intimidating looks or gestures to communicate their wishes.

Minimizing, Denying, Blaming

You hear some kids say, "Hey I beat up on my old lady." Seems like they're trying to be all big and bad for some reason. . . . "Yeah, she ain't gonna use me 'cause she went out with someone else."

—Ninth-grade boy

He knows that he needs help, and he was gonna go and get help, but he didn't.　　　　　　*—Twelfth-grade girl*

Teenage abusers mirror their adult counterparts in refusing to accept responsibility for their actions and in seeking to blame their victims for the abuse. Very often the boy's behavior is blamed on jealousy and almost any action on the girl's part is labeled as provocative, whether talking to another boy, not being home when he calls or going out with girlfriends (because he knows she'll "pick up guys"). Both high school and college-age students view jealousy as a major cause of dating violence (Makepeace, 1981; Roscoe and Callahan, 1985).

An abusive boyfriend seeks greater and greater control over his victim in the name of love. He loves her so much that he can't stand for her to spend time with others, especially other guys. He's jealous of her friends and her family; he wants to have her all to himself. Teens often feel flattered by these demands and view them as proof of passion, a view reinforced in our society. Jealousy is often accepted as an excuse for abusive behavior in relationships. In cases involving so-called crimes of passion, sympathy and sometimes leniency are accorded to the perpetrators, particularly when victims, usually female, have engaged in behavior likely to arouse sexual jealousy.

Sexual Abuse

He was a senior, a jock, the kind of guy to bring home to Mom, basically the all-American guy. We'd been dating for a few months; everything was fine. Then we went to a wedding in the small town he came from. I was really nervous 'cause it was the first time I had met his family. I didn't know anyone there, so I was quieter than normal, and he was getting upset with me 'cause I wasn't "performing." Then some guys I happened to know from a fraternity showed up which made me more comfortable 'cause there were finally some people I knew. He got mad, dragged me out and yelled at me. Then he drove me out into the country, driving crazy. Finally he stopped. I didn't know where we were; I was hysterical. I said, "What do you want from me?" He said, "I want you to suck my cock." And I did. What else could I do? I had never seen him like that. We had been intimate, but had never done that before.   —College sophomore

In several studies, teens reported that conflicts about sex often led to violence (Lane and Gwartney-Gibbs, 1985). Dating involves many negotiations around sexual behavior, for example, whether to have sex, which sex acts are acceptable, responsibility for birth control and safe sex to prevent AIDS. Although not always the case, abusive boyfriends are likely to use their power to coerce compliance in sexual matters as in other facets of their relationships.

Due to lack of experience and often limited education about sexuality, many teens are confused about what is appropriate sexual behavior in a relationship. It is often difficult for young women to identify sexual abuse in their relationships and to decide how to respond. The threat or use of physical violence often renders them unable to challenge the sexual abuse, which continues unchecked. An abuser may also try to manipulate or coerce his girlfriend into prostitution.

While the impact of ongoing sexually abusive relationships has not been studied with adolescent populations, research on adults found that compared to other battered women, sexually abused battered women were significantly more severely injured, frequently beaten, ashamed of their bodies, likely to have stress-related physical symptoms, likely to blame themselves for the abuse and most important, more in danger of being the victim or perpetrator of homicide (Campbell, 1987).

Isolation

At first it was pretty normal, nonchalant. The more I saw him, the more he decided he wanted these real strict things. I couldn't look at anybody; I couldn't talk to anybody, go out anyplace without him. I couldn't do anything unless it was with him or unless he knew about it.   —*College freshman*

Abusers devote exorbitant amounts of energy and time toward surveillance of their victims. In high school, a boy may rely on reports from his friends regarding his girlfriend's daily activities. He may also employ phone calls to keep tabs on her whereabouts or to force her to stay home, harassing or punishing a girl if she's not home when he calls, until gradually she restricts her activities to be there "just in case he calls" and thus avoid another fight.

This surveillance can be carried to extremes as demonstrated by the experience of a woman who, upon graduation from high school, enrolled in a small college halfway across the country in order to escape from her abusive boyfriend. Shortly after her arrival on campus, she was terrified to discover that the boy had not only enrolled there, but had also switched his major to hers— home economics. She endured a frightening semester, on guard at all times to avoid being caught alone by him. Although he did not attack her directly, his monitoring was constant. He was in almost all of her classes and followed her around campus. Luckily, he eventually stopped pursuing her and did not return after the semester break. However, she felt that her safety was so threatened by him that she did not return home to visit until years later after she was married.

The use of isolation increases the abuser's control in several ways. As other friendship ties are broken, the victim becomes more emotionally dependent on him. Without other perspectives to help her make sense of her experiences, she may come to accept his excuses and blame herself for the violence. When the couple is socially isolated, incidents of physical abuse are more easily perpetrated and hidden.

The end result of battering is that the victim's behavior eventually follows the abuser's guidelines, and she often must protect herself by acting as she thinks he wishes, even when these actions are not in her best interest. She may even deny the abuse to her family and/or friends. As a result outsiders often find it confusing and difficult to understand her behavior.

Reactions of friends may be supportive or may add to the victim's isolation. Friends may not be able to resist the abuser's efforts to isolate her from them. Friends may share the same expectations of relationships and the importance of keeping a boyfriend happy, leading them to expect her to tolerate and minimize the abuse and indicating that this is what is necessary to keep a boyfriend, and the importance of keeping him happy.

Intervention and Prevention

Parents go overprotective at that point. You work so hard to get your independence. One thing like that could just blow it all, and you'd have to start all over again. If you just leave it and don't tell your parents, you still have your independence. . . . If you get badly scared, like a person plays bad mind games on you . . . you can turn to someone else that won't take away your independence.   —*Eleventh-grade girl*

I know a lot of people who are in violent relationships, and they don't know what they should do; when they had the class [about dating violence], they had a chance to at least get some basic information about what they could possibly do.   —*Tenth-grade girl*

All battered women must overcome the emotional effects of victimization and the societal barriers that impede their escape in order to safely exit from a violent relationship. However, there are aspects of dating situations that pose unique problems, especially if the victim is legally a juvenile. The young women in these stories escaped the violence in their relationships in various ways. Often, ethnic, cultural and class differences affected their perceptions of options. Typically the girls told no adult. Sometimes friends or brothers of the abused girl beat up the boyfriend or warned him away from her. In some cases, new circumstances in the girl's or boy's life put physical distance between them. While these resolutions stopped the violence, they probably did little to change the abuser's behavior in future relationships. Often the girls endured the abuse for a long time, even after they recognized that they were being abused, because they simply didn't know where to turn for help. And often the abuse and harassment continue after the relationship has ended for the same reason. Many problems currently exist in our response, or lack of response, to violence in dating relationships.

When the victims and abusers in dating relationships are legally adults, they usually have access to the same legal and social services as married adults. Effective intervention strategies with victims incorporate education about battering, emotional support to counteract its effects and a practical plan offering as much protection as possible from further assaults. This can include use of emergency shelters, obtaining a restraining order, prosecuting the assailant, staying with friends and family, alerting one's employer, and so forth.

Interventions with the adult abuser usually rely on sanctions imposed by the community legal system, such as arrest or probation conditions. Batterer's programs can offer education and emotional support to reinforce egalitarian and nonviolent models of relating.

Intervening in violent relationships between juveniles poses unique problems for the adults most often concerned—parents, teachers, counselors and youth workers. The comment introducing this section illustrates one of the major difficulties. At this stage of development, adolescents are reluctant to confide in any adult, but particularly parents, fearing, rightly or wrongly, a loss of their independence. In one study, a quarter of the high school students told no one, only twenty-six percent told their parents and sixty-six percent reported the abuse to friends (Henton, et al., 1983).

If the couple attends the same high school, sometimes the only one in the community, the victim may feel trapped and vulnerable to further violence should she attempt to end the relationship. A victim may feel that seeking help from school counselors or administrators will be useless, particularly when schools have not publicly addressed this problem or communicated a willingness or ability to respond.

Juvenile victims who do seek assistance may not have access to the same legal or social services available to adults. Many battered women's shelters cannot house juveniles unless they are emancipated, usually defined as maintaining a separate residence from their parents or having a child. Temporary restraining orders may be unavailable to juveniles unless the application is made by their parents. Most communities fail to target young people in their outreach efforts and lack programs for juvenile victims that provide education about battering and emotional support. Likewise, juvenile courts and social services have paid little attention to adolescent abusers.

If we are to prevent further violence and promote early, effective intervention, communities must create solutions to the unique problems posed by violence in adolescent relationships. All adults in contact with teens—parents, teachers, school counselors, nurses, youth workers, religious leaders—must develop appropriate opportunities to provide education about the causes and effects of dating violence and to promote ethical development that rejects the use of violence to control others. It is important that social institutions with the greatest contact with adolescents, particularly schools, plan a response to adolescent victims and abusers in coordination with local community resources that maximize the victim's safety while confronting and stopping the abuse.

In the past ten years, curriculum materials and innovative programs have been developed to provide basic information on dating violence and promote egalitarian, nonviolent relationships (Dating Violence Intervention Project, 1988; Gamache and Weiner, 1988; B. Levy, 1984; R.A.P.P., 1986). Violence prevention projects have been instituted in many locations to introduce curriculum activities directly into junior and senior high classrooms in an attempt to reach all teens, as all are at risk. However, education alone will not be effective unless social arrangements that overtly or subtly support male domination are altered. An additional goal of many primary prevention projects is to challenge teens toward social action to change social policies that perpetuate violence.

Much is understood about the causes of violence in dating relationships; much can be done to prevent it. Young people who are involved in violent dating relationships express greater acceptance of violence in marriages (Cate, et al., 1982; Henton, et al., 1983). At present, little attention is paid to this social problem, and few communities have developed strategies to intervene with victims or abusers. This failure dooms many young people to needless suffering and injury. Serious efforts must be intitiated to confront this violence. By effectively responding to the abuse of power in adolescent dating, a community can influence the nature of adult intimate relationships as well as create a safer community for young people.

The Abused Black Woman:
Challenging a Legacy of Pain

Evelyn C. White

This article is excerpted from Chain Chain Change: *For Black Women Dealing with Physical and Emotional Abuse. In the book, Evelyn C. White wrote about the context of battering relationships for black women. Although written for adult women, her words are relevant for black teens as well.*

In addition, Barrie Levy asked Ms. White her views about the differences between teen and adult black women who deal with violence in intimate relationships, which is presented below as an introduction to the excerpt.

Levy: In general, what do you think are the key differences between adult and adolescent black women's experiences with violence in their relationships?

White: I think that a key difference between the experience of battering for black teens and for black adults is the loss of the age of innocence. Like all teenagers, black teenagers are romantic about their dreams and the possibilities for their lives, but their dreams often are crushed by violence. Adult black women have lived long enough to witness and experience the limits for black women in our society. For black girls, however, the experience of having their hopes and aspirations stunted by violence is terribly painful and disillusioning. For example, a fifteen-year-old black girl wanted to be a doctor and go to medical school. A goal like this requires a lot of support from others. She became involved with a young man who was verbally abusive, telling her she was "stupid" and that a "black girl can't become a doctor." At an impressionable age, this girl's self-doubts grew until they undermined her confidence, and she gave up her dreams.

I am using the term "girl" not to belittle black teens but to give them an identity they seldom have a chance to claim. So often, they are thrust into adult concerns and pains at an early age. This affects girls who also suffer the stresses and strains of poverty, but even middle-class girls are under enormous pressure. I want so much for black girls to have a girlhood—in the sense of being protected and carefree—and not be surrounded with adult fears and worries, such as, "How do I deal with my boyfriend who beats me?" or "Can I protect my sister from my mom's boyfriend who raped me?" I want to reclaim an age of innocence for black girls which they don't experience today.

Levy: Adolescence is a stage in our lives when we develop our identities, especially our identities as women. How do you think this identity development is affected by being a black young woman, and by the realities of black young women's lives? How does this affect young women's vulnerability to violence in their relationships?

White: Young black girls get conflicting messages about their identities. A girl's identity is not just based on who or what she believes she is, but also what society tells black girls they are. This is extremely painful because I believe that the first message black girls get is that they aren't good enough. I refer readers to Toni Morrison's novel, *The Bluest Eye,* for a good illustration of this. Morrison writes about the devastation a young black girl experienced because she was not born with blue eyes. I highly recommend that those wishing to counsel young black girls read this book in order to better understand the social context in which we grow up. It is the rare black girl who can develop her own identity outside the external societal forces, both black and white, that tell her what she should be. For instance, when I was thirteen I planned to be a prison warden when I grew up, even though my interest was in the arts. This decision was based on what I learned from society: that this job would be a way to help black people, the assumption being that most black people ended up behind bars. It was not until I got to college, away from the pressures of my environment, that I learned to develop my own sense of self. And lo and behold I discovered that I didn't want to become a prison warden but rather a theater lighting designer, which I did for several years with great satisfaction. I was lucky in that my true self was able to rise up from the messages I had been given. I think that this inability to find our own voice, our own being, keeps black girls vulnerable to the demands and expectations of others that are so prevalent in abusive relationships.

We are displaced people, displaced from our true heritage, our culture, our past. This is destroying us. We are African people who were made slaves; we were not born slaves. We had a long, proud history before slavery ever happened. Unfortunately, we have very little contact anymore with the black femaleness of royalty, regalness, being truly honored. Things would change if every young black girl could go to Africa, to see the achievements of black women. This is the road to healing; we must change how we see ourselves, and we must break the image imposed on black people that violence and being black are synonymous. We must help black girls begin to believe that they deserve better so that they can define and achieve their own dreams and aspirations.

Levy: In *Chain Chain Change*, you wrote about the impact of the ratio of marriageable black men to marriageable black women. Does this affect teens as well?

White: I think that young black girls are also affected by their awareness of the strains and stresses on black men. The concept of black men being an "endangered species" has been a major focus of the media and of sociological studies in recent years. This notion of black men being on the verge of annihilation essentially makes black girls make compromises in their relationships that they might not make under normal circumstances. I recently read in a Boston newspaper about a young black girl who, when asked why she had had a baby so young, responded, "because the guys in my neighborhood don't live to be twenty-five." This attitude is comparable to that of adult black women who have historically made compromises in their relationships because of the scarcity of black men.

Levy: Do you believe that relationships and communication between mothers and daughters is important in preventing dating violence for black teens?

White: It is absolutely critical that black mothers start talking to their daughters about the real and psychic violence that is visited upon black women. I think that there has been far too much silence about the reality of black female life. Too many black girls are growing up with a "Brady Bunch" image of life and are left utterly unprepared for the reality of being black and female. This is not to say that black mothers have to depict their lives as a cauldron of negativity and despair, because that is not the reality either. There are many magnificent, glorious and wonderful aspects of our lives. Not enough mothers tell their daughters about the true victories, how they have been able to overcome the obstacles. Not enough black children know their histories, what their parents have accomplished.

It is essential that we confront and talk about the impact of violence, racism, sexism, and the vast numbers of other societal inequities. We were taken from Africa, we were enslaved, we were beaten, we were forbidden to read or write—and, as Maya Angelou has said, still we rise. Look at what black women have accomplished with all these burdens—imagine what we could have done without the shackles. Our cultural situation today is that we live in a society that gives us negativity and distortions about ourselves. White society tries to convince us to replace what is missing in our lives with a culture that is not ours. But what is missing is the lost opportunities of our ancestors. We need to openly grieve with our families, we must acknowledge the real pain of oppression, and we must not be susceptible to the fake remedy for that pain; that is, the drugs and alcohol.

It is only when this generational silence around our pain is broken that black girls can begin their lives in a better position than their mothers. And isn't that, after all, what our ancestors died for, for us to be better off than they?

Black parents must talk to their children early, especially the girls, about self-respect and the negativity that is out there surrounding black life. We must do something about the fact that generation after generation of black girls grow up hating themselves because they do not have blond hair and blue eyes. Part of the task of confronting this problem is for black mothers to be honest about their own self-hatred, to admit that *they too* longed for blond hair and blue eyes when they were little girls. By revealing this and other self-hatreds early on they give their daughters greater chances to heal and become whole, to get the message that they are beautiful in their blackness at age three instead of thirty-three. It is important that a strong sense of self be developed in black girls at the earliest age possible. This can be done through black cultural activities, black-oriented toys, and by making sure that their sons and daughters see blacks in a positive light. The earlier that black children get the message that they are valued, the better the chances of avoiding intraracial violence. We have to come to grips with class and color issues in the black community that create divisiveness. We have to get real about the fact that this culture has taught us to hate ourselves and that, in combination with racism, contributes mightily to the pain and agony we suffer. And we must find ways to give black girls the strength to say to their young men, "I come from a history of women who have gone through real pain, not this TV 'bust 'em up' kind of pain. There is no place in my life for your violence."

Levy: Do you have any advice for people who work with black teens or for their parents?

White: My disaffection with many programs and services for black teens is that they are off the mark. What young black girls need is the chance to develop self-esteem. Young black girls and young black boys must be able to believe, like Jesse Jackson says, that they are somebody, that they have a future, that they can realize their dreams. With this the violence will stop. The more black teens value themselves, the less likely they are going to treat someone else badly. They must learn to take care of themselves, the way they protect their sneakers or their jeans. Black teens say, "Nobody's going to mess up my sneakers." They should be able to say the same thing about their lives.

. . .

(Excerpt from Chain Chain Change)

In 1928, black American writer and folklorist Zora Neale Hurston wrote an essay, "How It Feels To Be Colored Me." Today, nearly sixty years later, her words are still very much needed to help black women overcome the destructive images and unrealistic expectations that contribute to our physical and emotional abuse.

I am not tragically colored. There is no great sorrow lurking behind my eyes. I do not mind at all. I do not belong to the sobbing school of Negrohood who hold that nature somehow has given them a lowdown dirty deal and whose feelings are all hurt about it. Even in the helter-skelter skirmish that is my life, I have seen that the world is to the strong regardless of a little pigmenta-

tion more or less. No, I do not weep at the world. . . . I am too busy sharpening my oyster knife. (Hurston, 1976).

Images and Expectations of Black Women

The image of black women as long-suffering victims can keep us passive and confused about the abuse in our lives. Not only do we experience these feelings in our intimate relationships, but they impact our daily experiences as well.

In a contemporary parallel to Hurston's essay, noted black feminist scholar Barbara Smith points out, ". . . it is not something we have done that has heaped this psychic violence and material abuse upon us, but the very fact, that because of who we are, we are multiply oppressed" (Smith, 1983).

And who are we? Abolitionist Sojourner Truth, educator Mary McLeod Bethune, choreographer Katharine Dunham, playwright Lorraine Hansberry, astronaut Mae Jemison, tennis champion Zina Garrison, politician Shirley Chisholm, activist Angela Davis and academician Barbara Jordan are all part of our black female heritage. Yet too often are the images of black women reduced to the big-bosomed slave "mammy" or the wigged and high-heeled streetwalker with equally stereotypical "evil," "domineering" and "bitchy" images in between.

The often repeated reponse that black women are honored within our communities is far too simplistic. It does not address the reality of the many hardships that go along with being black and female. For instance, according to FBI statistics, we are at a greater risk of being raped than any other group; fifty-seven percent of us raise our children alone; because of the job discrimination we suffer, our children can expect to spend over five years of their childhood as "have nots" compared to the average white child who will spend only ten months of his or her life in poverty (Norton, 1985). We have been "honored" to endure these and other burdens that have often kept us from participating fully in life. And we have done so, not because we like being burdened, but because sexist and racist social systems have frequently given us little choice.

The images and expectations of black women are actually both *super-* and *sub-*human. This conflict has created many myths and stereotypes that cause confusion about our own identity and make us targets for abuse. Like Shug Avery in Alice Walker's *The*

Color Purple, black women are considered wild—but also rigid and "proper." We are unattractive—but exotic, like Vanessa Williams, the first black Miss America. We are passive—but rabble-rousing like political activist Flo Kennedy. We are streetwise—but insipid like Prissy who "didn't know nothin' about birthin' no babies" in *Gone With the Wind*. We are considered evil, but self-sacrificing; stupid but conniving; domineering while at the same time obedient to our men; and sexually inhibited, yet promiscuous. Covered by what is considered our seductively rich, but repulsive brown skin, black women are perceived as inviting but armored. Society finds it difficult to believe that we really need physical or emotional support like all women of all races.

These stereotypes about black women contribute to the confusion, inferiority and insecurity that we already feel because of the abuse in our lives. These negative and often conflicting images may make us wonder who we really are and what is really expected of us from our partner and society.

There are many passionate and celebratory aspects of our lives. Black women are as diverse in our ways of being as the rest of society. But this is easily forgotten, like many of our heroines, in the face of persistent messages that tell us our hair is too kinky, our behinds too wide and our tempers too quick.

The Abusers

Because of institutionalized and individual racism in American society, black men, in particular, have experienced much of the powerlessness, low self-esteem, feelings of ineffectiveness and insecurity that characterize many abusive men. In *The Third Life of Grange Copeland*, Alice Walker writes with eloquent, insightful passion about the devastating effects of racism on a Southern black family. She explains, but by no means excuses, the violent actions that some black men direct toward black women—the individuals *least* responsible for their suffering.

His crushed pride, his battered ego, made him drive Mem away from school-teaching. Her knowledge reflected badly on a husband who could scarcely read and write. It was his great ignorance that sent her into white homes as a domestic, his need to bring her down to his level! It was his rage at himself, and his life and his world that made him beat her for an imaginary attraction she aroused in other men, crackers, although she was not party to any of it.

His rage and his anger and his frustration ruled. His rage could and did blame everything, everything *on her.*

Clearly the experiences of slavery, lynchings, segregation, imprisonment and daily urban living have taken their toll on black men. Historically viewed by whites as rapists, pimps, hustlers, superstuds and superathletes, black men are some of the most exploited and mistreated members of American society.

Many black men feel, for good reason, that they have no power and little impact on the culture at large. Thus they are more likely to demand that their partners and family members treat them like a man and show them respect. Any challenge, any question from his partner can be interpreted as yet another attempt to chip away at his already insecure and fragile sense of self. For black men know that regardless of how hard they work, most will never become part of the power structure of American society. And the few who do pay a price for their "success" with increased physical and mental stress.

The early deaths, high unemployment rate and excessive imprisonment of black men are directly related to racism in this society. In addition, racism has contributed to a statistic with far-reaching implications for the relationships between black women and black men. According to a recent report from the NAACP Legal Defense and Education Fund, among blacks between the ages of twenty and twenty-four there are only forty-five "marriageable" males for every hundred females, largely because of unemployment and incarceration (*New York Times,* May 19, 1985). When one considers the existence of gay black men and those who choose to be involved with non-black women, the number of black men available for relationships with black women becomes even less. This situation is very significant in terms of the tensions that exist between black women and black men.

The average black man frequently struggles to provide his family with basic necessities. He looks for role models in the culture and finds, for the most part, athletes, entertainers, drug addicts, and armed robbers—the extreme successes and failures within society. The black man may decide that if nothing else he will at least control what happens in the home and within his family. He may behave abusively because, like most men, he has not learned how to express his pain, frustration, lack of confidence and insecurity about his impotence in the world. But abusing those he loves only serves to make him feel worse, not better, about himself. For he has confirmed the racist stereotype about the violent nature of black men. He may come to believe that he deserves to be feared as much as society fears him.

The Black Woman's Response

Black women live in the same racist society that black men do and therefore cannot help but be sympathetic to what they suffer. We know that the black family has been damaged by slavery, lynchings and systematized social, economic and educational discrimination. Though we have surely been divided as black men and women, our mutual suffering has prevented us from completely turning our backs on each other.

Black women have been conditioned to repair the damage that has been done to black families because we feel it is our responsibility to keep the family together at all costs. We have been willing to let our children grow up with even imperfect role models because black men are scarce in our communities.

The importance of even the facade of stability in family life was recently emphasized very poignantly by fifty-one black children in Chicago. They took out a newspaper ad begging their absent fathers to show up so they could be loved and honored on Father's Day (*Seattle Times*, June 15, 1985). In addition to the hardships we will endure for our children, we do not personally wish to give up the tenderness and affection that even abusive men express some of the time. Black women, like all human beings, desire love, attention and protection.

However, because we are sensitive to the effects of racism and the victimization of black men, does *not* mean that we should continue to endure abuse from our partners. As the late poet Pat Parker wrote:

> Brother
> I don't want to hear
> about
> how *my* real enemy
> is the system.
> i'm no genius,
> but i do know
> that system

> you hit me with
> is called
> a fist.

Black men will *not* heal their wounded pride or regain a sense of dignity by abusing black women. There are real pressures like poverty and discrimination that have contributed to the disruption in the black family over the last twenty years. But it is not until we begin to address these issues openly and take responsibility for what we can change within our families that we will move beyond our victimized status. Taking action does not mean that we want to emasculate men, but that we believe we have a right to a loving relationship. When a man learns how to treat his partner with care and understanding, he feels better about himself and his abilities.

The Context of Date Rape

Py Bateman

It has been estimated that over fifty percent of rapes are perpetrated against adolescents, with the vast majority taking place between individuals who know one another—that is, in an acquaintance or dating situation. Eugene Kanin, as early as 1957, reported that sixty-two percent of women surveyed had been victims of sexually aggressive acts during their last year of high school dating. In forty-four percent of those cases, the offender was either her steady boyfriend or fiancé. For twenty-one percent of those women, the sexually aggressive act was attempted or completed forced intercourse.

Twenty years later, Kanin and Parcell (1977) found that eighty-three percent of college women respondents reported having been victims of sexual aggression, sixty-one percent since beginning college. Twenty-four percent of these cases involved forced intercourse. These early figures are not much different from the recently publicized reports of the *Ms.* magazine study funded by the National Institute of Mental Health and conducted by Mary Koss (1987). Koss questioned 6,159 students at thirty-two U.S. colleges and universities. One-quarter of the women surveyed reported having been victims of rape or attempted rape, eighty-four percent of them by acquaintances. Fifty-seven percent of the acquaintances were dates. In another study (P. Levy, 1984), one out of ten young women interviewed stated that they had experienced forced sexual encounters while dating.

One of the major differences between the studies on courtship violence and those on date rape is that the former more frequently find similar rates of victimization for males and for females. Sexual aggression, however, remains an almost exclusively male province. Sigelman, Berry and Wiles (1984), who included two items on sexual violence on their modified version of Straus's Conflict Tactics Scale (1979), found only rare reports of female-committed sexual violence. More women reported having been victims of sexual aggression (thirty-five percent) than did men (twenty-one percent). Makepeace (1986) found that eight times as many females as males felt they were victims of forced sex.

Such figures suggest that the problem of sexual abuse constitutes a cultural phenomenon and that survivors of such violence, according to Courtois (1988), are the victims of "an endemic societal manifestation of the power imbalance between the sexes" where "men are conditioned into roles of power and dominance... and females... are conditioned to be passive and dependent." In other words, we live in a culture that condones sexual violence toward women.

Given this cultural context, it is not surprising that few young women report date rapes. Although accounts of the reporting rate for sexual assault vary, most investigators (for example, Koss, Gidycz and Wisniewski, 1987; Miller, 1988) agree that reports by adolescent date rape victims are rare. Furthermore, many adolescents do not even recognize that a rape has occurred.

This lack of recognition may be a result of a remarkable tolerance for or justification of sexual assault when it is associated with dating or "romantic" involvement. Miller (1988) reported that fifty-six percent of adolescent girls interviewed agreed that under certain circumstances, it is okay for the man to use force to obtain sex. In a study by Miller and Marshall (1987), one of every six women interviewed reported that they believed that when a man became sexually aroused it was impossible to stop him or for him to stop himself. Twenty-seven percent of the young women interviewed said that they had engaged in unwanted sex because of psychological pressure from their boyfriends. They saw these experiences not as rape, but as part of "what happens on dates." A study by Fisher (1986) demonstrated that women with more traditional values are more accepting of forcible rape as well as less sure of what constitutes rape. It is evident that women in our culture are socialized to believe that satisfaction of a man's sexual urges is a woman's reponsibility.

Acceptability of Rape

Several studies (for example, Koss and Leonard, 1984; Mahoney, Shively and Traw, 1985) indicate that men share in the belief that women are responsible for both stimulating and satisfying men's sexual urges, and that they hold other similar justifications for rape. Malamuth (1984) attempted to determine the likelihood that men would rape if they could be assured of not being caught and punished. Across seven studies, an average of thirty-five percent of men indicated some likelihood that they would rape. In another study, Briere and Malamuth (1983) investigated both the likelihood to rape and the likelihood to use sexual force and found that sixty percent of male college students "indicated some likelihood of raping or using force in certain (albeit hypothetical) circumstances" (p. 319).

One might explain this self-reported likelihood of rape by noting that perhaps young men think of forced sexual intercourse in terms of being "masterful," imagining themselves to be Rhett Butler carrying Scarlett O'Hara up the stairs. As Lieutenant Samuels said to Cagney and Lacey in one episode of the so-named television series, "I can't understand why when Rhett Butler does it, it's romance, and when some guy on the street does it, it's rape."

It has been suggested that what is required is that young women learn to better communicate with young men in courtship situations. While improved comunication will help, let us not excuse the offenders by blaming the victims for not saying what they mean. As Mary Beth Lacey replied to Samuels, "With all due respect, sir, if you can't tell the difference between romance and rape, you've got a problem."

Indeed, Kanin's (1967) study of male college students found that twenty-five percent admitted to physically forcing (or attempting to force) women to have sexual intercourse in situations in which the women responded by fighting or crying. Even if those women had not communicated more clearly, it takes a lot of distortion to interpret fighting or crying as consent.

So we see that not only do a significant number of young men think that rape is acceptable under some circumstances, and a majority report that they would force sexual intercourse if they knew they would not be caught, but a substantial minority admit to having committed sexual violence. These findings, and those describing the rate of physical violence in dating relationships, demand that we examine our culture, particularly our courtship customs, to discover the roots of this violence.

"Gatekeeper" Versus "Initiator"

It has been suggested by a number of authors that rape is a product of "overconformity" to masculinity (Kanin, 1985; Mahoney et al., 1985). Kanin (1985) reported that self-admitted date rapists reported greater peer pressure to be sexually active than nonrapists. He also documented the exploitive methods supported by peers that these rapists were likely to employ to force women to have sex. This suggests that the peer pressure to conform as a male may contribute to rape of intimates. It is also this aspect of courtship that makes it difficult for young men to set their own limits in their sexual exploration. The "custom" is that they must go as far as the girls will let them. The girls act as the "gatekeepers."

The source of this overconformity is that males are "supposed" to gain sexual experience, with a concentration on *quantity* rather than *quality*. Young men are not encouraged to consider the quality of the relationship in decision-making about sexual activity. It is the *doing* that is important. An example of this dilemma is evident in a problem that a boy brought to his high school counselor. He had gone out with a girl. As they were engaged in the sexual exploration common on dates, she told him to stop. He did. When he went to school, he heard from others that she had said that she did not mean for him to stop. She had expected him to push for more and was disappointed that he had not. He felt that he had "missed an opportunity." That feeling makes a lot of sense in the context of the male goal of "scoring." But if honesty and intimacy in relationships were the ideal, he would not feel disappointed, but relieved that he had withdrawn from sexual intimacy with someone who was not being honest.

The idea that "a real man doesn't take no for an answer" is related to the notion that "women don't mean it when they say no." If the boy does not initiate escalating sexual interaction until he is stopped by the girl in the gatekeeper role, he is seen as somehow falling short of the male ideal. The girl is caught between two ideals—one of the sexually reserved, "pure" madonna, the other of the sexually exciting "vamp" who can hold a boy's interest. She walks a fine line between being a "prude" and being a "slut." The opposing roles of initiator and gatekeeper set up an adversarial relationship in courtship. A belief that relationships between men and women are adversarial in nature is an attitude that has been linked to sexual aggression by authors Mary Koss and Kenneth Leonard (1984), citing a number of different studies.

If "real ladies" don't say yes, and "real men" don't take no for an answer, then they must find another way to communicate. They attempt to send and interpret various "signals" of sexual availability. Unfortunately the sending and interpretation of these signals is anything but an efficient system of communication. We find males attempting to interpret female behavior in light of the question of sexual availability, sometimes with success, but often with a fair amount of confusion and distress.

College students, asked about their assumptions about young women's willingness to have sex, indicated that the following behavior led them to conclude that she was willing to have sexual intercourse: her initiating the date, allowing the man to pay for the date or going to the man's apartment (Muehlenhard, 1988). They were asked if it turned out that she definitely did not want sexual intercourse, he would be justified in forcing it. Rape was rated as justifiable by 27.5 percent of the men and 17.5 percent of the women. The leap between assuming willingness to have sex and justifying rape is understandable only in the context of the adversarial view of sexual relationships, shown to be common among sexually aggressive males, but not exclusive to them.

Adolescents often overcome conflicts inherent in the adversarial view of relationships by interacting in ways that allow the male perception of what is required to maintain the relationship to prevail. The expectation that men are "entitled" to have sex with their partners is consistent with the expectation that men dominate and maintain power and control over "their" women. The acceptance of this expectation is evident in the tendency of young men and women to see possessiveness and jealousy as demonstrating "love." They are then confused if the jealousy becomes abusive and if the expectation of the young man to maintain control is enforced with emotional, physical and sexual violence. Sexual intimacy in this context can be used as a form of punishment. It is a source of humiliation and shame for its victim, as she struggles with the expectations of her gatekeeper role and her role as the caretaker of the relationship and at the same time feels responsible for her own violation by a person she loves.

Conclusion

Given the depth of social support for sexually aggressive behavior among males, it is clear that those of us who work to prevent dating violence and/or serve its victims must offer an alternative to the current set of "courtship customs." As a long-term goal we can hope to offer young women and men a model of relationships built on equality and mutual respect and caring. Thus we can begin to build a social environment in which date rape and other forms of dating violence will stand out from the "norm." In the short-term, the description of this ideal should give young women the ability to recognize and avoid date rape. Such an ability, combined with the resources for both verbal and physical resistance, should result in a reduction of completed date rape. Likewise, the recognition and condemnation among young men of sexually aggressive behavior should also result in fewer attempts at date rape. A date rape prevention program must address equally these immediate needs of recognition and resistance and, at the same time, challenge the cultural context of dating violence.

The author would like to thank Johanna Gallers for her contributions to this article.

Dating Violence: A Review of Contextual and Risk Factors

David B. Sugarman and Gerald T. Hotaling

Recently in a local newspaper, we saw a letter to an advice column from a young woman who was suffering violence at the hands of her boyfriend. At first, the assaults involved hair-pulling and an occasional hit, but her situation became more critical when her boyfriend beat her up. Still in the relationship, she expressed love for her assailant, but pled for assurance from the column's readership that she was not the only one to have gone through this horror and for advice as to how to cope with the situation.

This single cry for help signals a number of questions that social scientists and mental health practitioners must confront. How prevalent is this form of intimate violence? How should programs be organized to target most efficiently both the victims and offenders from these violent relationships? What form of intervention can best reduce the likelihood of future intimate violence and ameliorate possible secondary consequences, for example, lowered self-esteem and depression? Can prevention measures be implemented to abate this phenomenon, and what should the form or nature of these measures be?

The problem with answering these questions is that it requires a considerable understanding of dating violence. One needs to recognize not only the reliable findings that have emerged from the study of dating violence but also the gaps in this knowledge base. Consequently, the present paper serves two purposes: first, to review the dating violence literature with respect to various contextual factors and risk factors, and second, to offer potential implications of these research findings for prevention and intervention.

Defining Dating Violence

Since Makepeace's (1981) seminal article, social researchers have suggested a number of conceptualizations of dating violence. Thompson (1986), for example, suggested that courtship violence involves "any acts and/or threat of acts that physically and/or verbally abuse another person" (p. 166) in the context of "any interaction related to the dating and/or mate selection process" (p. 165). Carlson (1987) offered a definition that included "violence in unmarried couples who are romantically involved" (p. 17) and Puig (1984) defined courtship partner abuse to be "acts of physical aggression directed at one dating partner by another dating partner" (p. 268).

One problem that results from these varied definitions is how violence has been measured. Some studies have equated violence with injuries (for example, Makepeace, 1988). Some are limited to acts of physical violence (Puig, 1984), whereas others have included acts or threats of both physical and verbal violence (Thompson, 1986). A narrow perspective would define violence as those cases in which individuals suffer or inflict extreme injury (for example, being beaten, knifed, or shot). Broad definitions may include acts and threats of physical, verbal, sexual and psychological violence, regardless of their perceived severity. For the present purposes, a more moderate definition of violence is preferred: the use or threat of physical force or restraint that has the purpose of causing injury or pain to another individual.

This definition has several implications for this review. First, it focuses on either acts or threats of violence directed toward another individual regardless of whether injuries result. Second, it excludes acts of psychological abuse (for example, verbally demeaning or humiliating one's partner). Although recognized as a means to control another person, not enough work has focused on operationalizing psychological abuse in the dating violence research.

One additional definitional exclusion involves sexual abuse. Although sexual aggression between intimates can be conceptualized as an act of physical violence, many of the reviewed studies

do not include sexual aggression in their assessment of violent behavior (for example, Bernard and Bernard, 1983; Billingham and
Sack, 1987; Lane and Gwartney-Gibbs, 1985; Makepeace, 1981).
The omission of sexual dating violence from the present review
should not detract from its importance or revelance. Rather, it is
excluded as an attempt to focus narrowly on a single phenomenon
to facilitate the research review process. Similiar strategies have
been employed in reviews that concentrate on sexual dating violence and date rape (cf. Lundberg-Love and Geffner, 1989).

This decision to omit acts of sexual dating violence does have
implications for the conclusions derived from the present review.
First, by increasing the number of behaviors to be counted as dating aggression, the probability of higher prevalence rates also
increases. Consequently, the prevalence rates of dating violence
reported below may be perceived as underestimates in that they
exclude sexual violence. Second, because women report higher
sexual victimization rates than men do (Sigelman, Berry and
Wiles, 1984; Stets and Pirog-Good, 1989), the addition of sexually
violent behaviors to the research focus may increase the difference
between male and female overall victimization rates.

The association between physical and sexual violence in dating relationships has just begun to be examined. For example,
Stets and Pirog-Good (1989) noted a nonsignificant relationship
between sexual victimization and sustaining physical violence for
men, but a significant association between these two forms of victimization for women. Sigelman, Berry and Wiles (1984) reported
similar findings, and, further, reported a relationship between infliction of physical violence and sexual violence by men. Similiar
to the research on battered wives (Hotaling and Sugarman, 1986),
a link between male infliction of sexual violence and physical violence has started to emerge.

A second definitional problem surrounds the terms "dating"
and "courtship." Within the literature, these two terms are used
interchangeably and often are applied to a variety of dyadic interactions. Carlson (1987) suggests that these terms can be employed
to denote any romantically involved, unmarried couple while
Thompson (1986) emphasizes the process of mate selection as a
characteristic of "dating." Both of these definitions are insufficient because dating can involve married individuals (that is, ex-
tramarital affairs) and the functions of dating often involve more
than mate selection. We suggest that "dating" or "courtship" be

conceptualized as a dyadic interaction that emphasizes mutually rewarding activities that can enhance the likelihood of future interaction, emotional commitment and/or physical intimacy. It should be kept in mind, however, that dating involves a wide range of variation on these dimensions. This definition applies to homosexual as well as heterosexual relationships. A couple can date as "friends," or they may view the relationship as having the potential of leading to marriage. The relationship can be exclusive of other potential partners or not. There may be varying degrees of sexual intimacy. The couple may or may not be living together.

Prevalence of Dating Violence

Currently, over twenty data sets exist that can shed light on the extent of dating violence. However, methodological shortcomings and problems in data reporting undercut one's confidence in these numbers. For example, the widespread use of nonrandom college samples precludes generalizing about how much dating violence occurs in society-at-large. Furthermore, how much dating violence one finds can be affected drastically by how it is measured. Decisions about the type of violent acts to be included, the referent period of the survey (lifetime versus one-year estimates) and the role that the respondent had within the violent interaction (perpetrator versus victim) all affect prevalence rates.

Makepeace (1981) estimated that 21.2 percent of his college-age respondents reported that they had either engaged in or sustained violence within their dating relationships during their lifetime. Subsequent studies have uncovered a range of overall lifetime estimates from a low of nine percent (Roscoe and Callahan, 1985) to a high of sixty percent (McKinney, 1986a). These reported overall lifetime estimates present a picture of dating violence as a major social problem.

One would predict that estimates of minor assault rates should be higher than severe assault rates. This hypothesis appears confirmed (Arias, Samios, and O'Leary, 1987; Lane and Gwartney-Gibbs, 1985; Makepeace, 1983).

Patriarchy theory (Dobash and Dobash, 1979; Martin, 1976) would suggest that since men within Western culture are socialized to conceive of their partner as their property (even in a nonmarital relationship), higher rates of males inflicting violence would typify dating violence. A number of studies have compared victim and offender rates for male and female respondents. While three studies (Makepeace, 1983; McKinney, 1986b; Sigelman, Berry and Wiles, 1984) reported higher rates of males inflicting violence, a majority of the studies noted higher rates for women (Arias et al., 1987; Bernard and Bernard, 1983; Billingham and Sack, 1987; DeMaris, 1987; Lane and Gwartney-Gibbs, 1985; Marshall, 1987; Marshall and Rose, 1987; O'Keefe, Brockopp and Chew, 1986). Women also tend to report a higher prevalence rate of sustaining violence in a majority of the surveys (Bernard and Bernard, 1983; Billingham and Sack, 1987; Lane and Gwartney-Gibbs, 1985; Makepeace, 1983; Marshall, 1987; Marshall and Rose, 1987; O'Keefe et al., 1986). These studies suggest that women have higher levels of both inflicting and sustaining dating violence in contrast to men.

Overall, the preceding section serves several functions. First, it illustrates the extent of the dating violence problem in the United States. One can best guess that about twenty-eight percent of dating individuals were involved in intimate violence at some point in their dating careers. This statistic, however, is an estimate; the effects of specific study characteristics and methodological problems make firm conclusions difficult. Even with these shortcomings, this research is important and needed to direct prevention and intervention measures to ameliorate the problem of dating violence.

Contextual Factors and Risk Markers

Aside from estimating prevalence rates, the dating violence research literature offers information that can help clarify what goes on in specific dating violence episodes and who is more likely to become involved in such situations. This information can be grouped by (1) contextual factors and (2) risk markers.

Contextual factors offer the practitioner a modal description of a dating violence incident. They refer to those variables that are associated with the assaultive act and that can be assessed only if the respondent has been a participant (perpetrator and/or victim) in an act of dating violence. These are variables that offer a phenomenological perspective of the assault (for example, time and location of the assault, reported conflict that may have preceded the assault, victim's and perpetrator's interpretation of the violence and their relationship, actions taken by both parties after the violence occurred).

Risk markers are correlates of being in a violent dating relationship. Risk marker assessment mandates a statistical group comparison of individuals who are or have been involved in dating violence to individuals who are not or have not been involved in dating violence on a specific variable (for example, self-esteem). These variables can be related either to origins or consequences of the dating violence. Both types of risk markers are important because of their practical application. Etiological factors have implications for the primary prevention of the onset of violence whereas consequential factors are important because they can represent symptoms or outcomes that practitioners and clients often have to cope with during counseling. Caution should be taken with respect to these labels because risk markers are correlates and are not necessarily causes of dating violence.

Review of Contextual Factors

Much of the dating violence research is descriptive, presenting the reader with statistics that form a profile of the assault. Yet aside from offering a "who, what, when and how" litany of details, these data permit a study of the participants' social construction of the events that preceded and followed the assault.

Perception of why the violence occurred. Within this section, two categories of contextual factors are examined. The first factor involves whether the individual perceived that his or her role in the violent interaction was as an aggressor or as a victim. The second factor examines the attributions, perceived causes or explanations for this violent behavior.

Attribution research would suggest that people are more likely to label themselves as the victims of violence than as the initiators of violence (Tedeschi, Smith and Brown, 1974). This finding seems to be supported by the dating violence data. Across the reviewed studies, a majority of respondents (from seventy-five to one hundred percent) reported that they had not initiated the violent episode. Instead of taking sole responsibility for the violence, both men and women reported that either their partner was the initiator or that they were jointly responsible (Henton et al, 1983; Makepeace, 1986; Matthews, 1984; Roscoe and Callahan, 1985; Roscoe and Kelsey, 1986). However, when the question was more focused to assess whether they would have perceived themselves as being either the victim or the aggressor in the violent interaction, a sex difference emerged. Men were more likely to report being the aggressor, and women labeled themselves as being victims.

This contradiction may be open to a number of interpretations. First, when asked about the initiation of the violent episode, respondents may be reporting on their role with respect to the conflict that led up to the violence. Explanations such as "My partner was nagging me" or "We were having one of our typical arguments" may emerge as rationalization for the conflict. Second, respondents may be interpreting the roles of "aggressor" and "victim" with an emphasis on who did or did not initiate the violence and not the conflict. Third, it is possible that the respondent may be understanding the terms of "victim" and "aggressor" with respect to the violent interaction's outcome. The individual who loses the conflict (that is, is beaten up, gives in to the other's will) may be perceived as the victim whereas the triumphant individual will have the aggressor's role.

A second set of contextual factors relevant to grasping the phenomenology of a dating violence episode are the attributions that the participants employ to understand these interactions. Unfortunately, methodological differences make it difficult to compare findings across studies. Some studies used open-ended questions while other research employed a forced-choice format. In addition, it was not always specified whether respondents were making attributions for their own or their partner's behavior. Even given these problems, jealousy was reported as the prime reason for the violence when an open-end question format was used or when it was an option on a forced-choice item (Makepeace, 1981; Matthews, 1984; Roscoe and Benaske, 1985; Roscoe and Callahan, 1985; Roscoe and Kelsey, 1986). When jealousy was not among the options in a forced-choice format, "uncontrollable anger" was cited as the most frequent cause. Makepeace (1986) reported that jealousy and uncontrollable anger were perceived as the primary causes of dating violence for both men and women.

Another interesting point regarding the "causes" of the violent interaction was the admitted "instrumentality" of the males' violence. While women perceived that their violence results from uncontrollable anger, jealousy, self-defense and retaliation, they perceived that the male partner was motivated by sexual denial. Violent men reported findings consistent with this contention. Between a quarter to a third of men reported that their violence served the purpose to "intimidate," "frighten," or "force the other to give me something."

A number of studies examined the emotional labels placed on the violent acts. Anger and confusion were used most prominently to describe the emotional state of the aggressor (Cate, Henton, Koval, Christopher, and Lloyd, 1982; Henton et al., 1983; Matthews, 1984; Roscoe and Benaske, 1985; Roscoe and Kelsey, 1986). A sizable minority of respondents (from twenty-five to thirty-five percent) indicated that the violence represented love on the part of their partners. This melding of violence and love may signify that there is a normative confusion surrounding appropriate dating behavior (cf., Remer and Witten, 1988).

Overall, the research on these contextual factors indicates a number of points. First, men are usually perceived as the aggressor in these violent episodes. Second, the primary explanation for this violence tends to be jealousy or uncontrollable anger. Third, the violence may be tied to sexual issues and instrumental in its purpose.

Responses to dating violence. People emotionally respond to the trauma of relationship violence in predictable ways: Victims react with anger, fear and surprise (Henton et al., 1983; Matthews, 1984); offenders, on the other hand, exhibit sorrow. In the majority of cases, this trauma is described as mild. Makepeace (1986), however, reported that women outnumbered men by almost a three to one margin in those instances in which severe emotional trauma was reported.

Given the prevalence of relationship violence and the emotional trauma associated with it, one would expect that these episodes would lead to the seeking of professional help and relationship termination. Neither of these propositions has strong empirical support. With respect to seeking professional aid (that is, talking to a teacher, counselor, clergy member or law officer), victims underutilize these sources of support (Henton et al., 1983; Makepeace, 1981; Olday and Wesley, 1983). Instead, victims seek out friends and, to a lesser degree, family members for solace (Henton et al., 1983; Pirog-Good and Stets, 1989; Roscoe and Benaske, 1985; Stets and Pirog-Good, 1989). Pirog-Good and Stets (1989) reported a sex difference in help-seeking behavior in that women were more likely than men to talk to someone about the violent interaction.

Evidently victims of relationship violence, for the most part, do not consult individuals who aid in extricating them from the situation. Consequently one may suspect that they will act independently to cope with or terminate the relationship. Overall, the research findings across the studies offer a mixed picture: The percentage of the respondents that terminated the violent relationship varied from twelve to seventy percent. Further research is needed for the assessment of factors that would make termination of a violent relationship likely. Perceptions of the quality of the relationship among those who remained in relationships following the onset of violence was mixed. While about forty percent of the victims reported that the relationship worsened after the violence, the remaining majority perceived no change or an improvement in the relationship (Cate et al., 1982; Henton et al., 1983; Makepeace, 1981; Marshall, 1987; Matthews, 1984; Murphy, 1988; O'Keefe et al., 1986; Roscoe and Benaske, 1985; Roscoe and Callahan, 1985; Roscoe and Kelsey, 1986).

Overall, these data suggest that while physical violence within a dating relationship has been associated with emotional trauma, it is not a sufficient condition for relationship termination. Furthermore, the underutilization of formal helping agents suggests that victims either are unaware of available opportunities for aid or that they define the violence as normative, requiring either no intervention or simple reliance on their social network of peers.

Risk Marker Analysis

While an examination of contextual factors focuses on those variables that describe participants who have been involved in dating violence, risk markers attempt to identify those variables which discriminate persons involved in dating violence from those who are not involved.

Intrapsychic factors. This section examines three hypothesized correlates of dating violence: (1) attitudes toward intimate violence, (2) sex-role attitudes and (3) personality variables, particularly self-concept. Generally, one would predict that involvement in intimate violence is associated with greater acceptance of intimate violence, more traditional sex-role expectations and poorer self-concept.

With respect to attitudes toward both premarital and marital violence, a number of studies have supported the predicted association with dating violence involvement (Arias and Johnson, 1989; Cate et al., 1982; Deal and Wampler, 1986; Henton et al., 1983). However, this research did not examine whether these attitudes toward violence were more predictive of being victimized or being a perpetrator of violence or whether this relationship was moderated by the gender of the respondent. To investigate these issues, a number of researchers (Arias and Johnson, 1989; Burke, Stets and Pirog-Good, 1989; McKinney, 1986b; Stets and Pirog-Good, 1987a, 1987b; Tontodonato and Crew, 1988) did separate analyses for male and female offenders and victims. With one exception (Arias and Johnson, 1989), attitudes toward intimate violence did not discriminate female offenders from nonoffenders or female victims from nonvictims. For male respondents, however, this factor did differentiate between offenders and nonoffenders, and victims and nonvictims. Overall, this seems to suggest that attitudes toward intimate violence are associated primarily with the male partner's involvement in dating violence.

Patriarchy theorists of intimate violence (for example, Dobash and Dobash, 1979) have argued that the culture's norm of male dominance is a prime factor contributing to the existence of relationship violence. Consequently, it was predicted that those individuals who subscribe to these "traditional" norms would be more predisposed toward involvement in relationship violence than individuals who hold more liberal sex-role attitudes.

A series of studies that have examined this issue employing a range of sex-role identity measures have indicated highly inconsistent findings. For example, using the Attitude-Toward-Women Scale (Spence and Helmreich, 1972) has led to contradictory findings. McKinney (1986b) reported that women who held more liberal attitudes exhibited a greater likelihood of reporting that they sustained or exhibited violence in a dating relationship; however, no significant effects were indicated for men. Sigelman, Berry and Wiles (1984), on the other hand, reported that violent men showed more traditional attitudes than nonviolent men, and no effect was revealed for women. Bernard and Bernard (1983) revealed no significant differences between abused and nonabused women and abusive and nonabusive men.

This lack of consensus is reinforced by the two studies using the Bem Sex Role Inventory (1974). While Comins (1984) was unable to differentiate between violent and nonviolent respondents on this measure, Bernard, Bernard and Bernard (1985) found that violent men showed a higher level of masculine sex-typing than their nonviolent counterparts. On the other hand, victimized women showed a lower level of feminine sex typing than nonvictimized women. Finally, Tontodonato and Crew's (1988) multivariate analysis found that sex-role orientation was predictive of dating physical aggression for women but not men.

Three other sex-role attitude scales have been employed. Using the instrumentality and expressiveness scales of the Personality Attribute Questionnaire (PAQ) (Spence, Helmreich and Stapp, 1975), Stets and Pirog-Good (1987b) noted that (1) the instrumentality scale did not discriminate between assaultive individuals and nonassaultive individuals for either gender, (2) that assaulted men and women were more likely to have low instrumentality scores than their nonvictimized counterparts and (3) that low expressiveness scale scores correlated only with the male's likelihood of expressing or sustaining violence. In contrast to these findings, Burke et al. (1989) indicated that both men and women who perceived themselves as more feminine on semantic differential scales were more likely to express violence, and Deal and Wampler (1986) revealed that scores on the Osmond-Martin Sex-Role Attitude Scale (1975) did not correlate with the frequency of violent acts.

Overall, these results present quite a mixed picture. Examining only the findings that focus on discriminating violent men from nonviolent men, two studies uncovered the predicted relationship between assaultive behavior and "traditional" sex-role attitudes (Bernard et al., 1985; Stets and Pirog-Good, 1987b), five studies offered evidence of no relationship (Bernard and Bernard, 1983; Comins, 1984; Deal and Wampler, 1986; McKinney, 1986b; Tontodonato and Crew, 1988), and two studies reported significant findings in the opposite direction (Burke et al., 1989; Sigelman et al., 1984).

Even given these findings, sex-role attitudes may have an impact on dating violence. Instead of conceptualizing sex-role attitudes as an individual level variable, Sigelman et al. (1984) posited that dating violence would be more likely if the dyadic members held sex-role attitudes that were divergent. While the level of sex-role attitude divergence between partners did not differentiate assaultive males from nonassaultive males, women who reported that their sex-role attitudes were different from their partners' attitudes were more likely to be victimized than women who held attitudes similar to those of their partners. While this divergence of sex-role attitudes hypothesis is intriguing, further study is required. Another approach has been offered by Flynn (1990) who suggested that a woman's sex-role attitude may be more predictive of her termination of a violent relationship than a man's.

Self-concept and other personality constructs. A variety of other intrapsychic constructs have also been investigated. Four studies focused on self-concept and dating violence involvement and offered a very consistent pattern of findings. Assaulted individuals exhibited poorer self-concept as measured by the Rosenberg Self-Esteem Scale (1965) than nonassaulted individuals (Burke et al., 1989; Comins, 1984; Deal and Wampler, 1986; Stets and Pirog-Good, 1987a). However, no relationship was found between self-concept and assaultive dating behavior (Burke et al., 1989; Stets and Pirog-Good, 1987a). In addition, victims of dating violence exhibited higher levels of emotional distress (Comins, 1984). Deal and Wampler (1986) noted that victims had higher levels of overdependence and lower levels of self-confidence associated with higher levels of violence. Yet, feelings of inferiority were uncorrelated with the level of violence in the individuals' current dating situation (Arias et al., 1987). Lower social desirability scores (or the desire to give a socially acceptable response) on the Crowne-Marlowe Scale (1964) were predictive of only females reporting that they had either inflicted or suffered dating violence (Sigelman et al., 1984). Finally, Riggs, O'Leary and Breslin (1990) found that women who scored higher on an aggressiveness scale were more likely to inflict violence on their partners. This same measure did not discriminate violent men from nonviolent men. In summary, the only consistent association between these personality measures was the association between lowered self-concept and being a victim of dating violence.

Alcohol usage. In their review, Hotaling and Sugarman (1986) noted that the male's use of alcohol was a consistent risk marker for husband to wife violence; consequently, a similar effect was expected in the dating violence literature. A number of studies have implicated alcohol usage as a contextual factor of dating violence (Bogal-Allbritten and Allbritten, 1985; Brodbelt, 1983; Comins, 1984; Laner, 1983; Makepeace, 1981; Matthews, 1984; O'Keefe et al., 1986), but this variable's status as a correlate of intimate violence in this context is unclear. Makepeace (1987) reported an association between self-reports of having a drinking problem and experiencing dating violence. Tontodonato and Crew (1988), on the other hand, did not uncover a significant relationship between college students' alcohol usage and either their actual involvement in dating violence or their willingness to use force in a dating situation. This lack of association remained even when separate analyses for each gender were conducted.

Experiencing and witnessing violence in the family of origin. While violence in the family of origin has found consistent association with husband-to-wife violence (Hotaling and Sugarman, 1986), the dating violence literature presents a less consistent picture.

Focusing on the relationship between experiencing childhood violence and inflicting violence, seven studies reported a significant positive relationship (Bernard and Bernard, 1983; Comins, 1984; DeMaris, 1987; Laner and Thompson, 1982; Marshall, 1987; Marshall and Rose, 1988; Sigelman et al., 1984) whereas five others noted no significant association (McKinney, 1986a; Murphy, 1988; O'Keefe et al., 1986; Stets and Pirog-Good, 1987a, 1989). Attempts to predict dating violence victimization have produced an even split. Although some studies revealed a significant positive association with experiencing childhood violence (DeMaris, 1987; Laner and Thompson, 1982; Marshall, 1987; Marshall and Rose, 1988; Sigelman et al., 1984), the remainder failed to uncover a significant relationship (Comins, 1984; Murphy, 1988; O'Keefe et al., 1986; Stets and Pirog-Good, 1987a, 1989).

Nonsignificant findings appear to be even more common when examining the impact of witnessing violence in one's family of origin. Four studies supported the hypothesized effect (Bernard and Bernard, 1983; Gwartney-Gibbs, Stockard and Brohmer, 1987; Marshall, 1987; Sack, Keller and Howard, 1982); seven studies did not (DeMaris, 1987; Marshall and Rose, 1988; Murphy, 1988; O'Keefe et al., 1986; Sigelman et al., 1984; Stets and Pirog-Good, 1987a, 1987b).

This mixture of findings offers only minimal support for the "intergenerational transmission of aggression" hypothesis (Makepeace, 1981). Caution, however, has to be taken not to dismiss this hypothesis prematurely. First, the reported findings confound the respondent's role in the dating violence (that is, perpetrator, victim) and their gender. Based on the marital violence research, these factors may be more predictive of male aggression than female aggression (see Hotaling and Sugarman, 1986). Breslin, Riggs, O'Leary and Arias (1990) found that men in dating relationships who reported witnessing maternal violence against their fathers were more likely to self-report inflicting dating violence. Violent women reported higher levels of witnessing general interparental violence in contrast to nonviolent women. Consequently, researchers need to be more sensitive to the potential impact of these markers.

A second possibility is that divergent findings can arise from the same data set depending upon the statistical analysis performed. For example, Gwartney-Gibbs, Stockard and Brohmer (1987) reported a significant univariate relationship between witnessing violence in the family of origin and men's reports that they inflicted or suffered dating violence; however, a multivariate analysis resulted in the disappearance of these effects. Consequently, further research needs to test whether the observed significant findings are spurious or whether violence in the family of origin is a distal (that is, long-range impact) causal factor whose effect is mediated through more proximal (that is, immediate) mediating causes (for example, attitudes regarding the use of violence in intimate situations).

Interpersonal factors. A number of measures have been used to assess the relationship between the level of interpersonal commitment and dating violence. These include relationship phase, measures of love and liking, length of time in the relationship, number of dates with the partner and living arrangements.

A review of descriptive statistics would suggest that a majority of the dating violence incidents (between forty-seven to eighty-six percent) occurs during either the steady or serious dating phase of a relationship (Cate et al., 1982; Henton et al., 1983; Makepeace, 1989; Olday and Wesley, 1983; Plass and Gessner, 1983; Roscoe and Benaske, 1985; Roscoe and Kelsey, 1986; Sigelman et al., 1984). The correlational research, on the other hand, has presented little evidence for an association between relationship phase and either suffering or inflicting dating violence (Arias et al., 1987; Billingham, 1987; Billingham and Sack, 1987; Deal and Wampler, 1986). The one exception (Laner, 1989) found higher levels of male combative behaviors in more serious relationships. However, this operationalization of combativeness included both physical aggressive acts (for example, slapping one's partner) as well as nonphysical aggressive acts (for example, belittling one's partner).

Two explanations can account for these contradictory results. First, the reported descriptive statistics may simply represent the distribution of relationship phases among the dating population. Essentially, violence is more prevalent within steady relationships because steady relationships are more prevalent in the samples studied. A second explanation is based on the finding that violent relationships tended to be perceived as more intimate than nonviolent relationships (Comins, 1984). Consequently, respondents may be misperceiving the degree of commitment that the relationship entailed due to the presence of the violence.

Measures of loving and liking for one's partner were employed by Arias et al. (1987), who found that level of loving was uncorrelated with violence involvement for either gender. Violence-involved women reported that they held higher levels of dislike of and more negative feelings toward their partners than women not involved in violent relationships. No relationship was found for men on the liking scale.

Six studies used either the length of time in the relationship (Arias et al., 1987; Marshall and Rose, 1987; Rouse, Breen and Howell, 1988; Stets and Pirog-Good, 1987b) or a composite measure that combined the length of time and the number of dates (Burke et al., 1989; Stets and Pirog-Good, 1987a) as a measure of relationship commitment. A relatively consistent pattern for men emerged. Men exhibited higher rates of dating violence as the commitment level increased (Arias et al., 1987; Burke et al., 1989; Marshall and Rose, 1987; Rouse et al., 1988; Stets and Pirog-Good, 1987a, 1987b). However, only two studies reported significant associations between either inflicting or sustaining dating violence by women and these measures (Arias et al., 1987; Burke et al., 1989). Finally, male victimization was related to length of relationship in only a single study (Burke et al., 1989).

Living arrangements have been assessed in six studies. Stets and Straus (1989) revealed that cohabiting couples had a higher rate of assault and more severe violence than either married or dating couples. This replicates earlier findings by a number of researchers (Lane and Gwartney-Gibbs, 1985; Rouse et al., 1988; Sigelman et al., 1984; Yllo and Straus, 1981). However, Billingham and Sack (1987) did not uncover any significant differences between cohabitating and noncohabitating respondents.

The marital violence literature has suggested that the equal distribution of power and resources within a relationship would result in a lower rate of relationship violence (Allen and Straus, 1980). This contention receives only limited support from the dating violence literature. Although there is an absence of significant effects for men, lowered rates of both inflicting and sustaining violence were associated with a more equal split of power for women (Sigelman et al., 1984). However, this power-violence relationship may be moderated by attitudinal variables. For example, DeMaris (1987) noted that higher inflicting and sustaining violence rates occur with men when two conditions are met: (1) the men believe that they should control the relationship, and (2) their partners have greater resources than they do. Women, on the other hand, show higher rates of inflicting violence if they have a belief in female relationship control, regardless of actual resource distribution.

Implications for Prevention and Treatment

After a decade of dating violence research, our knowledge base offers researchers and practitioners only the most preliminary understanding of the factors associated with this phenomenon. In fact, it is disconcerting that the associations between dating violence and a number of factors presumed to be important remain nebulous. For instance, Makepeace (1981) conceptualized courtship as a mediating step between an individual's family of origin and family of procreation. Consequently, witnessing or experiencing violence in one's family of origin would be expected to be associated with dating violence involvement. The research findings on the intergenerational transmission of aggression hypothesis are ambiguous. Similarly, the impact of sex-role attitudes and stress is uncertain. Finally, the research has investigated only superficially a range of important factors (for example, alcohol and drug usage, or family income).

Even given the overall paucity of firm research findings, consistencies do emerge. First, a more positive attitude toward the use of violence in intimate situations has been related to a greater likelihood of inflicting dating violence, especially for men. Second, victimization is related to a lowered sense of self-esteem or self-concept, particularly for women. Finally, violence involvement tends to be more characteristic of longer relationships and relationships involving cohabitation. Each of these findings has prevention or treatment implications for dating violence.

The first implication focuses on selecting target populations for prevention services. If this were a "perfect" world without scarce resources, prevention services would be directed at all population members; however, resource limitations require concentrating on that segment of the dating population that shows a higher level of risk for violence. In particular, violence prevention efforts should be aimed at young people in long-term dating relationships and relationships involving cohabitation. Both relationship types involve factors that may increase the likelihood of violence. First, they entail deeper and more intimate knowledge of the partner. Second, these relationships usually include higher levels of interaction frequencies. Third, the likelihood of complications due to sexual jealousy increases. Consequently, outreach programs need to focus their instructional and counseling efforts on these dyads.

Granted that certain populations should be targeted for services, the next logical question would be what services seem to be required. The present review points to a number of both preventive and interventive services. High schools and universities can play an important role in teaching about close relationships. Seminars, workshops and lectures on conflict resolution strategies should include sections on dating relationships. There is clearly enough known about dating violence to guide this process. Any program developed to work with couples should emphasize the following issues: (1) the nonviolent management of interpersonal conflict, (2) means for coping with anger and jealousy, especially sexual jealousy and (3) altering the attitude that violence is an acceptable means of conflict resolution.

The issue of a positive attitude toward the use of violence in dating relationships offers insights into the normative nature of this behavior. There is an apparent lack of social stigma attached to the behavior by participants. In the reviewed studies, substantial numbers of males are quite explicit about the instrumental nature of their violence. They report that they use violence against their female partners in order to "intimidate," "frighten," or "force the other person to give me something." The violence is perceived as an appropriate means to obtain a desired goal. These claims are much bolder than those who use violence against women in other contexts. Violent husbands, for example, rarely admit that their aggression is manipulative but rather rely heavily on a set of "out of control" reasons such as alcohol, drugs, anger or stress (Dutton, 1986). In fact, a large minority of victims of dating violence interprets the violent actions of their partners as signifying love. Overall, these findings provide evidence that this monumental tolerance of dating violence constitutes normative approval.

The high prevalence of dating violence combined with the casual attitude about its occurrence points to the need for a massive educational effort. This effort should comprise a number of components. First, even though it is clear that dating violence occurs among persons of many ages, awareness of the problem should be directed at high school and college-age students. The goal is not only to influence the members of the violent dyad but also to alter the peer group's support of this violent behavior. Both victims and offenders of dating violence talk to friends about their experiences. In fact, males who use violence in dating relationships communicate this behavior to the peer group and appear to receive support for it (DeKeseredy, 1988). The transmission of information about dating violence in the form of pamphlets, lectures, class discussions and films or through other means should emphasize what role the peer group can play in withholding support of the use of violence in dating relationships.

Health and counseling personnel in secondary school settings should explicitly question students about violence in dating. Resources should be made available on campuses to offer assistance to persons involved in abusive relationships, and efforts should be made to assure that the availability of these services is publicized to increase the likelihood that they will be utilized. Once again, the role of the social group is important. Since individuals involved in dating violence tend to seek out peers for assistance with respect to this issue, efforts should be directed at informing the peer group about the availability of intervention programs.

After examining the research in dating violence, a quandary presents itself. On the one hand, the research literature offers only the barest insights into the causes and consequences of this form of behavior. Yet, on the other hand, the problem is of pandemic proportions. Hence, there is a desire to intervene in order to ameliorate this social problem; yet, the knowledge base does not indicate clearly how one should intervene. This situation requires that practitioners and researchers create an alliance to further both goals of understanding the phenomenon and reducing its occurrence.

Bonding with Abusive Dating Partners: Dynamics of Stockholm Syndrome

Dee L. R. Graham and Edna I. Rawlings

This article presents a theoretical model for viewing the responses of young women to abusive dating partners. This model was inspired by the political hostage literature and developed by noting parallels and differences in the responses of victims to a broad range of other "hostage" groups. Therapeutic recommendations that grow out of this model are briefly described.

Bonding to an Abuser as a Survival Strategy

A number of researchers argue that complex combinations of factors contribute to the likelihood that a young woman will continue a relationship that becomes physically, sexually or emotionally abusive. Lack of power as a female, gender role expectations, social pressure to be "coupled" during adolescence, the need to establish independence from the family of origin and the influence of violence in the family of origin are several of these factors. In contrast, we view the factors affecting whether a woman will remain in an abusive relationship as arising from the *situation* to which she is exposed *while in the relationship*.

Noting parallels in the predicaments of hostages and women in abusive relationships (see, for example, Graham, Rawlings and Rimini, 1988), we propose that it makes no more sense to attempt to explain why particular women get into abusive relationships (while others do not) by analyzing their childhoods or personalities than to attempt to explain why particular Americans are aboard an airplane that is skyjacked (while other Americans are aboard airplanes that are not skyjacked) by examining their child-

119

hoods or personalities. Following the same analogy, it makes no sense to attempt to explain why battered women have tremendous difficulty escaping from their abusers by referring to the women's backgrounds and/or personality characteristics. Although the backgrounds and personalities of the *captors* (or *abusers*) might be useful for understanding why hostage-taking events progress as they do, the focus of this paper is on the relationship between the forces coming to bear on hostages and the survival strategies of those hostages.

Bonding to one's captor (abuser) has been viewed as a survival strategy when the victim is a hostage (Kuleshnyk, 1984). The phenomenon of bonding with one's captor has been called Stockholm Syndrome, referring to a bank holdup in Stockholm, Sweden, in 1973 in which three women and one man were held hostage for six days by two men. During that period, the four hostages and their captors bonded bi-directionally. The hostages even came to see their captors as protecting them from the police! When one of the captors was later asked why he did not kill one or more of the hostages, when doing so would have helped him in his negotiations with the police, he reported that he had grown too fond of them to kill them (Lang, 1974). Following the release of the hostages, one of them reportedly became engaged to one of the captors (Hacker, 1976). Such bonding is no longer considered unusual by professionals who negotiate with hostage-takers. In fact, they encourage its development, for it improves the chances of the hostages surviving (Kuleshnyk, 1984; Ochberg, 1982), despite the fact that it means the officials can no longer count on the cooperation of the hostages in working for their own release or in later prosecuting the hostage-takers (Kuleshnyk, 1984).

Graham (1987) examined the psychological literature on nine different "hostage" groups to ascertain whether there was evidence that a Stockholm Syndrome-like response (bonding to an abuser or captor) occurred in other "hostage" groups as well. Such a response was found for all hostage groups studied: concentration camp prisoners (Bettelheim, 1943; Eisner, 1980), cult members (Alexander, 1979; Atkins, 1977; Bugliosi and Gentry, 1974; Mills, 1979; Yee and Layton, 1981), prisoners of war (Hunter, 1956), civilians in Chinese Communist prisons (Rickett and Rickett, 1973; Schein, Schneier and Barker, 1961), procured prostitutes (Barry, 1979), incest victims (Hill, 1985), physically and/or emotionally abused children (Alexander, 1985; Coleman, 1985; Finkelhor, 1983) and battered women (Dutton and Painter,

1981; Ehrlich, 1989; McGuire and Norton, 1988). The seemingly universal nature of this phenomenon suggests that bonding to an abuser (Stockholm Syndrome) may be instinctive and thus play a survival function for hostages who are victims of interpersonal abuse.

Although there is not a universally accepted definition, Kuleshnyk (1984) argues that Stockholm Syndrome is present if one or more of the following feelings is observed: (1) positive feelings by the captive toward his/her captor; (2) negative feelings by the captive toward the police and authorities trying to win his/her release and (3) positive feelings by the captor toward his/her captive. Graham (1987) has attempted to more fully ascertain the parameters of this syndrome by compiling a list of responses of persons to different hostage situations and subjecting them to empirical test. Aspects of victims' psychology observed in the various "hostage" groups were viewed by Graham as potential aspects of Stockholm Syndrome. To date, sixty-six different potential aspects of Stockholm Syndrome have been identified by Graham.

Because Graham found bonding to an abuser or captor to occur in all the "hostage" groups mentioned, she proposed that Stockholm Syndrome describes a unitary phenomenon observed whenever the following four conditions—hypothesized *precursors* of Stockholm Syndrome—co-exist: (1) perceived threat to survival and the belief that one's captor is willing to carry out that threat (2) the captive's perception of some small kindness from the captor within the context of terror (3) isolation from perspectives other than those of the captor and (4) perceived inability to escape.

Psychodynamics Underlying Stockholm Syndrome

Graham hypothesized that the following dynamics take place in a hostage or battering situation. An abuser (or captor) traumatizes a victim, who cannot escape, by threatening her (physical or psychological) survival.* As a result of being traumatized, the vic-

---

* Abusors and captors are most often male and their victims may be female or male; battering most commonly victimizes women. Therefore, we will refer to the abuser as "he" and the victim as "she."

tim needs nurturance and protection. Being isolated from others, the victim must turn to her abuser for the needed nurturance and protection if she turns to anyone. If the abuser shows the victim some small kindness, this creates hope in the victim, who then denies her rage at the terror-creating side of the abuser—because this rage would be experienced as overwhelming—and bonds to the positive side of the abuser. With the hope that the abuser will let her live, the victim works to keep the abuser happy, becoming hypersensitive to his moods and needs. To determine what will keep the abuser happy, the victim tries to think and feel as the abuser thinks and feels. The victim therefore (unconsciously) takes on the world view of the abuser. Because so much is at stake, namely her survival, the victim is hypervigilant to the abuser's needs, feelings and perspectives. Her own needs (other than survival), feelings and perspectives must take second place to the abuser's. Also, the victim's needs, feelings and perspectives can only get in the way of the victim doing what she must do to survive: they are, after all, feelings of terror. Therefore, the victim denies her own needs, feelings and perspectives. She sees the captors as the "good guys" and those trying to win her release (for example, parents, police or therapists) as the "bad guys," as this is the way her captor sees things. The victim projects the anger of the abuser onto the police, whom she sees as more likely to kill her (or get her killed) than the captors. If the victim is subjected to these conditions for a prolonged period of time (for example, months or years), even her sense of self comes to be experienced through the eyes of the abuser.

If the victim is given the opportunity to leave the abuser, she will have an extremely difficult time doing so. Having denied the violent, terrifying side of the abuser as well as her own anger, the victim sees no reason to leave him.

At the same time, intense, unconsciously driven "push-pull" dynamics characterize the victim's orientation to the abuser. These dynamics involve powerful, survival-based feelings of being *pulled* toward the abuser (because it is the mutual bonding between the victim and abuser that has convinced the abuser to let her live) and of being *pushed* away from him (because he is threatening her survival, even though this may be recognized only unconsciously). "Pull" forces are expressed as feelings of wanting to help the abuser because he needs her, of feeling that she is the only one who really understands him, and of wanting to protect him as she perceives that he has protected her. These feelings also help the victim to feel she is in control. They are her source of power in this life-threatening relationship. "Push" forces are expressed as terror and anger, though this anger is almost never expressed toward the abuser out of fear of retaliation.

A number of mechanisms make it difficult for the victim to separate from the abuser, physically and/or psychologically, following prolonged captivity. Two such mechanisms are fear of losing the only positive relationship available to her and fear of losing the only identity that remains—namely, her self as seen through the eyes of the abuser. These fears are expressed as fear of abandonment—of being lonely or of not being able to live without the abusive partner—and as fear of not knowing who one is, feeling empty, and so on. In the case of child victims, this view of self may be the only sense of self the victims have ever experienced. In the case of adult victims, this view of self may have replaced a previous sense of self. Regardless, living without her abuser, and thus without a sense of self, is experienced by the victim as a threat to psychic survival. The more difficulty a victim has with these issues, the greater is the damage to her sense or self. Both loss of her only friend (the abuser) and loss of self as experienced through the abuser's eyes require that the victim take a leap into a terrifying unknown. Leaping into the unknown is sufficiently frightening to be difficult even for people in healthy environments and it is considerably more difficult for someone whose survival depends on the fragile feelings of predictability and control produced by cognitive distortions and the whims of a terrorist.

Feelings that the abuser may return to "get" the victim once again, and that this time the abuser might not be so "nice" to the victim (that is, might not let her live), serve to keep the victim loyal to the abuser long after the ordeal is over and the victim appears safe to outsiders. The victim *knows* the abuser could get her again—after all, he has done it before, and that is proof that it could happen again. She might live the rest of her life fearful of showing any disloyalty, preparing for the time when the abuser might catch up with her again, and thus never fully separate from the abuser psychologically. Because the abuser does not want the victim to be apart from him (for his dominance over the victim is his source of power), the released victim lives in fear of her physical survival, for being apart from the abuser is seen as a form of disloyalty. The fears persist even if the abuser dies or is sent to prison.

The need to master the terror created by the hostage-taking

experience may keep the victim in the terrorizing situation longer than would otherwise be necessary. Mastering the terror created by the trauma involves the victim (1) processing her (positive and negative) feelings surrounding the life-threatening ordeal and (2) developing feelings of control (for example, recognizing survival strategies that she used and that could be used again if needed). Only if the victim masters the terror will her fear of being reterrorized subside.

Indicators of Stockholm Syndrome

The following are aspects that one would expect to be present if an individual had developed Stockholm Syndrome:

• The victim and abuser are bidirectionally bonded.
• The victim is intensely grateful for small kindnesses shown to her by the abuser.
• The victim denies the abuser's violence against her, or rationalizes that violence.
• The victim denies her own anger at the abuser.
• The victim is hypervigilant to the abuser's needs and seeks to keep the abuser happy. To do this, the victim tries to "get inside the abuser's head."
• The victim sees the world from the abuser's perspective; she may not have her own perspective.
• In accordance with the indicator above, the victim sees outside authorities trying to win her release (for example, police, parents) as "bad guys" and the abuser as "good guy." She sees the abuser as protecting her.
• The victim finds it difficult to leave the abuser even after her release has been won.
• The victim fears the abuser will come back to get her even after the abuser is dead, in prison, and so on.
• The victim shows symptoms of Post-Traumatic Stress Disorder.

Relation to Borderline Personality Disorder

Graham and Rawlings (1987) identified four outcomes of prolonged Stockholm Syndrome: (1) splitting, (2) intense push-pull dynamics in relationships to others, (3) displaced anger, and (4) lack of sense of self. Noting the correspondence between these and

Borderline Personality Disorder (BPD), they proposed that prolonged Stockholm Syndrome eventuates in Borderline Personality characteristics and, in the more extreme cases, in BPD itself. Graham and Rawlings theorized that prolonged exposure to the four precursors at any age after approximately eighteen months of age would lead to the generalization of abuser-victim psychodynamics to relationships with persons other than the abuser, which would appear as Borderline Personality characteristics or BPD.

Therapy With Young Women in Violent Dating Relationships

Therapists can increase their effectiveness in working with young women in violent dating relationships—and reduce their own frustration—by keeping in mind the survival value of the clients' "symptoms" within the terrorizing context in which they emerged. It may be that it is necessary for clients to view their symptoms within this context before they can judiciously assess what they want to do with each symptom. For example, they might choose to continually "use" the symptoms to help guarantee their continued safety or to use them only when in other abusive relationships or contexts of terror. Understanding the psychodynamics of the client's relationship to her dating partner and the ways in which those dynamics may have generalized to her relations with others can thereby help both the therapists and her depathologize her behavior and empower her in future relationships.

In this section, we will describe how, in our work with young women at the University of Cincinnati's Psychological Services Center, we apply Graham's theory of Stockholm Syndrome. Due to space limitations, we will discuss what we believe are the major therapy issues that come out of using a Stockholm Syndrome perspective with young women who are or have been in violent dating relationships. Although many of the procedures we recommend are similar to techniques used by other therapists who work with abused clients, our approach is unique in that it is grounded in a coherent theoretical framework. The therapy principles articulated here are in a developmental stage, and we would appreciate getting responses to our ideas from other therapists working with young women in abusive relationships.

Creating a Safe Therapeutic Environment

The client is (or has been) in a relationship in which her physical and/or psychological survival is threatened by an abusive dating partner with whom she has emotionally bonded to reduce terror. As discussed above, intense push-pull dynamics develop with respect to the abuser, and these are later generalized to other relationships, including the therapeutic relationship. To make the therapy environment safe, the therapist must establish a relationship in which the boundaries between the client and therapist are demarcated and the expectations for each are specified. Limits and expectations can be negotiated and may vary based on the clinical state of the client, the stage of therapy and the strength of the therapeutic alliance. The therapist can expect much testing by the client of the therapeutic limits. The therapist can predict to the client that testing will take place, and when it does, label it as a survival strategy: "I'm glad you are not trusting me at this point; it tells me you are looking after yourself in this relationship, and I want you to do that." Abuse victims may seem to re-create abusive relationships within the therapeutic context. The therapist needs to model maintaining firm boundaries—neither being abusive to the client nor accepting abusive behavior from the client.

Helping the Client Understand Her Experience

For the client, having the relationship described in terms of Stockholm Syndrome theory creates meaning out of chaos and removes the victim-blaming that further weakens self-esteem already damaged by bonding with an abusive partner. We introduce Stockholm Syndrome theory to the clients in two ways. First, we administer the Dating Relationships Questionnaire (Graham, Foliano, Latimer and Rawlings, 1990) to clients after rapport has developed and provide feedback about where they stand on the Stockholm Syndrome precursor scales and factors relative to an undergraduate, normative female sample.* Discussion of the findings inevitably leads to a discussion of Stockholm Syndrome theory and its relevance to the client. We have learned to present

---

* Therapists interested in administering the Dating Relationships Questionnaire to their clients should contact the first author. If the client will sign a release form and the therapist will return the client's answers to us, we will mail the therapist a computer printout of the client's scores relative to an undergraduate female sample.

questionnaire findings and theory cautiously early in therapy, as the client can be overwhelmed if too much is presented at once. This is particularly the case when the client is currently in or has recently left an abusive relationship (see next section). Second, we give clients some brief written material pertaining to the theory (for example, a copy of Graham, Rawlings and Rimini, 1988) if they express interest in learning more about it. Even when clients do not initially connect the theory with their experiences, introduction of the material gives clients an opportunity to express their perspective on their relationships as well as to examine a different perspective. Almost all the clients we have worked with have been able to connect to some aspects of the theory, and the aspects they reject are opportunities for dialogue. We have found that the language of Stockholm Syndrome provides useful metaphors in therapy (for example, consider the implications of viewing a relationship as one between hostage and captor versus one between lovers).

Table 1

Cognitive Distortions Reframed in Terms of Stockholm Syndrome

Cognitive Distortion	*Stockholm Syndrome Explanation*
Denies partner's violence against her and focuses on his positive side	An unconscious attempt to find hope (and thus a way to survive) in a situation in which she would otherwise feel powerless and overwhelmed
Feels shame for abuse done to her	Reflects client's having taken abuser's perspective (namely, that she caused his abuse of her and thus that the abuse was deserved).
Resents outsiders' attempts to free her from abusive partner	Client knows partner is likely to retaliate against her for any disloyalty shown toward him, so she resists others' attempts to free her or to hold partner accountable for abusing her.
Identifies with the victim in the partner	Represents the projection of client's own victim status onto partner; enables client to feel sympathetic and caring toward partner.
Believes partner's violence against her is deserved	Represents an attempt to feel she controls when and whether violence is done to her and thus permits her to believe she can stop the abuse.

Rationalizes part-ner's violence against her	Is an attempt to maintain bond with partner (and thus hope of survival) in the face of behavior (violence) that otherwise would destroy that bond (and hope).
Uses partner-as-victim explanation to account for partner's abuse of her	Represents an effort to see partner in a positive light so as to maintain bond (since bond provides client her only hope of surviving).
Feels hatred for that part of her that partner said led to her abuse	To improve chances of survival, client internalizes partner's perspective, including stated reasons for abusing her.
Fears partner will come to get her, even if he is dead or in prison	Client knows partner is willing to "get her" because he has done so at least once before; remains loyal in anticipation of his return.

Reframing abused clients' cognitive distortions in terms of Stockholm Syndrome reveals their survival function. For example, cognitive distortions found by Graham et al. (1990) to underlie Stockholm Syndrome in young women involved in violent dating relationships are shown in Table 1. Alongside each cognitive distortion is listed the survival function that the distortion serves within the Stockholm Syndrome framework. Educating clients about the dynamics of Stockholm Syndrome and having them examine the abusive episodes from that perspective can aid in reframing some of their distortions. Techniques of cognitive behavior therapy (for example, Ellis, 1962) are also useful in working with cognitive distortions. Group therapy with other abuse victims is particularly useful because the women can recognize these distortions in others more easily than in themselves.

Therapists' Countertransference Behaviors

Conceptualizing the clients' predicaments within the framework of Stockholm Syndrome theory keeps us as therapists from becoming abusive (victim-blaming) to clients who are or have been involved in an abusive relationship. It also keeps us from becoming frustrated with women who exhibit push-pull behavior both in the therapeutic relationship and in their relationships with their abusive partners.

Since the client is bonded with the abuser and that relationship is stronger than the therapeutic relationship, attempts to persuade the client to leave the abusive relationship, no matter how well intended, will disrupt the therapeutic relationship, often causing the client to flee therapy. Many adolescent women in abusive relationships come to view parents who oppose the boyfriend or the relationship as interfering. Young women, because they are in a separating-from-parents life stage, may be more likely than older women to transfer their attitudes toward their parents (of being interfering) to their therapists. The therapist should make it clear that it is not her/his intention to rescue the client from the relationship, but, instead, to help the client reach a point of personal strength where she can decide what she needs to do for herself. In *Games People Play*, Eric Berne's *"rescue triangle"* shows that protectors (for example, therapists) may take the role of the abuser if the victim refuses to be rescued.

Young women who are still in an abusive relationship often take breaks from therapy since they can tolerate only so much of the affect that therapy stirs up in them. When a women client breaks off from her abuser, therapists should not be too invested in the client's staying out of the relationship, since it may be difficult for the client to continue therapy if she does resume her relationship with the abuser.

Validating Both Love and Terror

Acknowledging the polarities of love and terror helps the client integrate both feelings toward her partner. Within the safety of the therapeutic environment, the therapist should work to help the victimized client integrate the loving-violent split that has enabled the bond. ("It must be confusing to you when this man who is kind and loving to you in so many ways treats you in such a mean, uncaring way.") Helping the client integrate both the terrorizing and loving sides of the abuser will assist her in giving up her dream that the relationship will become the type of relationship she had hoped it would be. This integration requires that the therapist be willing to validate both the positive and negative aspects of the abuser and encourage the client to express both her anger and love for him. A distinction between feelings and behavior is often important in this respect. The therapist can point out that the client can feel love for the abuser without acting on that love if the relationship is destructive to her.

Discriminating Between Different Ego States

Almost every therapist who has counseled a client who is in an abusive relationship has witnessed that client vacillating between a logical, rational state, in which she makes statements such as "I'm angry at him; I'm going to break up with him," and a helpless, powerless emotional state in which she feels she cannot leave the abuser. We have observed clients flip-flop between these two states within minutes. Many therapists, perhaps erroneously, consider having their client spend more and more, if not all, of her time in the logical, rational state to be a desirable therapeutic outcome.

We hypothesize that this split represents two dissociated states. Therapists frequently assume that realizations available to the client while in the cognitive state are also available to her while in the emotional/hostage state. If the split is truly dissociative, the cognitions and affect of one state are not available to the client when in the alternate state.

To reduce this splitting, the therapist can help the client become aware of her emotions when she is in the cognitive ego state. When the client is in the affective ego state, the therapist can empathize with the underlying feelings (terror, sadness, rage, hopelessness, and so forth) being expressed and aid her in connecting these feelings to the abuse she has experienced. Helping the client to become aware of the different states and eventually to label them can be useful in helping her to discriminate when and how the psychodynamics of abuse are affecting her (for example, identifying the triggers for each of the ego states). Eventually, the therapist can begin to confront the client with cognitive inconsistencies while the client is in an affective ego state. The ultimate goal is to integrate the (cognitive-affective) split that these states represent.

Lessening the Conditions That Produce Stockholm Syndrome

Weakening the conditions that produce Stockholm Syndrome should also weaken the need to bond. Interventions with respect to the four conditions should begin with those conditions that appear most susceptible to change. Because the conditions are highly correlated, weakening one may weaken the others as well.

Isolation. Isolation factors often offer the therapist a good place to start, since the client's coming into therapy has somewhat reduced her isolation. Helping the client discover and develop a supportive network is important. Self-help groups or group therapy (especially if the group is a feminist one) can be a useful adjunct to one-on-one therapy. The Stockholm Syndrome framework, women's studies classes and feminist organizations and writings can help reduce ideological isolation. The client needs support in questioning her internalized societal myths about women's traditional role in relationships. Caution should be exerted in encouraging her to talk to important others in her life about the abuse until the therapist is confident that she will get support from these sources or at least that she can stand up to criticism or rejection from these sources if they are not supportive toward her.

Violence. As a psychic defense against terror, women in abusive relationships minimize the abuse and often do not label themselves as abused. It may be necessary to ask directly about different types of violent behavior, without labeling it violence at this point, in order to get a reasonably accurate picture of the abuse within the relationship. Because clients will take on the perspective of the abuser (who will not see himself as abusive), many clients are confused about what constitutes abuse. The therapist will need to help clients recognize abusive aspects of their relationship without pushing to break down the clients' denial (a needed defense, particularly if the client is still being terrorized). Many young women are also confused about what is acceptable male behavior within the dating context. This is particularly true in regard to sexual abuse.

Confusion also exists because emotional abuse is often subtle and difficult to recognize. When the abuse is primarily emotional, we have successfully taught emotional detachment to some clients by helping them separate their partners' emotionally abusive behavior from their own reactions to it. For example, when dating partners are verbally berating or putting down clients, the clients can at least silently remind themselves, "That is only your opinion. I disagree."

It is important to reduce the client's denial of physical violence at a pace that is comfortable (not overwhelming) to her. To do otherwise will cause the client to experience *the therapist* as abusive and, because of the important function served by the client's denial of the abuse, possibly cause the client to leave therapy. One way to encourage a client to acknowledge the terrorizing aspects of her situation (a way that keeps her working with, and not against, the therapist) is to insist that she develop a well-rehearsed, overlearned escape strategy that fits with her experience of the abuser's violence patterns. The therapist should provide information about shelters, crisis hot lines, and so forth, so that the client will know how to obtain protection in the event of an emergency. In this way, without increasing the client's defenses, the therapist is communicating that she or he views the physical violence as very serious and is concerned for the client's well-being. The decision regarding if and when to implement an escape plan remains in the client's hands.

Inability to escape. Conditions that prevent escape should be carefully assessed. Helping the client discover alternatives she was previously unaware of (because high anxiety causes perceptual constriction) can enable some clients to eventually leave abusive relationships in which they feel trapped. For example, Ellen, who felt trapped in the upper-floor, one-exit-only apartment selected by her abusive boyfriend, Ralph, followed her therapist's suggestion that she check with a moving company regarding a safe way to move out. She learned that the moving company could move all of her belongings in a few hours while Ralph was at work. Although Ellen did not move out immediately, she had additional information that she could use when she was ready to act.

Kindness. Small kindnesses or promises from the abuser can create disproportionately high hopes in the client that her partner will change. The therapist must be patient as the client's hopes rise and fall over time. When the client is away from the abuser, she may crave his love and attention. At those times, she is not in touch with her feelings of terror, due to her dissociation of those feelings. Encouraging the client to develop alternative sources of nurturance and caring will help her be less dependent on her partner's attention and kindness. However, patience is needed even here, for the client may initially view this move as a form of "disloyalty" to her partner.

Following abuse, the client will experience a compelling need to have the abuser signal that he is no longer angry at her and, in fact, loves and cares for her. It is possible that this period has addictive qualities (cf. Dutton and Painter, 1981; Kenrick and Cialdini, 1977; Solomon, 1980). Having nonabusive others available to provide nurturance to the client at this critical time is extremely important. Since few therapists are available around the clock, the therapist should help the client identify sources of supportive intervention (for example, hot lines, crisis centers, shelters, friends or family) she can turn to immediately after abuse occurs, so that the abuser is not her only source of nurturance and care at that time.

Reducing Denial Defenses

Since denial of abuse is central to Stockholm Syndrome, the client needs to be reminded of the violence of the abuser, preferably in ways that do not make the therapist responsible for the reminder. Ways of keeping the abuse in focus in therapy are to encourage journal keeping, autobiographical writing, dream work, and so on. Reading and discussion of firsthand accounts written by battered women or viewing and discussing films that deal with abuse may be helpful to some clients. We have respect for clients' defenses and have found that clients will avoid those activities they find too distressing.

The adolescent whose family of origin is abusive may view her dating relationship as a "way out" of life with her parents. Questioning the dating relationship can create panic in the young woman if she sees life with her parents as the only alternative to her dating relationship. Panic may also ensue if she realizes that she cannot trust her parents *and* she cannot trust her dating partner. She may begin to feel that she will never be able to trust anybody and to wonder what's wrong with her.

Anger and Grief

As denial of the abuse begins to weaken, the client will begin to experience the anger toward her abuser that she previously split off and repressed for survival reasons (expressing anger toward an abusive partner can be very dangerous). These feelings should be validated, and the therapist should help the client vent her rage in a safe way. Anger not expressed verbally or physically will be expressed psychosomatically. Use of the Gestalt exercises involving the "empty chair" or fantasy are initially safe ways of expressing anger. Some clients will want to write a letter expressing their angry feelings to their abusers, which they may never intend to mail.

Burtle's (1985) "anger therapy" also provides safe ways for clients to express anger. Burtle notes that women have been socialized to view their anger as a destructive force that is hurtful to others. Certainly women who are or have been in abusive dating relationships have good reason to view anger as destructive. The abuser's anger, because it is coupled with violence, demonstrates to the woman the destructive nature of anger. In addition, having taken the abuser's perspective, the client sees anger toward the abuser as destructive because *he* sees it that way. Furthermore, expression of anger toward the abuser can provoke the abuser's violence. Burtle suggests that the therapist begin by reframing anger as energy that "can be used for appropriate self-assertion, maintenance of good relationships and creativity" (p. 75).

Giving up denial of the abuse also involves giving up the dream of what the relationship might have been. This often produces grief and mourning for the lost dream of the relationship. At this time, therapists need to do grief work with the client.

Repairing Psychological Damage

Clients who have experienced abusive dating relationships may have symptoms of a diagnosis that resembles Borderline Personality Disorder, even though their symptoms may not completely meet the Diagnostic and Statistical Manual III-R criteria for this diagnosis. In the clinical literature, a diagnosis of BPD leads to an extremely poor prognosis, perhaps because the dynamics underlying BPD have not been understood. Viewing BPD within the context of Stockholm Syndrome theory leads to a more hopeful prognosis, since this theory presents BPD as survival responses to a pathological situation. For example, this context helps us understand borderline clients' supersensitivity to rejection, their push-pull dynamics, lack of sense of self, displaced anger, and so forth, and the survival functions played by these "symptoms" within the abusive relationship.

Although it is terror that leads women to bond to their abusers, this bond is experienced by women as a void inside of them that can be filled only by their partner. Rather than saying they fear what their partner will do to them if they leave him (for the abuser often has threatened to kill them should they leave), they report that they fear the pain or emptiness created by the loss. These statements are indicative of the loss of sense of self that has resulted from hypervigilance to another's needs and indicate the extent to which loss of sense of self fuels the desire to maintain a bond with the abuser.

For a woman to stay separated from her partner, then, she must develop her own sense of self. Much of the early phases of therapy is directed toward this end. To accomplish it, the client should be encouraged to focus on her own feelings and needs and to develop her own perspective, apart from that of the abusive partner.

As a woman begins to heal, she may express fear that she cannot trust herself to recognize a potentially abusive partner. Abuse victims often feel *not attracted, but (unconsciously) "pulled"* to be nice to persons they recognize as abusive, so as to prevent future abuse. Thus, they are more likely to establish bonds with abusive persons whom others would ignore or avoid. Educating clients about this dynamic helps them to understand why they may find themselves in other abusive relationships that could have been avoided early on; this understanding helps them avoid repeating that pattern. In addition, therapists should educate clients about characteristics of healthy relationships.

Conclusion

Stockholm Syndrome theory views bonding to an abuser as a survival response shown by a wide range of hostage groups under conditions of inescapable terror. Given empirical support obtained by Graham et al. (1990) for Stockholm Syndrome in young women in violent dating relationships, therapeutic recommendations include using Stockholm Syndrome theory as a framework for helping therapists and clients to understand the clients' experiences, current "symptoms" and cognitive distortions; acknowledging and validating both the good and bad sides of the clients' abusers; identifying and discriminating different split-off ego states; and breaking down the Stockholm Syndrome precursors as a means to breaking down Stockholm Syndrome itself.

The authors wish to thank Dr. Robert Stutz for granting the first author release time to do research and writing, and Dr. Roberta Rigsby for editorial suggestions regarding this article and ideas regarding therapy.

Violence During Teen Pregnancy: Health Consequences for Mother and Child

Judith McFarlane

Each year, one of every ten American teens becomes pregnant. In 1986 (the latest year of available data) 472,081 births occurred to women younger than twenty, some 12.6 percent of all births (Hughes, Johnson, Rosenbaum and Liu, 1989). Among all age groups, teens are the least likely to receive early prenatal care. Inadequate prenatal care, combined with low socioeconomic status, places teens at increased risk for complications of pregnancy, including hypertension and anemia, as well as jeopardizes the viability of the infant (Hofferth and Hayes, 1987). Infants born to teens are significantly more likely to have low birth weight and suffer increased risk of morbidity and mortality (Hughes, Johnson, Rosenbaum, Butler and Simmons, 1988). Pregnant teens who are abused by boyfriends are at even greater risk for health problems.

This article examines the prevalence of physical abuse during teen pregnancy and the associated health effects for the mother and her child. Efforts to document and prevent battering of pregnant teens are described, including a multisite longitudinal research study—the nation's first effort to study the patterns of violence during teen pregnancy and document the impact of the violence on the health of the young woman and her child—and a primary prevention education and training program.

Violence During Pregnancy

Studies of battered women have reported that forty to sixty percent of the women were abused during pregnancy (Fagan,

Stewart and Hansen, 1983; Stacey and Shupe, 1983; Walker, 1979, 1984). Reports of abuse during pregnancy include blows to the abdomen, injuries to the breast and genitals and sexual assault. Many battered women report miscarriages, stillbirths and preterm deliveries following a battering incident (Dobash and Dobash, 1979; Gelles, 1975; Hilberman and Munson, 1978; Martin, 1976; Straus, Gelles and Steinmetz, 1980).

An in-depth study of 542 battered women in a Dallas shelter found forty-two percent to have been battered when pregnant. Eight percent reported complications. Most of the battered women reported that battering became more acute during the pregnancy and the child's infancy (Stacey and Shupe, 1983). Interviews by Fagan, Stewart and Hansen (1983) of 270 battered women revealed forty-four percent of the women to have been abused during pregnancy, with injuries during pregnancy being more severe. Similarly, Campbell (1986) found battering during pregnancy to be associated with increased severity and frequency of abuse and risk of homicide.

Most reports on battering during pregnancy have been secured from battered women, usually women in shelters. Two notable exceptions are the Helton, McFarlane and Anderson report (1987) and the Hillard report (1985). Both studies interviewed a healthy population of pregnant women. Helton, McFarlane and Anderson randomly sampled and interviewed 290 pregnant women from public and private clinics in a large metropolitan area with a population exceeding three million. The 290 black, white and Hispanic women ranged in age from eighteen to forty-three years. Most were married, and eighty percent of the women were at least five months pregnant. Nine abuse-focused questions were asked of each woman. Of the 290 women, eight percent reported battering during the current pregnancy (one out of every twelve women interviewed). An additional fifteen percent reported battering before the current pregnancy. Battering did not vary as a function of demographic variables. Of the women battered during the current pregnancy, 87.5 percent had experienced prior abuse by the male partner with whom they were presently living, indicating that pregnant women are more likely to be abused during the pregnancy if they were abused before. One-third of the women battered during pregnancy had sought medical attention for injuries sustained from the abuse, and twenty-nine percent reported the abuse had increased following knowledge of the present pregnancy. One-fourth of the women battered during pregnancy had been assaulted during the first trimester. All of the abused women were living with the batterer.

Hillard screened 742 prenatal patients. One abuse-focused question was asked. Hillard reported that eleven percent of the women were abused in their present or a past relationship and four percent were being abused during the current pregnancy. The abused women tended to be older and have greater parity and a lower educational level than nonabused respondents. Emotional problems were noted in forty-three percent of the abused women as compared to five percent of the nonabused women; twenty percent of the abused women had attempted suicide.

To ascertain the prevalence of physical abuse during teen pregnancy, Bullock and McFarlane (1988) conducted an informal survey among pregnant adolescents in several large metropolitan areas. Of the more than two hundred pregnant teens surveyed with a questionnaire, twenty-six percent reported they were in a relationship with a male partner who was physically abusive. Of those females being abused, forty to sixty percent stated that the battering had either begun or escalated since discovery of the pregnancy. Even more alarming was the fact that sixty-five percent of those abused had not talked with anyone about the abuse, and no one had reported the abuse to law enforcement agencies.

Health Consequences of Violence During Pregnancy for the Infant

Violence affects not only the pregnant teenager but also the health and viability of her unborn child. Birth weight is the most important determinant of survival and healthy growth and development for children.

To determine if an association exists between battering before or during pregnancy and infant birth weight, 589 postpartum women at a private and a public hospital were interviewed and asked if they had been physically abused (Bullock and McFarlane, 1989). Each woman was classified, according to self-report, as positive or negative for physical abuse. The percentage of women battered for the total sample was 20.4 percent. At the private hospital, the percentage of battered women delivering a low-birth-weight infant was 17.5 percent as compared to 4.2 percent among nonbattered women. At the public hospital battered women delivered a higher percentage of low birthweight infants than the nonbattered women, but the difference was not statistically significant. When analyzed by private versus public client status, battered women at the private hospital were four times more likely to deliver a low-birth-weight infant.

For the total sample of 589, 12.5 percent of the battered women delivered a low-birth-weight infant compared to only 6.6 percent of the nonbattered women. The difference was highly significant. When variables associated with low birth weight (that is, tobacco and alcohol use, age and race) were mathematically controlled, a strong connection was still seen betweeen battering and low birth weight. The implications were clear: Violence is highly stressful to the pregnant woman and may affect the birth weight, and subsequent health, of her child.

The Study and Prevention of Violence During Teen Pregnancy

Battering during teen pregnancy is potentially a major adolescent health problem, jeopardizing adolescent and infant health. Research, early intervention and primary prevention are important to reducing this health risk.

The Surgeon General's Workshop on Violence and Public Health (1986) recommended screening and treatment for physical abuse during routine prenatal care. It is only during pregnancy that healthy women have regular, scheduled contact with health care providers. The recommendations advise that abused pregnant women be classified as high-risk for health complications during pregnancy. In January 1989, the American College of Obstetricians and Gynecologists (1988; 1989) sent information about battered women to its twenty-eight thousand members for the purpose of facilitating identification and follow-up. Despite increased awareness of violence toward pregnant women, there is minimal surveillance, risk group identification and risk factor exploration (Centers for Disease Control, 1988, 1989; Mercy and O'Carroll, 1988).

Injury in America (1985), a National Research Council and National Academy of Sciences report on the number of Americans affected by unintentional (accidental) and intentional injury, recommends longitudinal epidemiologic studies to establish high-risk populations, including types of injuries sustained, consequences of injury and circumstances of injury. To this end, the first longitudinal study of violence during pregnancy in this country was initiated in January 1990. Twelve hundred pregnant women, representative of teens and adult women, will be followed during pregnancy to establish the pattern and severity of any injuries sustained during pregnancy and associated consequences on maternal health and infant birth weight. The women will be interviewed repeatedly and assessed for physical and emotional abuse as well as risk factors of homicide. Each woman will be asked to keep a calendar to chronicle any physical abuse. Health parameters of pregnancy will be monitored, and the health and viability of the infant will be measured. Preliminary data will be available in 1991. Gathering data about intentional injury to pregnant women and their children is the first step required for violence surveillance, control and prevention. Pregnant women and their infants are the human resources for the next generation; protecting their physical safety is a national priority.

A second step is primary prevention and educational strategies targeting pregnant teens. To prevent violence during teen pregnancy, a communitywide educational program has been funded by the March of Dimes. Its aim is to increase awareness of the problem of abuse (McFarlane, 1989). Initially, an eleven-minute video was designed to educate adults working with teens about the problem of battering. The video is divided into two sections: The first part discusses normal adolescent development, teen pregnancy statistics and reasons teens may be at increased risk for abuse during pregnancy. The second portion is devoted to educating the health care provider or adult working with teens on ways to respond to abuse during pregnancy, including assessment methods, counseling dialogues, and teaching skills for relating without violence. To accompany the video, pamphlets and bookmarks were developed that list community resources for teens, including the telephone numbers for police and sheriff's departments, ambulance, shelters, counseling, runaway hot line and children's protective services agencies. The pamphlets also include specific information for teens about the cycle of violence and risk assessment facts. The materials are disseminated through workshops, conferences and communitywide violence prevention programs. Additional educational materials to prevent violence during pregnancy and evaluation data are described in several articles (Bullock, Maloney and McFarlane, 1990; McFarlane, 1989; McFarlane, Anderson and Helton, 1987);

Conclusion

Violence in an intimate relationship frequently occurs during pregnancy. Four to eight percent of adult women interviewed in two studies reported battering during the present pregnancy, and eleven to fifteen percent reported battering that began prior to the current pregnancy. Twenty-six percent of pregnant teenagers interviewed in a third study reported physical battering. Physical abuse is clearly associated with negative health effects for woman and child. In addition to the injuries sustained, negative health effects are visible in low infant birth wieght. In a sample of 589 women, the percentage of low-birth-weight infants was twice as high among battered women compared to nonbattered women. The social and health costs of violence in relationships are enormous.

The cycle of violence can be interrupted, and the health and safety of women and children protected. The first step is public awareness, and the second step is assessment for abuse of all teenagers, pregnant and nonpregnant, followed by counseling, education and referral. Relationships without violence can be a reality.

Talking with Incarcerated Teens about Dating Violence

Kenneth M. Greene and Cathleen E. Chadwick

This article focuses on dating violence histories of a group of teen-age women incarcerated for various crimes, including prostitution, drug offenses and assault. Although the total number of teens included here is not large (twenty), their individual and collective experiences relate important information about how and why violence has been a part of their lives.

The twenty teenagers, ages fourteen to eighteen, who contributed to this project live in a locked, medium-security facility in San Diego County, California. The group included three black, seven Hispanic and ten white young women. Their sentences range from three to eighteen months.

Services in which the teens participated included weekly educational support groups/workshops that covered child abuse, parenting, decision-making skills, values clarification and other information, discussion and support. One of the authors devoted three of these sessions to the issue of violence in their dating relationships.

The sessions included showing the video *When Love Hurts* (produced by Marin Abused Women's Services, San Rafael, California) and a tape of a television documentary on violence against women (*Eye on L.A.: War on Women*, KABC, February 4, 1985). To stimulate discussion, the young women were given a questionnaire about types and amounts of violence they had experienced in dating relationships. The questionnaire, taken from Claudette McShane's *Warning! Dating May Be Hazardous to Your Health!* (1988), includes four sections addressing physical, sexual, verbal and emotional abuse. The young women were also given a set of questions to respond to in writing about their personal histories of dating violence. All of the activities over the three-week period were prefaced and followed by discussions. They were encouraged to discuss their thoughts and feelings about the general issue and specific incidents that came up and to consider ways to deal with dating violence should it happen to them in the future.

The information shared by these teens was profound. Of the twenty, nineteen told the group they had grown up in homes where they witnessed violence by one parent against another. Sixteen of the twenty completed questionnaires. Their responses were full of stories of dating violence. Of the sixteen who responded, fourteen reported physical abuse, twelve reported sexual abuse, sixteen reported verbal abuse and fourteen reported emotional abuse by a dating partner. One teen reported having been verbally abused only, while another reported almost every specific type of abuse in all four categories as having been a daily occurrence for two years. The remaining fourteen reported the entire range of dating violence histories from verbal to severe physical abuse.

At least half of the young women reported having been pushed, shoved, slapped, punched or beaten. The most frequent kind of sexual abuse reported was the use of force or violence to have sex (seven reported this). Twelve of them reported the following types of verbal abuse: being humiliated in front of others, being accused of things they didn't do, having their partner explode into a jealous, angry outburst over something that never happened, having their partner swear at them or call them names. At least ten of the teens reported they were emotionally abused when their partner belittled their feelings, broke promises and then denied it, or led them to believe that there was more to the relationship than there was.

In addition to the McShane questionnaire, the authors developed a series of questions to which the young women could respond in writing. The questions follow:

1. Has anything like this (dating violence) ever happened to you?
2. How old were you?
3. What happened?
4. Why do you think it happened?
5. How did you feel?

6. What would you do if it happened again?
7. Do you think you could prevent it? How?
8. Were drugs or alcohol involved?

Seven of the young women wrote responses to these questions. Three of the stories are included here in their entirety. Excerpts have been taken from the other four.

The Stories

Valerie: In response to the question "Has anything like this ever happened to you?" Valerie wrote, "Not really. I just got pushed and slapped before, and he got slapped right back." If it happened again, Valerie would "get someone to beat him down."

Deidre: "I've never been beaten by a guy, but I've been thrown around a couple of times. I've gotten a busted lip from being thrown around, but that was the most. I got hurt more emotionally.... I felt really let down because he always said he would never hurt me. I cried a lot because I loved him. Two months later, I went back to him."

Donna: "It didn't get into beating, but, yes, he did slap me one time.... Now and then he tried to hit me, but I told him that as soon as he does, he better just forget about me because I'm the kind of girl that doesn't take that stuff from anybody, especially from somebody that's going to be using me as his punching bag.... He is the real jealous type. He doesn't want me talking to anyone. He trusts me, but he says it looks wrong." After they had broken up, "I went partying, and he knew I was going to be there, so he went too.... He came up to me and said for us to go home. I ignored him and he told me again in a stronger tone of voice. Then he grabbed me and took me outside, and he said that we were going home. I refused, so he put me inside the car and began giving me this big old lecture about me and him. Then he brought up the guy I was talking to and asked me who he was, and I told him. Then he didn't believe me, so I started laughing. It made him more angry, so he slapped me. It wasn't with force, but I knew he wished he gave it to me with force. So then I became really angry and gave him a lecture that if he would ever even try to harm me in any way that he would regret it badly, and he said that he was sorry, that he really didn't mean it. I know him, and ever since then, he has screamed at me but never lifted his hand at me once."

Cheryl: "I was fifteen, sixteen, seventeen when this occurred in my life. I could estimate this happened to me about two hundred times with a total of two different boyfriends. . . . He would beat my butt, kick me in the ribs, and he stabbed me one time. . . . I felt scared, angry most of the time. I just literally wanted to kill him and, at times, came very close." Cheryl thought she might be able to prevent this from happening to her again "by choosing someone who is not on drugs and treats people with respect."

The statements from Valerie and Deidre are good examples of the relativity of the term *abuse* for adolescents. Both young women report being physically assaulted, yet both feel their experiences do not really count as violence. Donna and Deidre have both taken strong, outspoken positions in their relationships regarding the consequences of further abuse. Donna goes on to say that although her boyfriend screams at her, he has not hit her since she set a verbal limit with him. Both Catherine and Beverly, whose accounts are given below, also believe that taking a strong verbal stand against violence when it first happens would be effective in stopping it. Cheryl is very clear about the extreme dating violence she has experienced and that her response has been fear, anger and feelings of vengeance. Her idea that she might be safer with a non-drug-using partner who "treats people with respect" shows some awareness of the effect of drugs in exacerbating a problem with violence.

Jackie: "Yes, dating violence has happened to me. It has happened numerous times; I can't even count. It is still an issue with me. It began when I was sixteen—I'm eighteen now. I was bitten by my boyfriend, on the face, kicked, hit, burned (third degree) and sexually assaulted. He used foreign objects such as bananas and beer bottles with stale cigarette butts in them, while having sex. I think these things happened because I was so insecure about myself; I felt that negative attention was better than no attention at all. At this point I feel scared. I can't believe that I put up with such insanity. After I was in these relationships for such a long period, I seem to feel comfortable in them. I was expecting these things out of the relationship. Sometimes I feel out of place if the guy doesn't get angry with me because I feel he is holding back his feelings. Everyone gets angry; it's normal. Sometimes I even miss violent relationships because of the excitement. (I don't miss getting hurt though!) If this happened again, I could see myself falling back into the old pattern again. That's why I'm scared. I guess I could prevent it by moving on. I don't have to stay with that person and can avoid the situation."

Jackie's feeling that a violent relationship was better than no relationship reflects her own low self-esteem and the importance our society places on women having relationships with men to prove their value. At only eighteen years old, she shows wisdom in her awareness that although she took no pleasure in the actual violence, the excitement of the violent relationship attracts her. This also makes her afraid. She also recognizes that she has come to equate anger with violence. Because anger is normal, it follows that violence is as well. She now finds it hard to trust a nonviolent partner for fear that he is holding back his "true" feelings.

Beverly: "It all started when I was fifteen. I was living at home with my mother. I just got out of drug rehab. I met a real nice, sweet, understanding guy. We started to go out for a week, then we were engaged to be married. Things happened real quick. I moved out of the house to live with him and his uncle. That's when it really began. We started to use drugs again. That's when I found out he used needles. However, it never stopped me from loving him any less. We started to argue about how much drugs we were using. It kept our neighbors up all night. We started to get into serious crimes. That's when he said I was cheating on him, and he started to slap me around. Then his uncle kicked us out of the house, and we lived on the streets. Finally we moved in with my mom. She put up with him because she did not want to lose me. After his extended use of needles, I began to fix it for him. I would inject the needle into his arm because he was too lazy to do it himself. He started to talk to his dad in New York, and he asked me if I wanted to go live there. He promised never to hit me again or use drugs ever again. It sounded so great! I said yes, so we ripped off my mother's house to get the money to go to New York. We sold all the stuff we stole, and we sold our car. My mother was in the hospital when my boyfriend and I left for New York. When we got there, the first two weeks were great. We got married. I loved it. I was sixteen now. He was keeping his promise to me, and his dad was real nice. Then at the beginning of the third week, I came in from work and saw my boyfriend's father raping his own wife. I was scared. I stayed in my room most of the night. When my boyfriend came home from work, he started to beat me because I saw what happened. Then he raped me. I could not believe this was happening to me! The next day my boyfriend's father came in and started to beat on me. When he was done, he raped me. I tried to tell my boyfriend, and he called me a liar. Then he beat me real badly. I fell down two flights of stairs and broke three of my ribs. I called home, and the next day I left without a word. On the way back on the Greyhound bus, I miscarried two babies. I got a divorce, and I was free of that life. I never talked to him again. Almost every day of the last year with him, I was beaten. The first thought that came into my head was 'What will I do without him?' I THINK I'LL LIVE!!!!'"

Beverly's story of a truly nightmarish experience makes several important points. She became isolated from any support and became the victim of the intergenerational cycle of violence that is so common for batterers. The father rapes his wife, the son rapes his wife, then the father rapes the son's wife. It is also interesting to note that as Beverly tolerates her boyfriend's behavior because she loves him and doesn't want to lose him, Beverly's mother also puts up with him because she fears losing her daughter. Again, the social message to women is that their own self-worth is defined by their success at maintaining relationships, even if violent and even at great personal cost.

Catherine: "It has happened to me a number of times over a period of two years. Not exactly by a dating partner, but by my ex-boyfriend. It went on from the time I was fifteen through seventeen. We met in high school and had a good relationship for about six months, and then we started doing drugs. He was going out on me, and then I started going out on him. After a while it was like a competitive love-hate relationship. There were times all through the relationship when I didn't have anywhere to go and only had him to depend on. I suppose since he was taking care of me and helping me out in my time of need he felt he had dominance over my life, that the only way to keep me in line was to beat me. He must have really brainwashed me because I wasn't raised to live that kind of life, and after a while I really started believing that is how it was supposed to be. I felt I needed someone like him. Like it was healthy. It really wasn't. My reasons for staying with him, I see, were very stupid reasons. I found myself hanging on the boy-friend I had met at first, the nice one, instead of realizing that this might be a different person now—a drug addict. This one beat me up. I guess I just wanted to hang on to the nice one. I see reality now.

"I think it happened because we spent most of our time being jealous instead of trusting each other and because my going back to him most likely made him think he could do it again and again, sure that I wouldn't leave him. I also think that the drugs played a pretty big part in it.

"After a while I felt like it was normal. Now that I have more knowledge about it, I should say that if it ever happened again I wouldn't be masochistic as I was in the past. I would leave with-out feeding into the situation and stay gone.

"I don't know about totally preventing it, but I could proba-bly help prevent it by not letting him know about my past of being abused because that sometimes will tell a man that since I let someone else beat me, so can he. Also tell them, 'Look, you want someone to use to let out your aggression on and abuse, then find someone else.' Let the person know you refuse to take abuse from anyone at the first sign of it.

"Almost every occasion it was under the influence of either al-cohol or cocaine or both combined."

Catherine's story is filled with insights about her experience in a violent relationship. Just as so many adult women want to be-lieve in and hang on to the "goodness" in their partners, so did Catherine. Both she and her partner accepted the sense of entitle-ment society has frequently given men over women. She felt that because he was "helping her," he had the right to treat her as he pleased. She also believed he felt it was up to him to keep her "in line." Catherine says, in retrospect, that her staying with him gave him more permission to continue his violent behavior and that taking a firm stand against violence "at the first sign of it" might prevent its frequent occurrence. Catherine also makes some valuable points about communication in relationships. As she de-scribes him "going out on her" and her "going out on him" in re-taliation, it seems clear that she was not able and/or did not feel safe enough to tell him how she actually felt about his behavior. She later concludes that telling him of her past abuse gave him permission or encouragement to abuse her, so she should not disclose this in the future. Catherine has concluded from her own experience that honest communication can be dangerous. She also acknowledges the effect of drugs in her situation, a common theme among these young women.

Conclusion

The young women included here represent what many would label a high-risk population. The fact that they are incarcerated indicates that they are already struggling to establish socially acceptable ways of living. Factors in their lives that have contributed to their criminal behavior may also make them more vulnerable to abusive behavior. The teens' family settings and social environments often discourage self-respect and self-responsibility and limit their sense of empowerment and control over their environments. As young women embarking on lives with increasing independence from adults, they are inexperienced, yet "street wise," vulnerable yet "tough." Because these factors are also present for many young people who have not committed criminal behaviors, it is probably safe to conclude that dating violence is part of life for many more teens than those in the type of population described here.

Involvement with drugs and alcohol is described by most of the girls in this discussion. The exposure to drugs and alcohol and the social norms related to drinking and using drugs add to the vulnerability of the adolescent. The use of drugs and alcohol by both the abused teens and their abusive partners may represent attempts to avoid the emotional pain often present in their lives even before the violence begins. It also becomes a contributing factor to the violence by reducing inhibitions, increasing tolerance for pain (physical and emotional) and providing a rationalization for violent behavior.

Several other issues present in the violent histories of these teens closely parallel those described by adult battered women. For example, there is great variation in what is perceived as violence or abuse. Statements that they were "only slapped" or "only pushed" or that their partners only lied to them and insulted them on a daily basis indicate that they do not identify their experiences as violent and that they often minimize it. As with many adult abused women, these young women often equate anger and love with violence. They may believe that violence is the direct (and sometimes only) expression of anger and that violence indicates how important they are to their partner, that is, how much he loves them.

As with many adult abused women, the teens seem to feel strong pressure to continue their relationships subsequent to the violence, based on the importance of forgiving, the fact that their partner can be and has sometimes been good to them, the woman's feeling that she "needs" the man emotionally, the woman's isolation as a result of the violence in the relationship and her sense of responsibility to help or change her partner. These factors are closely related to social expectations for all women: Women have primary responsibility to nurture and maintain relationships; the value of a woman is measured by her ability to establish and maintain a relationship; and men have the right to treat their partners however they wish.

In spite of the vulnerability of these young women, they have strengths worthy of recognition. Several of them indicate that dating violence is a past, not current, situation for them. Given some of their insights about avoiding partners who use drugs or treat others disrespectfully and the importance of setting limits with their partners about abuse, there is reason to expect that at least some of these young women can avoid violence and abuse in future relationships.

The opportunity to articulate their attitudes and feelings and to discuss their experiences with one another may contribute to the sense of self-respect so essential for healthy violence-free lives. The impact of family, institutional and social attitudes toward sexuality, male-female relationships and violence is also evident. Adolescence is a time when these are discovered, explored and practiced. Changes in the social context of adolescent violence, confrontation of violent behavior and support for survivors are crucial to decrease violence experienced by teens in their intimate relationships.

III

Intervention Strategies

Coordinating a Community Response to Teen Dating Violence

Laura Prato and Regina Braham

The Jersey Battered Women's Service (JBWS) is a private, non-profit agency that provides services for battered women, their children and abusive men. In 1987, JBWS developed the Teenage Dating Violence Program. Its sole purpose was to educate high school students, their parents and teachers about the cause, scope and consequences of violence against women in intimate relationships. But as teens became more aware of abuse or the threat of abuse by their boyfriends, they began calling the JBWS hot line for help. They needed more than a prevention education program. They needed protection.

"I'm trying to break up with him, but he won't let me," is how Lisa Clarke explained what was happening between her and her boyfriend, Eric.* During the months to follow, we all learned how aptly this simple explanation described the situation in which this sixteen-year-old high school student found herself.

The following description of Lisa's situation highlights many of the issues confronting victims of dating violence, as well as the role of a dating violence program in coordinating a community response that ensures protection of victims.

Background

Detective Hill, a local police officer, referred Lisa to the JBWS Dating Violence Program in March 1988 after school au-

---

* "Lisa Clarke" and "Eric" are pseudonyms chosen to protect their confidentiality.

thorities informed him about a series of "scenes" that had occurred between Lisa and Eric. A high school junior, Lisa was attempting to end a year-long relationship with Eric, a senior at the same high school. Alternating between tearful pleading and angry threats, Eric was determined the relationship would continue.

In his initial referral call, Detective Hill described Eric as physically large and imposing, with a history of a "temper" that intimidated teachers and students. In fact, Eric was on probation as a result of assault charges filed against him by his father and stepmother during a family conflict. Detective Hill also noted that Eric's father had a past history of violence toward Eric's mother. Eric's recent performance on the football team and his relationship with Lisa had provided him with an acceptance and status that had previously eluded him. Though his poor academic skills and occasional aggressive behavior had long been of concern to school personnel, his recent "successes" were seen as progress, and indeed, one of his teachers labeled the fall of Eric's senior year as his "reconstruction."

Lisa felt that Eric's harassment was escalating. Detective Hill and school personnel felt that Lisa appeared to be sending "mixed messages" in response to Eric's repeated approaches at school. At times, she appeared friendly and attempted to reason with Eric ("We can be friends"); at other times, she ignored him. In either case, the result was the same. Eric insisted they were "in love" and accused Lisa of betraying him ("How could you do this to me?"). As their confrontations became increasingly volatile and disruptive, Lisa found herself screaming at Eric in response to his accusations. The principal of the high school met several times with both teenagers and Detective Hill to resolve the problem.

After discussing safety options with Lisa, Detective Hill contacted both JBWS and Lisa's mother. He told Ms. Clarke about the JBWS Dating Violence Program and obtained permission for a counselor to contact her.

Reaching Out

Ms. Clarke was extremely receptive to the counselor's telephone call. She said that Lisa had been trying to "break up" with Eric for weeks, but he wouldn't let her. Although initially she didn't understand what her daughter meant, she was becoming increasingly concerned.

Ms. Clarke had received a call from two of Lisa's girlfriends. They decided to contact her following a recent dating violence presentation by JBWS to their health class. Responding to questions listed in a brochure distributed to students, the girls identified Lisa as a victim of abuse. They confided to Ms. Clarke that they were worried about Lisa and knew of incidents in which Eric had pushed and threatened her.

When Ms. Clarke confronted her daughter with her knowledge of the abuse, Lisa began to sob, expressing her confusion and fear. Ms. Clarke became especially alarmed when Lisa disclosed that, a few days earlier, Eric had chased her into the girls' restroom and shook her by the neck as she screamed for help and attempted to flee. She reported that Eric repeatedly verbally abused her in the school hallways, calling her a bitch or whore and accusing her of betraying him. Ms. Clarke expressed frustration that school officials had not informed her of these incidents and feared for her daughter's safety.

The counselor helped Ms. Clarke to develop "safety plans" with Lisa. Ms. Clarke would drive Lisa to and from school; Lisa would travel in the halls only with a friend; and she would alert a teacher if Eric threatened her in any way. These plans would be reviewed and revised dozens of times during the next few months.

Meeting With Lisa

Lisa came to the guidance office to meet with the JBWS counselor the next day. She sat down with her hands nervously clutching her books. Although she tried to speak calmly, her voice trembled and she cried as she spoke of her relationship with Eric. She really cared about Eric and didn't want to see him hurt. She described Eric as jealous and moody and said she had thought about breaking up with him many times. Lisa related several incidents in which Eric shook her or pushed her against the wall during arguments. Afterward, he was sorry and explained that he only became upset because he loved her so much. Sometimes she would buy him cards and write notes to reassure him of her love. Although that would seem to calm him for a while, the problems would soon begin again. According to Lisa, during the past few months they were arguing more often and she was upset much of the time.

When the counselor asked what she would like to see happen, Lisa didn't hesitate. "I want to break up with Eric. I just want this to be over." She acknowledged the confusion she felt about how to respond to Eric when he approached her at school. She explained that when she said hello to him and entered into a conversation with him, Eric assumed they were "back together." If she ignored him, he became angry and created scenes in the hall which embarrassed and humiliated her. Many of their mutual friends felt sorry for Eric and blamed Lisa for upsetting him. One girl even asked her, "Why are you trying to mess up Eric's life?"

The counselor supported Lisa's right to end her relationship with Eric and helped her see Eric as responsible for his reaction. They developed safety plans for traveling to and from school, attending school activities and on weekends at the restaurant where she was a waitress. Lisa decided to avoid any situation in which she might find herself alone with Eric.

Two Months Later

During the next several months, Eric's harassment and threats to Lisa persisted. Through phone calls and letters, he warned her that he'd be her "worst enemy" and repeatedly pledged that she'd never have another boyfriend. Eric made it known in school that he did not want anyone else to date Lisa and slashed a boy's tires in retaliation for his friendship with her.

Clearly, Lisa was at risk and not able to stop the abuse alone. In addition to providing counseling for her and her mother, the Teenage Dating Violence Program advocated for a coordinated community response that involved Lisa, her parents, her peer group, her school, the police department and the court system. Only through their combined efforts did Eric finally stop abusing Lisa.

A Coordinated Community Response

The Police Response

Detective Hill, a juvenile officer, was a familiar sight in the township's high school—both in the hallway and the classroom. He learned about the JBWS Dating Violence Program when the counselor presented the topic to the senior health classes. The counselor and he subsequently collaborated on programs for the school's peer leadership training seminar. Because Detective Hill understood the problem of dating violence, had the respect of the school administration and knew how to use the legal system, he became an important link in coordinating Lisa's protection. He identified Lisa as a victim of abuse and referred her to JBWS. Detective Hill's continued involvement in the case communicated the serious nature of Eric's threats and harassment, and validated Lisa's need for protection.

Court Response

As difficult as it is for (adult) battered women to find protection through the legal system, for teenagers the system is even less accessible. In New Jersey, the Prevention of Domestic Violence Act is the civil remedy that provides protection to victims. It does not include minors, with the exception of those who have been declared emancipated by the court. Obviously, this excludes the vast majority of teenagers involved in violent dating relationships.

In Lisa's case, the issue of Eric's violence entered the court system through a "back door." Eric was on probation as a result of assault charges filed by his father and stepmother. When Detective Hill identified Eric as physically abusive to Lisa, he contacted Eric's probation officer. The probation officer brought this problem to the attention of the judge, who in turn asked Lisa to appear in Family Court for a probation review hearing.

The JBWS counselor helped to prepare Lisa and her mother for the hearing and accompanied them to court. At the hearing, the judge asked Lisa to state whether she wanted to continue a relationship with Eric. She repeated no to each of the judge's variously phrased questions.

The judge ordered Eric to refrain from all contact with Lisa, including phone calls, letters and messages from friends. Despite the inclusion of this matter in the probation process, Eric's harassment of Lisa was a peripheral issue for the court. Although the court hearing was highly emotional for both Eric and Lisa, the matter was treated with a lack of serious regard or understanding about the potential risks to Lisa. The judge chided Eric that "a handsome boy like you can find a new girlfriend any time."

Eric blatantly ignored the restrictions imposed by his probation, which included a curfew, strict school attendance, a psychosocial evaluation and no contact with Lisa. His parents were unable to provide the support and structure needed to enforce these conditions, and the legal system was unable to impose sanctions that conveyed the message that Eric's behavior was wrong and would not be tolerated.

Five months after Lisa initiated the breakup of their relationship, Eric reached eighteen years of age. At this time, he was still sending Lisa "love letters" to the restaurant where she worked part-time and calling the Clarke home to make threats against Lisa ("I'm going to get you alone... ") and her new boyfriend. Lisa was increasingly anxious and fearful that Eric would eventually find a way to hurt her.

Though reluctant to anger Eric further, the Clarkes decided to file a complaint of harassment against him. Because of his adult status, the case was heard in a municipal court. The judge issued a temporary restraining order and warned Eric that he faced a jail sentence if the order was violated. The judge ordered a continuance and review of the case in six months.

At about the same time as his municipal court appearance, Eric became involved with someone else. Perhaps because of the combination of events (the threat of severe consequences and another love interest) Eric's harassment of Lisa decreased in frequency and intensity. Although she reported that he "stared" at her in school, he stopped making overt efforts to contact her. This was eight months after Lisa had told Eric she wanted to end their relationship. Because there were no further threats of abuse toward Lisa, the judge dismissed the harassment charges at the six-month review hearing.

The School's Response

Schools often function like "islands," settling disputes and negotiating conflicts within their system. This approach can be advantageous since it allows for flexibility and efficiency. However, it can also serve to insulate an abusive student from more serious legal consequences.

School officials initially responded to the loud angry "scenes" between Eric and Lisa by calling them both into the office to "talk it out." When the JBWS counselor met with the school principal and Eric's guidance counselor, they characterized the problem as "just a volatile teenage dating relationship." They minimized the severity of the problem and therefore never notified Ms. Clarke of some of the abusive incidents.

Although school officials acknowledged that Lisa repeatedly stated that she wanted to "break up" with Eric, they maintained a belief that Lisa provoked the conflict by sending "mixed messages" to Eric about her interest in continuing their relationship. However, when asked how Lisa *should* respond when Eric approached her in school, they held differing views, from "absolutely ignore him" to "be friendly and courteous." The counselor used this to illustrate the difficulty a sixteen-year-old girl would face in responding to Eric and how easily Lisa's confusion and varying attempts might be interpreted as a mixed message.

When Lisa obtained an order restricting Eric from having contact with her, the JBWS counselor supported Ms. Clarke's request that the administration notify all teachers of this order. At first, the school administrator expressed some uncertainty as to what extent the order applied to school grounds. However, once the JBWS counselor clarified this issue, the information was spread throughout the school and schedules were changed to ensure that Lisa and Eric would not be in the same classroom.

The JBWS Dating Violence Program played an important role in helping school authorities to redefine the problem, protect Lisa and hold Eric accountable for his verbal and physical abusiveness. Over a span of several months, school authorities became aware of the potential risk Eric posed to Lisa and were more involved in protecting her.

The Parents' Response

Ms. Clarke was consistently available for and supportive of Lisa. She maintained regular contact with the school and local police and worked closely with the JBWS counselor for several months. A major thrust of her discussions with the JBWS counselor focused on Lisa's immediate need for safety, that is, developing clear, specific and realistic "safety plans" on a daily basis. With the support of Detective Hill and the JBWS counselor, she eventually filed a criminal harassment complaint against Eric.

In addition to dealing with the immediate, concrete demands of this crisis, Ms. Clarke identified several issues of concern to her:

• "I shouldn't have let her date him. I knew he had some

'family problems' and had been in trouble. I believed he was a sad, confused young man. My daughter asked me to give him a chance." At times Ms. Clarke blamed herself for allowing Lisa to become involved with Eric. She believed that perhaps she should have been able to prevent the emotional trauma and physical danger her daughter was experiencing.

• "I should have known something was wrong earlier. They seemed happy in the beginning. But more recently I noticed that Eric was unpredictably moody and Lisa was often in tears." Ms. Clarke questioned why she failed to recognize that Lisa was being abused before the risk to her daughter escalated.

• "There's never been abuse in our family, but a friend of mine said that Lisa might *look* for this type of relationship again. Is there something *wrong* with my daughter that will attract her to abusive men?" With education about violence against young women in dating relationships and emotional support, Ms. Clarke was able to confront her own self-doubts and avoid "victim-blaming"—holding herself or Lisa responsible for Eric's actions.

Mr. Clarke remained somewhat peripherally involved throughout this crisis. He was employed by a utility company and often worked long hours. Ms. Clarke assumed most parenting responsibilities. Though it appeared that Lisa and her mother kept Mr. Clarke informed about Lisa's efforts to end her relationship with Eric, Mr. Clarke did not communicate directly with school officials, police or JBWS. On several occasions, Ms. Clarke remarked that her husband was "getting impatient with all of this" and sometimes thought he should resolve the situation "his own way."

Peer Response

When Lisa initially broke off her relationship with Eric, she felt condemned and misunderstood by her classmates. Many of their mutual friends sympathized with Eric and blamed Lisa both for his emotional pain and disruptive behavior. They did not understand her fears or her right to leave the relationship. In fact, an "underground" school newspaper featured the couple and chastised Ms. Clarke for failing to "mind her own business"—adding to Lisa's intense embarrassment.

Her peers' reaction contributed to Lisa's self-doubt and confusion. Perhaps it *was* her fault. . . should she try to work things out? How could she do this to Eric?

Eric, too, was influenced by his peers' expectations that he take "control" of this emotional situation. He couldn't allow Lisa to date other boys—he was compelled to protect his "ownership" of Lisa, his "rights." Rather than express his disappointment, even his fear of being without Lisa, he could only show his friends his rage.

JBWS Response

The JBWS Teenage Dating Violence Program has three components—education, counseling and advocacy. The significance of each of these is readily apparent in Lisa's case. Without the education component, for example, Lisa may not have been identified as a victim of dating violence and referred to JBWS for help. Although JBWS has an established counseling program for battered women and despite the common roots of violence against teen and adult women, teenagers, like Lisa, need a specialized program.

The JBWS Dating Violence Program uses a short-term, problem-solving counseling approach and integrates an understanding of violence in intimate relationships with the many unique developmental, emotional, social and legal issues confronted by teenagers. The program's philosophy (clearly communicated to teenage clients) is consistent with that of our counseling services for adult battered women. It states that 1) each of us has a right to live free from violence; 2) the abuser is solely responsible for his violent behavior; and 3) restrictive sex-role expectations create a power inequality between men and women that perpetuates violence against women in intimate relationships. Counselors provide information about dating violence and support the teenager's work toward her goal, whether it is to explore her relationship or to end a violent relationship safely.

It is often helpful to encourage teens to disclose their experience with dating violence to adults in their lives, beginning with their parents. This communicates the importance of seeking support from others in solving problems one cannot handle alone. Some teens have valid reasons to resist disclosing their contact with a counselor to a parent (for example, child abuse or a potentially violent reponse). For others, such as Lisa, parents are a primary source of protection and support.

Educating, enlisting and coordinating the involvement of resource people available to teenagers requesting assistance is an important advocacy characteristic of our program. With the teenager's permission, the counselor attempts to create a network of understanding adults (for example, parents, school administrators, teachers, police officers, guidance counselors and school nurses). Although Lisa was initially reluctant to tell her mother and other adults about Eric's abuse, clearly their knowledge of what was happening was critical to Lisa's safety and emotional well-being.

Conclusion

The JBWS Dating Violence Program played a critical role in protecting Lisa from further abuse. It empowered Lisa to safely end her relationship with Eric by (1) affirming that she was at risk; (2) teaching her self-protective skills; (3) encouraging and facilitating communication with her mother; (4) identifying, educating and coordinating resource people; and (5) assisting her through the legal process.

The key to a successful coordinated response to dating violence is a strong education program. Dating violence, like domestic violence, is surrounded by misconceptions that create victim-blaming. Through formal presentations and individual consultations with the resource people involved, JBWS helped them to redefine Eric as solely responsible for his abusive behavior and Lisa as a victim at risk. Educating each individual involved in Lisa's case was an ongoing process throughout the entire nine-month intervention. Although time-consuming, it was essential in ensuring a unified response that supported and protected Lisa.

This response, however, failed to stop Eric from assaulting his new girlfriend. Although Eric was given the strong message to stay away from Lisa, he never suffered any serious legal consequences for his abuse nor did he receive counseling. JBWS urged his probation worker to make batterer's counseling a mandatory condition of probation. Instead, he was ordered to a juvenile treatment program for an evaluation and counseling. He never attended; yet his probation was not revoked.

Eric, like so many juvenile offenders, "slipped through the cracks" of a complicated system. As a result, his violent behavior has only worsened. He has recently assaulted his new girlfriend and faced an aggravated assault charge for using a lead pipe to beat her male acquaintance. Because this was his first recorded offense as an adult, he received a sentence of one year's probation and (at the urging of Detective Hill and JBWS) mandatory counseling.

Felicia: Working with a Teen Mother in an Abusive Relationship

Bonnie Zimmer

Felicia* and I met at the prenatal clinic of a hospital in a white working-class community in July 1987. It was my first day on a new job, and she was my first client. I introduced myself and asked if she'd ever spoken with a social worker before. She laughed at me. "You're number twenty-three," she reported as her eyes finally met mine in a challenging stare. Our relationship had begun.

Over the next few months, Felicia and I were to develop a close, even intimate, working alliance. We visited several times a week at my office, her home or the local donut shop. We spent time at the welfare office, the bank and the prenatal clinic. We would talk about fashion, hairstyles, soap operas, our favorite foods. I would lecture her about the importance of using birth control, and she would lecture me about keeping my notoriously cluttered and filthy car clean. Eventually, Felicia told me about her thirteen years as a foster child and her history of school failure, physical and emotional abuse and attempted rape. We discussed intimate details of her life: her pregnancy decision-making (she was keeping her baby), her contraceptive decisions, her feelings about her changing body as the pregnancy progressed. We developed so much trust that Felicia asked me to be her labor coach and I was an honored guest at the birth of her daughter.

What Felicia didn't (or couldn't) tell me until six months after we'd met was that she was being battered. Two years later,

---

* "Felicia" is a pseudonym chosen to protect the client's confidentiality.

Felicia agreed to collaborate with me on this article. We met in our kitchens and talked about our work together and about Felicia's experiences with abuse. Ours is a story of a "professional" and a "client" working together to help one woman and child escape from the violence in their lives. We hope that it may speak to other workers and young mothers as well.

Felicia feels it is important for readers to know something about her past, in order to understand the context of her life at the time the violence occurred.

My real mother was an alcoholic, heavy on drinking, doing drugs, not responsible enough to be on birth control. She had ten kids. Her first child was at the age of sixteen. Her sixth child, being me, was at the age of twenty-three. My oldest sister, who's twenty-seven now, took care of me and my sisters... she brought us up until we were put into foster homes. I have no memories at all of ages one to five. I hear stories... that I used to get locked in the closet... that I used to get beat on... things like that I do not remember... who knows, maybe in time I will remember.... Anyway, they put me in a foster home for what was supposed to be three months... and that became six months, nine months, all the way up to thirteen years. I got pregnant in February 1987 and I threw my past up into my own face.... My exact words were, "I'm being just like my mother. I'm young, I'm unmarried. I'm on welfare. I'm heading right in the same direction as her."

The Legacy of Victim-blaming

Felicia learned early that people would blame her for her misfortunes. Here, she describes her experiences in school in which she was blamed for things that were beyond her control.

I was probably one of... ten foster kids in the whole school, so I would be more or less... picked on... ruled out. It was like, it was my fault that I was put somewhere. They'd say... if you can't stay with your family you must be no good, a nothing. I was picked on, and it made me feel like a little, small person. And I was held back, too, on account of I couldn't read. But my counselors told me that was because my mother drank when she was pregnant with me, so I had a learning disability.

Felicia claims that her involvement with protective service and mental health professionals replicated her schoolyard experiences of victim-blaming and added to her sense of personal responsibility for her problems.

I was constantly in counseling, 'cause that's what everyone said was good for me, which I really resented them for. . . . I hated going to counseling. . . . I felt I was being picked on . . . AS AN INDIVIDUAL . . . people prying into my business . . . it was like it was my fault again. . . . I'd say, "Why are they ruling me out? Why don't they go talk to my mother." She's the one who needed counseling.

The social workers wanted to know everything—when you breathed, when you went to the bathroom, everything. They just wanted to know your whole life story. It was just their attitude, that since you're in foster care we can lay anything we want on you, make you feel guilty. We were considered to be state children, so the state, they'd say, had every right to know what was going on.

Repeatedly asked questions about her sex life, the status of her relationship with her partner, the quality of her family life, Felicia felt that these questions never had her best interests in mind. As a child, she had learned not to reveal much about herself for fear of losing even more than she had already lost. Now, as a teenage mother herself, she depended upon the very systems that had failed her as a child. She developed a stony stance toward social workers in general.

There were several opportunities for me to personally witness the angry, judgmental treatment by her caseworker when I accompanied Felicia to the welfare office. After her worker told her she was a liar, we agreed that she would attend her required meetings only when I could accompany her because Felicia said she was treated more respectfully when I was with her.

Felicia explains the impact of her lifelong involvement with social service providers on her self-image and her growing feelings of helplessness. Felicia's depression began to escalate during her junior year in high school.

I sometimes thought about killing myself because I felt like such an outsider, and I couldn't talk about my problems. I couldn't do anything. I was slow in school, and I just began to think "What am I doing here?" My foster parents brought us up that God put us here for some reason: some to succeed and some to fail . . . I figured I was going to fail.

And then, in her senior year of high school, Felicia was kicked out of her foster parents' home following an argument at a family party. She felt desperate.

Like many of the young women I met during my years working with pregnant and parenting teens, Felicia opted out of suicide. She found what she considered to be a more positive solution to her desperate situation. Felicia met a new boyfriend. Within a few short months, she was pregnant.

I got pregnant in February 1987 because I wasn't careful and one thing led to another... and in my head I think I wanted to get pregnant. Probably to spite what happened in my family [getting kicked out]. I guess I could have given up the baby, either with abortion or adoption, and I thought about it, being eighteen and not having anyone there for me, like a mother or father. But I decided to keep the baby. I told my boyfriend, and things went... [Felicia whistles] whew!!! just right downhill.

During the sixth month of her pregnancy, when she finally began to show, the abuse began.

At the age of eighteen, when I was pregnant, it was pretty much when I started experiencing it... being verbally and physically abused.... He told me I was a bitch. Then he started beating on me, telling me I'm not allowed to leave the house, being pushed, strangled, just a lot of stuff. But you know it was more or less the verbal abuse that killed me most. I just felt like I was no good, I was trash, the things he used to say to me... that I would never get another boyfriend in my life, that I'm a bitch, a whore. And then things got even worse. I started getting hurt. I put my hand through two windows when he was beating on me. He wasn't letting me out the door, and he punched me in the nose. My nose was bleeding, and I put my hand right through the window to try to get out. I split it right open. So here he was beating on a seven-month pregnant girl, and I thought to myself that if anyone was mentally disturbed at the time it was him.

Felicia tells us what feminist writers have emphasized in recent literature: that physical violence, while terrifying and dangerous, is also only one dimension of the complex pattern of control and domination that we call battering (NiCarthy, 1986; Schechter, 1982; Yllo and Bograd, 1988).

We have used the terms *battered* and *abused* interchangeably. Felicia, in fact, prefers the term *abused* since she says that *battered* is not a word she attributes to her own experiences. However, many services remain titled "battered women's services." We agreed, therefore, to refer to Felicia's personal experiences as abuse and to apply the term *battered* to more general references.

Attempts to Seek Help

Felicia was beginning to consider that perhaps her boyfriend, not she, might be responsible for the violence. But several failed attempts at getting help led her back to the victim-blaming that helps to trap so many battered women in self-hatred. I asked her about her attempts to seek help and escape from the violence.

I tried telling his parents. His father said I was lying, that his son couldn't be hitting me.

Another time his mother was right there [during a beating]. The only way I could get her to help was . . . I picked up a bottle of aspirin, and I threatened her that I would take them all. . . . I had them right there in my hand. Then she called the hospital, but all they were worried about was whether I'd hurt the baby. They thought I was crazy, and they didn't talk about that he had been beating on me. They were worried . . . would I abuse the baby?

Once though, when that guy tried to rape me when I was twelve years old, I told my parents, and my father was going to kill the guy. [At the age of twelve, Felicia was stopped by a man posing as a policeman while bicycling home from school. He lured her into his car and attempted to rape her. She was able to escape.] There was something clearer cut about that. You can't blame a twelve-year-old girl for riding her bike home.

Though no one could "blame a twelve-year-old girl for riding her bike home," she knew all too well that many would blame a pregnant eighteen-year-old woman for being involved with a violent partner. Felicia began to see that she was no longer seen as a "worthy" victim.

Felicia also tried therapy. Her boyfriend was in counseling, and she was asked to come to a couple's session.

She [the therapist] was more or less shocked when I told her that it was happening. So she asked me if I nagged him too much. I told her I did everything in the world for him. And then I just shut my mouth because she was saying it was my fault.

Building Trust With Teen Mothers
Who Are Abused

I wondered why Felicia had decided to tell me about the violence at all? Why would she risk disclosure after so many disappointments throughout her life with twenty-two previous social workers?

You told me you weren't from DSS and that helped. [The Department of Social Services is the child protective agency in Massachusetts.] But even so, when I first met you I was afraid that if I did something wrong my baby would be taken away. Because that's what the state does. I got over being afraid, though, after about six months . . . actually less, 'cause I asked you to come in and help me deliver my baby so I guess I trusted you then.

You were the first person I told. 'Cause you weren't like a social worker. You always listened. [She laughs.] You know, it's supposed to be that the social worker listens and the client talks, but I would find it would usually be the other way around, with social workers talking and talking at me. But you really listened. And if I needed you, you'd come right over. And you wouldn't blame me . . . for being pregnant or for him beating on me. . . . My foster parents would say, "One night in the sack, and this is what happens; it's your fault." You didn't do that.

I asked Felicia what it was like to finally tell me about the violence and to share her feelings about it with a social worker.

It was . . . a relief. . . to let it go, because no one else believed it was happening. But I knew it was happening because I was the victim. I told you because I was sick of it, and I found I could talk to you about it.

But it was also hard. It hurt a lot to talk about it with you. It made it . . . that it was really happening. That someone I had a kid with was doing this to me . . . talking to you was different. I had thought, more or less, "No, it's not real, it's just my imagination." I thought I was too happy of a person for this to be going on. But deep down inside, I was really a miserable person . . . a really hurt person. And when I told you, I believed it.

As professionals we need to remind ourselves of how much courage it takes to reveal one's pain to another human being. And being in an abusive relationship is a profoundly painful experience. In addition to finding the inner strength to face her own pain, Felicia needed outer reassurance that, unlike the others, I would not hurt her with the knowledge of how wounded she felt, inside and out.

She also touched on some issues that I found to be common among the teen mothers I knew.

For battered women in Massachusetts, the fear of losing one's baby is very real. Too often when women go for help, protective workers fail to see the woman as being in need of services. Instead they focus exclusively on the protective concern for the child. The assumption they make is if the woman can't protect herself from violence, she won't be able to protect her child. They often decide to remove children from the home. As a result, younger women, already scrutinized because of their age, retreat from services in an effort to keep their families intact.*

The other common thread in Felicia's account is the disbelief that "someone I had a kid with" could be a batterer. Like their adult counterparts, teens who become parents often embrace dreams of escape into a "happy family" of their own creation that may heal the injuries of their often painful personal histories. To admit that their baby's father is battering them means relinquishing the dream that sustained them through pregnancy, childbirth and the difficult adjustment to parenting. Further, beyond the psychological resistance lies the reality of welfare dependence and poor future employability owing to limited educational opportunities and lack of adequate child care, job training and flexible work schedules, which make up the real worlds of most single teen mothers.

Despite this, Felicia decided to tell her twenty-third social worker about the abuse. She struggled with her boyfriend for many more months as the violence escalated. She eventually ended up at the emergeny room of the local hospital with a leg injury. She didn't tell the hospital personnel how she sustained the injury for fear of losing her baby. She did, however, call me. We discussed all her options, including leaving him, seeking shelter with the local battered women's group, obtaining a restraining order and changing her telephone number and the locks on her doors. Through many months I listened as Felicia struggled to accept the reality of her boyfriend's violence. They were reunited several times.

During this same time period, Felicia also began working on some long-range goals for herself and her baby. She enrolled in a state-funded job-training program that provided child care. She studied hard and prepared for her high school General Equiva-

---

* A unique alternative to traditional social service models can be found in the AWAKE program at Children's Hospital in Boston. Founded by battered women's advocates, the program provides advocacy for the mothers of abused children. (See Straus, Schechter, Grace and Michalek, 1987.)

lency Degree (GED) exam while pursuing a training program in automated bookkeeping. Her learning disability has made the GED exam a difficult task, but Felicia has taken the exam repeatedly and increased her score steadily each time. Though she is still falling short of a passing grade, she is confident that she will someday receive her equivalency certificate.

As professionals working with young mothers who may be abused, what can we do to encourage trust, to empower women and to help them escape violence? My work with Felicia and other abused teens was difficult work. I had to be available for crises (which were many). I had to educate myself about the services to battered women in my area, become familiar with the courts and learn how to walk a woman through the process of obtaining a restraining order or pressing criminal charges. I also sat in on an open support and education group at the local shelter.

Having supportive supervision and peer support is also essential. Working with abused women can evoke feelings of helplessness at times, and it is this sense of helplessness that too often leads to victim blaming by well-meaning professionals. Working with teen mothers can present difficult ethical dilemmas stemming from our role as both advocate for the young abused women and mandated reporter in cases of suspected child abuse or neglect. Skilled supervision and close consultation with battered women's advocates can help ensure a balanced response that does not ignore women's needs in favor of children's.

I asked Felicia what had made the difference for her.

A lot of counseling and a lot of friends telling me I was not a bad person. I had to hear it a lot of times, lots of times, QUITE A FEW TIMES, but then I heard it. And graduating from my bookkeeping course and working on my GED.

I have more confidence in myself that I can do anything I want to do. Being able to talk to people, open up, show my expressions, not to hide them . . . just being able to be myself, not try to be somebody else. . . . Now I'm able to be honest with myself and who I am and what I can do to change myself, not have people change me. Because that's the way life is.

Overcoming Post-Traumatic Stress Disorder in Adolescent Date Rape Survivors

Johanna Gallers and Kathy J. Lawrence

During the last fifteen years, there has been mounting evidence that being raped or battered causes considerable psychological trauma months or even years after the victimizing experiences have occurred. Kilpatrick, Saunders, Veronen, Best and Von (1987) found that 57.1 percent of all rape victims developed Post-Traumatic Stress Disorder (PTSD) sometime after the rape. According to a literature review by Steketee and Foa (1987), some of the most common responses following rape or battering are fear and anxiety, depression, disruption of social functioning, problems in sexual functioning, suicide attempts, sleep disturbances, hostilty, somatic complaints and obsessive-compulsive symptoms. Additionally, according to Janoff-Bulman (1985), survivors often experience shock and confusion combined with feelings of helplessness and powerlessness.

Janoff-Bulman describes a cognitive response in terms of a shattering of basic assumptions that many women experience after rape or battering has occurred. These assumptions make up "one's overall theory of reality... which is used as a means of recognizing, planning and acting" in the world. The first assumption is the belief that we are invulnerable. In order to function in a potentially dangerous and hostile world, one needs to believe that terrible things happen only to *others*. The second assumption is that the "world is meaningful and comprehensible." One believes that the world "makes sense," that there is justice and that people who are harmed are getting what they deserve. The third assumption is that "we see ourselves in a positive light." That is, one feels that one is a worthy, decent person who can cope with whatever happens in a mature, self-assertive fashion. People believe that they have power and can control their own lives. When one is raped, the world suddenly becomes a frightening, incomprehensible place where all notions of justice are overturned. A survivor's sense of her ability to protect herself and function autonomously is destroyed, and she is left feeling helpless, powerless, needy and out of control.

This new self-perception reinforces negative images of oneself as bad and weak. With such massive loss of self-esteem, it is easy to see how many survivors blame themselves for the rape or battering. First, because they feel bad about themselves and second, if they accept some responsibility for their victimization, many survivors feel they can reestablish some control over their lives. If they believe that they have some responsibility, then they also have some control. They are not as helpless and powerless as they were made to feel. Therefore, survivors are often in a terrible bind. If they acknowledge their helplessness and powerlessness in preventing their victimization, they reinforce negative self-images. But if they accept some responsibility for the outcome, then they cannot be legitimately angry with the perpetrator. They internalize blame as a means of saving their self-esteem, but then try to live with the guilt of their own complicity.

Teenagers who have been raped or battered suffer from additional difficulties. For many survivors of sexual assault or battering, there is a feeling that one's sense of personal integrity has been violated. According to Everstine and Everstine (1989), four dilemmas are experienced by adolescent rape survivors. First is a "sense of loss of personal integrity or wholeness which can be particularly devastating to an adolescent who is still in the process of defining who she is and separating from her parents." The developmental task for adolescents, according to Erikson (1950), is to establish a separate identity in the world apart from their family identity and ties. When an adolescent is raped or battered, this work is interrupted and there is often a regression back to the safety of earlier stages of development.

Second, teenagers have a need to believe that they can begin to control their environments. Rape or battering upsets a teenager's "perception of her ability to control her environment." Furthermore, a teen's sense of trust in the world is disrupted, forcing

her to reconsider her parents' earlier warnings about the danger-
ousness of the world and her newly found belief that she can
handle such dangers.

A third issue is the damage to the adolescent's emerging sexual identity. Teenagers may not be able to clearly distinguish between rape and consensual sex because of lack of experience.
Therefore a rape experience may have serious repercussions for
subsequent sexual encounters in that later sex may be tinged with
the feeling of violation.

A final issue deals with the damage to the adolescent's self-
esteem. Teenagers are by nature narcissistic, which means that
they ascribe causality to themselves. An adolescent, then, is much
more likely than an adult to internalize blame for the rape or battering. False assumptions, such as "I am bad" or "I deserve to be
raped or battered because I was with him," reinforce an already
shaky and underdeveloped sense of self and can lead to severe self-
esteem problems.

Symptoms unique to adolescent survivors, according to Hilberman (1976), are sudden personality changes, drop in school
performance, withdrawal from usual school or social activities,
flagrant promiscuous behavior, sudden phobic behavior, self-
destructive or risk-taking behavior, drug or alcohol abuse, development of eating disorders such as bulimia or anorexia and sudden alienation from peers or family.

Diagnosing PTSD in Adolescents

The diagnostic category most frequently used by psychother-
apists to explain the trauma associated with rape, battering and
sexual abuse is Post-Traumatic Stress Disorder (PTSD), first described in 1980 in the American Psychiatric Association's third
edition of the Diagnostic and Statistical Manual (DSM III).
PTSD is defined by (1) the existence of a recognizable stressor
that would evoke significant symptoms of distress in almost anyone; (2) the reexperience of the trauma either through (*a*) recur-
rent intrusive recollections, (*b*) dreams, or (*c*) sudden feelings
(emotional lability); (3) a numbing of responsiveness or reduced
involvement in the external world indicated by diminished interest in activities, feelings of estrangement from others and con-
stricted affect; and (4) at least two of the following symptoms: hy-
peralertness, sleep problems, survival guilt, problems with mem-

ory or concentration, avoidance of activities or the intensification of symptoms when exposed to stimuli related to the traumatic event.

However, rape or sexual assault is not a unitary experience. Such factors as age and developmental stage at the time of the trauma as well as whether the violence was one experience, part of chronic exposure to violence or one episode superimposed on a history of chronic abuse need to be part of the diagnostic determination. PTSD symptoms vary across survival situations.

David Finkelhor (1988) points out that the DSM III overlooks symptoms such as fear, depression, self-blame, anxiety and sexual problems, which clinicians working with survivors of chronic abuse almost universally find to be present as well. In fact, Kilpatrick and colleagues (1987) found in one survey that only thirty-six percent of survivors of childhood sexual abuse ever experienced any of the PTSD symptoms described in the DSM III. The more classic PTSD symptoms delineated in the DSM III are more prevalent in adolescent or adult survivors of a *single instance* of violence or trauma.

Flooding

Many clinicians and investigators, such as Marshall (1985), Foy, Resnick, Carroll and Osato (1990), Saigh (1987), Frank, Anderson, Stewart, Dancu, Hughes and West (1988) and Fairbank, Gross and Keane (1983) to name a few, agree that one of the most effective psychotherapy treatments for PTSD involves reexposure to the memory of a traumatic event or situation. There are several ways that therapists do this; systematic desensitization, flooding or implosive therapy, and stress innoculations are the most widely used by clinicians. However, it is important to stress that such reexposure is viable only when the client is out of the traumatic situation. Reexposure is not suitable, for example, in treating adolescents who are still being abused by their partners because these young women need their defenses intact in order to continue to survive. Once they are safe from the battering, then they can afford to deal with the more intrusive symptoms of PTSD. Until that time, it may be more adaptive to remain emotionally numb.

PTSD symptoms are a defensive reaction to an abnormal situation. According to Levis (1980), the symptoms are functional for traumatized individuals in that they help alleviate or limit anxiety associated with the memory of the traumatic event. By repeatedly being presented with the memories of the most traumatic events, the survivor unlearns the fear of both the memories of the violence and the stimulus cues associated with those memories.

Flooding is a behavioral therapy technique that allows survivors of violence to access memories stored in the affective state present at the time that the trauma occurred. These memories can be fully retrieved only when that state is simulated. Disassociation of the affective component of a memory from its cognitive component is common in survivors of all ages who have not been able to talk about or emotionally process their feelings about a traumatic experience right after it has occurred. With teenagers, the disassociation is even more pronounced. Adolescents are actively dealing with identity formation issues. Any assault on their self-esteem and sense of emerging autonomy throws them into a crisis. Instead of feeling a cohesive sense of self, the self seems diffuse and fragile after a trauma. All the gains made toward becoming autonomous individuals seem lost. Adolescents feel humiliated and ashamed of their helplessness and powerlessness. In their own eyes, they once again seem like a child trying to negotiate an incomprehensible universe. Adolescent rape and battering survivors, according to Lyons (1987), either become very compliant and withdrawn in response to the disruption of the identity development process or become aggressive and act out sexually or with drugs or alcohol.

Joy

Joy, a nineteen-year-old college student had been raped by a young man she had been dating while she was an exchange student in Paris. After meeting him in a park near the university, they began seeing each other for "coffee and philosophical discussions at first." Being shy with men as well as sexually inexperienced, Joy enjoyed the platonic aspects of the relationship and believed that Jean understood her fears about becoming physically intimate. One day, he invited her to his apartment, in Joy's words:

. . . just to show me where he lived and to make me lunch. I accepted because I trusted him and believed him when he told me that we would just eat and then he would bring me back to the dormitory. We had a nice lunch and I drank more wine than I should have. I got sleepy and he told me I could lie down on

his bed and take a nap. I felt funny doing that, but I was very sleepy, so I closed his bedroom door and went to sleep with all my clothes on, on top of the covers. I awoke to find Jean lying next to me, wearing only his shirt and sweater. He had his hands on my breast, and he kept saying it was okay. It wasn't, and I was scared. I said no, but he rolled over on top of me, pinning my body to the bed. He was hard, and his penis pressed into my side. He pulled up my skirt and pulled down my underpants. I didn't fight. Lying there, I thought that I must have made him do this because I was here and I just wanted him to get it over with as soon as possible.

Afterward Jean acted as if nothing had happened. According to Joy, he even offered her some more wine and seemed genuinely surprised that she wanted to go back to her dorm "so soon." Joy started to cry, and Jean told her that it was okay. She stopped and began to wonder if she wasn't "just making a big deal out of nothing." Continuing to see Jean for coffee and conversation as well as more afternoons and evenings in his apartment, it did not dawn on Joy that she had been raped. She never enjoyed sex with Jean and even dreaded the encounters, but she thought that maybe this is what "sex is all about" and she would "learn to like it some day with enough practice." Jean always initiated the sex, and Joy would "just lie there."

Joy stayed in Paris for another three months. Paris, however, was not the same after that first afternoon in Jean's apartment. Eventually feelings about the experience began to intrude into her awareness. She started having nightmares, was plagued by intrusive thoughts about sex and violence that made concentration on her studies impossible. Finding Paris to be an alien and rather hostile city, she decided to cut short her year abroad and come home.

Joy came from a warm, supportive family. Her mother was familiar with issues relating to rape and PTSD and consequently was understanding and validating. Her father and brothers were appropriately outraged and protective. She had no history of emotional, physical or sexual abuse prior to this. Joy was a good student who before the rape had been outgoing with friends and very self-confident. It was her strong belief in herself that enabled her at nineteen to make the decision to live in another country by herself for a year. In developmental terms, before the rape, she was dealing with normal adolescent issues of separation and individuation, feelings of empowerment in the world apart from her family and the need to begin to establish an identity as an autonomous human being.

During the months after the rape and her relationship with Jean, Joy began to develop classic PTSD symptoms as a means of coping with the emotional turmoil engendered by the assault and her subsequent relationship with the perpetrator, which had reinforced her feelings of helplessness, powerlessness and self-hatred.

Joy was treated for seven sessions with a combination of flooding and cognitive restructuring. By repeatedly presenting the memory of the rape scene to Joy, she unlearned her fear reaction to both the memory of the rape and the stimulus cues associated with that memory. Her anxiety decreased dramatically, and she was able to again participate in activities that had become anxiety-provoking after the rape, such as studying, being alone in a strange place or going out with friends.

Joy had been consciously in shock during the rape and had had other reactions during and immediately after the rape about which she was not aware. She had been "frightened, felt humiliated and ashamed, betrayed and dumb." As time passed, these feelings became more isolated from the cognitive memory of the event, so when Joy finally did talk about the rape to her parents, she described the event quite factually and unemotionally as if she were reading a story aloud from a book.

Joy's assumptions about herself and the world were shattered, so as time passed she withdrew emotionally from her former life to protect herself from the anxiety that stemmed from the shattering of those assumptions. She learned to avoid any cues that reminded her of the rape, such as being alone in an enclosed space with a man, being alone in a strange situation or being in class with many other students, thus minimizing her anxiety about feeling so powerless to protect herself. However, intrusive symptoms such as nightmares and panic attacks did manifest themselves, and she came to therapy for help.

During the intake session, she talked about the rape in detail in a rather detached, unemotional fashion. When she described her PTSD symptoms, especially the nightmares, she showed a bit more feeling because, as she put it, nightmares "happen when something is frightening you." The therapist and Joy talked about the rape and the negative assumptions that women often develop about themselves after a rape, especially when it has been perpetrated by a man they have been dating. Flooding as a means of alleviating the intrusive PTSD symptoms was also discussed during the initial session, and although she was hesitant to emotionally relive that first afternoon in Jean's apartment, Joy said that she would try it. The therapist explained some of the possible side effects to flooding: increased level of anxiety, more intense nightmares for a few days, other sleep disturbances and increased emotional lability.

The flooding began the following session. Joy was asked to lie down on a couch and to face away from the therapist and close her eyes to prevent any interaction with the therapist. The therapist took Joy through a progressive relaxation exercise to help her get outside the grounding of the day's events and go back to that afternoon in Paris. At the end of the exercise, she was asked to keep her eyes closed and to start describing the rape. As she did, the memory of the event intensified. As the memory became more vivid, she started to feel anxious. But, now, she did not defend herself against the feelings associated with the memory, and she began to relive it emotionally as well as cognitively. The feelings present at the time of the rape returned. As she remembered the rape, she started to cry. It was only the second time she had cried about it.

As Joy recounted the event, the therapist began to challenge whatever false assumptions she had about her culpability. For example, Joy maintained that she hadn't really been raped because she had gone to Jean's apartment "willingly." She had lain down on his bed "willingly," and therefore she had led him to believe that she "wanted sex." This idea was challenged. Did she not say no when she awakened to find him fondling her breast? She agreed that she had said no. The therapist responded that Jean had no right to touch her without her permission. As she saw that her right to say no had been violated and that she had been raped, she began to feel less ashamed and guilty. Other assumptions were similarly challenged whereas the terrible nature of the rape and her feelings about it were validated.

During the second flooding session, Joy again recounted the rape. This time she became more visibly upset and cried more freely. Joy talked about the feelings of shame and humiliation she experienced, about feeling powerless to stop Jean and about her "loathing sex." The therapist told her she had been in shock, and her reaction was normal. One does not expect a trusted boyfriend to commit such an act. Joy continued to restructure her assumptions about the rape.

During the third and fourth flooding sessions, Joy's pain broke through her defenses and she was able to rage at Jean and cry for her betrayed self. She left the sessions alternately sad and mad and went home after each session to take a nap, after which she awakened feeling "lighter." She stopped having nightmares after the third session and began to feel generally more peaceful after the fourth session. She underwent one more flooding session where she again was able to reexperience her anger toward Jean. This time, the emotion was pure anger, untinged with guilt or shame. She met two more times with the therapist. The work involved some final cognitive restructuring about the feelings she had about herself. She left therapy saying that she "felt like herself again."

Jamie

Teenagers who have been physically or sexually abused as children and who then experience sexual abuse or battering in a dating relationship manifest different psychological responses to the experience than do adolescents who experience rape or battery once. Jamie was physically and psychologically abused as a child and then as an eighteen-year-old was raped by a young man she was dating. Jamie's mother had been physically abused, neglected and finally abandoned when she was a child. With little or no positive modeling to teach her how to be a loving, nurturing parent, Jamie's mother perpetuated her own bleak and painful childhood in her relationship with Jamie, who she alternately physically abused and psychologically terrorized. Jamie was an extension of her mother's need system as well as a target for her mother's projections of her own self-hatred. Growing up with such an abusive parent, Jamie not only never learned how to express her own feelings and, in fact, learned that it was futile to have feelings at all.

Jamie started using alcohol, drugs and food as means of self-medicating her emotional pain during her early adolescence. Her involvement with boys was similar to her involvement in other aspects of her life: "I did what everyone expected me to do." Later on she studied nursing for the same reason, because it was what her family had decided she should do.

When she was eighteen she met Michael. He was a cousin of a friend of hers, and she was "attracted to his strong body." Being very shy and insecure, Jamie did not have much experience with boys, nor had she learned how to measure her reponses to others. After dating Michael two or three times and seeing him on several other occasions at her friend's house, she felt "he was probably okay to be with" and started to settle into a dating relationship with him. One night the couple went for a drive and stopped to "park and pet" in a rather deserted section of Jamie's neighborhood. They started kissing, which was "just fine" with Jamie. "Then all of a sudden, he was on top of me, pinning me to the back of the car seat. At first, he was too nervous to get inside of me, but he kept trying until he did. It hurt. According to him it was my job to help him maintain an erection, and he got angry when I didn't. I believed him, but I couldn't bring myself to touch his penis. When he got off me, he laughed and said I had worn him out. I felt strange, but I thought that I had done something to make him do that to me. Afterward, we both acted as if nothing had happened. We continued to date for a while. I didn't even know that I had been raped. I thought I had participated because I knew him. I thought that I was stupid and that my body did not have any value. Anyone could do anything they wanted with it."

Sometime after this relationship, Jamie came into therapy because a relationship in which she was involved was ending and she "needed to talk to someone to find out why." Initially, Jamie talked about her confusion about the present relationship. When asked about her past relationships, she talked about the incident with Michael as if it had no special importance in her life. Similarly, she reported three other date rapes with three other young men. In all three cases, she had been in similar situations where she was in a car "talking or making out with a guy I knew from before" when they grabbed her and forced her to have sex. She did not think that any of these situations constituted rape because she had been with these young men voluntarily and "rape is when a stranger grabs you."

Jamie was extremely anxious and socially withdrawn to the point where she would not look at the therapist throughout the entire session. Jamie experienced some intrusive symptoms, such as difficulty concentrating, chronic anxiety and intense social fears bordering on panic whenever she was in a new social situation dealing with strangers or people she did not know well. Her anxi-

ety and fears were diffuse and pervasive. Developmentally, Jamie
was egocentric, manifesting little awareness of others in relation to
herself, unaware of how her often socially idiosyncratic behavior
affected others.

Jamie's experience of the rape was framed by her long-
standing emotional orientation to a world that she found frightening, painful, lonely and in many ways incomprehensible. Jamie
appeared to be dealing with developmental issues associated with
childhood rather than adolescence. At the same time, it was clear
that she was suffering from a severe psychological reaction to the
rapes that was colored by her earlier abusive experiences. In
Browne and Finkelhor's Traumagenic Dynamics Model (1986),
Jamie's cognitive and emotional orientation to the world had been
altered by her earlier experiences of neglect and abuse so that her
"self-concept, world view and affective and cognitive capacities"
were distorted. Emotionally, the rapes were experienced as just
one of many betrayals and traumas. Consequently, her psychological reaction to the rape was not particularly intense or well defined. Developmentally, she was dealing with issues of basic trust,
autonomy and functionality. The work of therapy, therefore, dealt
not only with feelings and memories connected to the rapes, but
with all the negative assumptions she had about herself and the
world. The therapeutic work was more long-term than Joy's and
focused not only on a reexposure to the traumatic event so Jamie's
emotional reactiveness would be extinguished, but on issues of
trust, self-esteem development and the development of her cognitive and affective capacities as well.

Jamie also underwent flooding, with the same sequence of
procedures as did Joy. However, she had a number of memories
related to earlier childhood traumas on which she needed to work,
and the flooding part of her therapy took longer. Helping Jamie to
alter her false assumptions about herself also took longer. Her
world had never been a safe and secure place, so consequently
Jamie had never learned to feel good about herself in it. The work
she and her therapist did was restitutive, helping her to begin to
develop, in part through their relationship, a different self-concept
as well as an alteration of her basic assumptions about the world.
To Jamie, the rapes and abuse she had suffered were "normal occurrences" that happened in a world that is basically unsafe, one
in which an individual is reactive, never active, and needing to
constantly monitor her environment. She learned that the world

was not the unsafe, lonely place of her earlier years, but a place where one could be loved and respected.

Conclusion

Flooding and cognitive restructuring help survivors to integrate traumatic experiences into the context of their current lives, enabling them to live more fully in the present. Once survivors can reexperience the emotional content of a traumatic memory with someone who cares, someone who can listen to and validate their pain, the meaning of the outcome changes. This time they are not going to be hurt. This time they are not alone with their terror and rage. This time they can begin to integrate and master these feelings, which in turn lose their power to cause them to feel so intensely anxious and fearful. Both Jamie and Joy after treatment were able to live freer and more fulfilling lives. Their responses were more dynamic, rather than reactive, making their worlds more joyful and joyous.

Dating Violence in Asian/Pacific Communities

Mieko Yoshihama, Asha L. Parekh and Doris Boyington

The Asian/Pacific population is the fastest growing minority group in the United States.* Asian/Pacifics numbered over 3.7 million in the 1980 U.S. census, making up 1.5 percent of the total population.† According to expert estimates, Asian/Pacifics made up about 2.1 percent of the total U.S. population in 1985, or 5.1 million in number (Gardner, Robey and Smith, 1985). This increase of 48.5 percent in a half decade reflects, among other factors, an increasing number of refugees, primarily from Southeast Asian countries such as Vietnam, Cambodia and Laos. In 2080, Asian/Pacifics are predicted to make up approximately twelve percent of the U.S. population (Bouvier and Gardner, 1986). This growing population makes it important to address the dimensions of a social problem such as adolescent dating violence in the Asian/Pacific community and the resulting impact on and needs of the community.

The "model minority" myth, maintained through a collusive alliance between the majority culture and the Asian/Pacific community, is a stereotype that allows serious problems such as dating violence to go unaddressed. It perpetuates an image of Asian/Pacifics as homogeneous and successful people without the social

---

* The term *Asian/Pacific* incorporates many cultures and refers to immigrants and refugees from countries with different historical and cultural backgrounds, specifically, but not limited to, Bangladesh, Bhutan, Cambodia, China, Guam, Hong Kong, India, Indonesia, Japan, Korea, Laos, Malaysia, Mongolia, Myanmar, Nepal, Pakistan, Philippines, Samoa, Sikkim, Sri Lanka, Taiwan, Thailand, Tibet and Vietnam.

† U.S. Department of Commerce, Bureau of Census, 1980 Census of Population.

ills that are commonly associated with other minorities (Gould, 1988). Frequently, Asian/Pacifics utilize the model minority label as a survival mechanism to prevent more damaging stereotypes and gross generalizations regarding our communities. Although this stereotype does not reflect the reality of the diversity and the social problems within the Asian/ Pacific community, it is easily accepted because it does not clash with our cultural value systems, which emphasize harmony at all costs.

The evolution of the sexual assault and domestic violence movements in America has created a heightened awareness regarding the realities of rape and, to a lesser extent, dating violence. In spite of this growing awareness, the realities of violence against women remain invisible in the Asian/Pacific communities, creating an illusion that violence against women does not exist.

Frequently Asian/Pacific teenage victims of dating violence choose to remain silent regarding their experiences because of the invisibility of this problem in their community. Those young women who do speak about their problems and seek help often are assaulted with a "second injury" (Symonds, 1975) because of the insensitivity and discriminatory behavior of their families and their communities as well as the professionals they turn to for help.

Simply by coming together to address this topic, we are challenging a commonly held myth in both Asian and non-Asian communities: that is, that dating violence does not exist in Asian/Pacific communities. Although each of the authors has worked with Asian/Pacific adolescents who have been victims of dating violence, it was only with the validation that we provided each other through our discussions that we were able to acknowledge that this is a problem that must be written about.

Cultural Issues

Because of our work with Asian/Pacific teenagers, we were able to identify the influences of culture on their vulnerability and on their perceptions and experiences of dating violence. We view perspectives and values for young women that stem from their cultural histories and beliefs as strengths, even when they add to their vulnerability. For example, young women's allegiance to their families and to maintaining their families' respectability may cause feelings of shame and reluctance to seek needed help, but can also create a sense of strength, support and meaning beyond their immediate experience. The cultural values must be viewed as presenting a conflict rather than as a source of judgment about the culture.

Immigration Experiences

The past history and immigration experiences of a family significantly affect the way they respond to dating violence. For example, the experiences that family members have had with authorities in their native country often influence their wish to avoid any entanglement with law enforcement or other agencies in the United States. The family may have witnessed or been subject to law enforcement officers who accepted bribes, exploited the oppressed, carried out oppressive practices, including unjust accusation, arrest and torture, and generally created a deeper feeling of helplessness for those individuals the law is supposed to protect.

The immigration status of the victim of dating violence and her family members may also affect their willingness to report incidents to the authorities. With the exception of Japanese-Americans, over three-fourths of whom were born in the United States, the majority of the Asian/Pacific population in the United States are foreign-born (Gould, 1988). Among these are a considerable number of undocumented immigrants as well as those who do not have permanent residency or citizenship status. It is not uncommon for undocumented immigrants to decide against filing a police report regarding dating violence incidents because they fear their illegal status may be discovered. Even those who do have legal status—for example, those on student visas—may be fearful of the possibility of deportation and, thus, avoid any contact with authorities.

Immigrants from war-torn countries such as Vietnam, Laos and Cambodia may deny the seriousness of relationship violence because it may not be as severe as their other experiences, whether of war, oppression or the flight from their homelands. For many immigrants, the harsh reality of escape was a treacherous journey that involved risking their lives and experiencing many vulnerabilities and horrors beyond the realm of normal experience. According to a study conducted by the United Nations in 1980, approximately forty percent of female Vietnamese refugees who traveled by boat had been raped by pirates at sea, sometimes repeatedly and brutally. Eleven percent of these women were between the ages of eleven and twenty (Le, 1982).

Both witnessing and experiencing this violence have a devastating impact on the coping mechanisms of refugees. Thus they may deny or choose to "ignore" dating violence or minimize it as easily coped with after all they have been through (Kanuha, 1987). Even the second-generation members of a family (the first of their families to be born here)—who have not had these horrifying experiences—may be deeply affected by the stories of their parents and may have a similar perspective: anything difficult that happens to them here cannot be serious compared to what their families have experienced. But perspectives within a family may differ among individuals and generations, and thus create conflict between family members.

Sex Roles and Power Differences

Asian/Pacific family structure is patterned by a hierarchical, patriarchal model based on generation, age and sex. Interdependence among family members is highly valued. The man is clearly the head of the household. Men are taught to be authoritarian, and women are raised to value obedience and submission (Li-Repac and Fong, 1985). Thus there exists a clear power difference between men and women in Asian/Pacific cultures, and young women are at the lowest level, subordinate to dominant father-husband-brother-son (Chow, 1985). Frequently the intensity of that difference varies among individuals, based on family-of-origin acculturation, immigration and urbanization experiences (Li-Repac and Fong, 1985). From the authors' experience with Asian/Pacific teens, it is apparent that young women internalize these expectations and attitudes even though they may rebel against them, consciously and unconsciously.

Contact between Asians and Americans within and outside the United States contains a long history of exploitation of Asian/Pacifics as economic units of labor, but Asian/Pacific women have been further exploited as sexual commodities. Through various wars, Asian/Pacific women were used as "prostitutes and sexual objects who provided rest and recuperation from the war zones" (Chan, 1988). Currently, this continues near military bases around the world. The American media further reinforce this stereotype of Asian/Pacific women, portraying them as exotic, subservient, passive and sexually attractive. The

Asian/Pacific mail-order bride business highlights the objectification of Asian/Pacific women as submissive sexual servants (Chan, 1988).

These myths, stereotypes and values about Asian/Pacific women also make them vulnerable to victimization by non-Asian men, who may subtly force them to behave according to the stereotypes. Often women internalize the expectation to be subservient and sexually indulge men, which leaves them at high risk to be abused (Chow, 1985).

Dating and Sexuality

Although sexuality is not openly talked about in Asian/Pacific families, a woman clearly learns that her worth and her family's reputation depend on her being a virgin at marriage. The young woman may be explicitly taught how to behave with propriety in the company of men. The lesson includes the requirement that she accommodate the requests and demands of men. Men who seek domination and control may view the highly valued virgin young woman as a prize to conquer. Perplexing feelings arise for the woman, who is divided between duty to her family values of virginity and accommodating the man she is dating.

The value of virginity is conveyed by stories of "good" and "bad" women and by the way that "bad" women are treated or talked about by community members (Li-Repac and Fong, 1985). The Asian/Pacific unmarried young woman may feel responsible to not bring shame to her family in the eyes of their community by being nonsexual. The importance of virginity in some Asian/Pacific cultures (for example, Vietnamese, Korean, Indian) is so powerful that it has a pervasive effect on young women's thoughts, feelings and behavior. Complicated feelings the Asian/Pacific young woman may have about sexuality in general may conflict as she assimilates and tries to conform to social expectations of her American peers.

In most Asian/Pacific cultures, dating issues are considered as taboo as sexuality, and not discussed by teens with their parents. In others, the acceptability of dating varies. For example, in contemporary Japan, dating is a much more common practice than in Thailand. One of the authors, while working in a Los Angeles high school with a group of teenage women from China, Vietnam and Korea, heard the young women express traditional Asian values regarding dating practices. They stated that they

planned to wait until they had gotten a good education before engaging in dating activities. It was difficult to know if they experienced any conflicts. However, from the experience of the author,
these students attended school with a large majority of non-Asian
students, making it likely that they experienced some peer pressure in this area. Teenagers may date but keep it a secret from
their parents, because of the disparity between the values of their
American peers and the traditional Asian family.

A young woman who has been dating or has been sexually active loses her respectability according to the traditional values of
her community, which puts her at higher risk for violence in intimate relationships. When violence occurs in a secret dating relationship, there is additional stress from keeping both the violence
and the dating relationship secret from the parents. The secrecy
associated with dating intensifies the teenager's feelings of being
responsible for the violence. The Asian/Pacific young woman is
more likely than other young women to feel isolated as a result of
dating violence. There is fear not only of the violence but also of
the parents' reactions. She may have greater difficulty turning to
her family for support because of the shame she experiences following the violence (National Institute of Mental Health, Center
for Prevention and Control of Rape, 1977). The abusive
Asian/Pacific young man may make accusations that she is worthless and threaten her with exposure, possibly with lies. This gives
the abuser the control he seeks with a rationalization that his
abuse is sanctioned by their community. Sexual violence further
shatters the young woman's feelings of self-worth that were tied to
her value as a virgin (Li-Repac and Fong, 1985; Tam, 1983).

Disclosure

The authors have worked with Asian/Pacific teenagers who
did disclose dating violence against them, but for each of these
young women, the decisions and feelings about telling families,
friends or authorities were overwhelming. They were fearful that
their families and others (including the authors) would not believe
them, and they expected to be blamed (Li-Repac and Fong,
1985). This was especially true in situations where dating occurred without parental consent or knowledge.

Their fear of disclosure was intensified because of their feeling
that they were bringing shame and humiliation to their families
(National Institute of Mental Health, Center for Prevention and

Control of Rape, 1977). They did not have any idea about how to tell their families about their conflicted and taboo experiences with dating, violence, sexuality and sexual abuse, thus they were even more vulnerable without their most important support system.

Disclosure may represent an acceptance of responsibility for their actions, for something they believe they have done wrong. In some situations, disclosure may also represent a minimization of the responsibility of the abuser.

Young Asian/Pacific women may believe that there is no point to talking about the victimization. They may feel that they and their families, friends and others can do nothing to change the circumstances, especially if the abuser is of the same cultural background. They may believe that taking any action or telling anyone will only create problems by bringing shame to their families—and not solve anything. Because of their situation, Asian/Pacific women experience a greater sense of isolation than other dating violence victims (Li-Repac and Fong, 1985).

Endurance

A cultural value that is shared by most Asian/Pacific cultures is that of enduring and suffering without complaint. Men and women alike value silence and acceptance as a way of handling difficulties with pride. There is pressure to keep silent, to save face and to prevent family shame. Immigrants from Southeast Asian countries, influenced by Buddhist and Confucian philosophy and the concept of determinism (*karma*), may believe they need to accept life's tragedies whether societal (war) or personal (assault) and move through life with honor, pride and tolerance (Kanuha, 1987). Adding to this is a powerful belief in the unimportance of the moment in relation to the centuries of family ties to ancestors and the past and future of the family. This leads to an acceptance of the "pains" of the moment since the pains diminish in time and the strength of the family endures for generations.

This presents a conflict for adolescent women for whom the pains and concerns of the moment are demanding, as is natural for this stage of development. The self-centeredness of adolescence makes it difficult to endure the immediate pain for the sake of generations of family. The Asian/Pacific young woman may feel conflicted about her "selfishness" and believe that she should not be reacting so intensely to her trauma.

The Experience of Fong

Fong is a sixteen-year-old Chinese girl who immigrated from Taiwan a year ago. Due to her exposure to the American culture in school, Fong assimilated more rapidly than her parents. Much to her parents' dismay, Fong began dating. Although her boyfriend, Mark, was also Chinese, he had been living in the United States for twelve years. As their relationship developed, Mark began to pressure Fong to have sex. Fong, who was having difficulty being sexual with Mark because of her upbringing, was also becoming increasingly curious about sex and experiencing pressure from her peers. The strong influence of her culture as well as her romantic interest in Mark created an ambivalence regarding sexual intimacy. Being tired of having his sexual advances rebuffed, Mark was verbally abusive and condescending. In addition to her own ambivalence, Fong became doubtful about herself, believing Mark's accusation that she was a failure as a woman. He continued to make sexual demands, pushing Fong, until he forced her to have sex with him. Although Fong was in agony, she felt she could not tell her parents since they did not even approve of her dating. She felt guilty because of her ambivalence regarding sex, since she knew she was expected to be a virgin. She felt she loved Mark, but felt confused because she felt both disrespected by him and also unworthy of him. When she discovered she was pregnant, Fong confided in her parents.

Although both Fong and her parents had been living in the United States for more than a year, they were at different stages of the acculturation process because of their different exposures and experiences. Mark had been living in the United States for most of his life. All of these individuals had different perceptions and reactions to dating and dating violence. Exposure to mainstream culture, developmental stages, length of stay in the United States, and generational position are all variables that affect the degree of acculturation of young Asian/Pacific women and their family members.

Mark identified more closely with his American peers and their expectations of dating and sexuality. At the same time, he drew on the influence of Chinese culture in his life and expected that Fong would not say no to a man and would strive to make him feel comfortable. Because of this, he had difficulty understanding Fong's ambivalence. Fong was caught between two cultures with different views on dating and sexuality. She was also at the developmental stage where she was exploring the issues of identity, sexuality and intimacy. Even if Fong knew clearly that she did not want to have sex, Mark's pressure presented a dilemma regarding her customary accommodation to men. Furthermore, Fong was not prepared to deal with the issues of sexuality and dating because of her lack of socialization and experience in these areas.

After disclosing the pregnancy to her parents, Fong was told she no longer belonged to her family. Her family felt she had brought disgrace not only to them, but to their community as well. Fong's parents relinquished custody of Fong, and she was placed in a residential treatment setting. Months later, Fong disclosed to her social worker the sexual assault and abuse in her relationship with Mark. She felt that the assault, the pregnancy and being disowned by her family were her fault for disobeying her parents. Through counseling, Fong learned that her life was not predestined to fail. Fong did sever all contact with her boyfriend. Unfortunately, she never reconciled with her family and is now living independently as an emancipated minor.

Implications for Intervention and Prevention

The problem of teen dating violence in Asian/Pacific communities remains invisible. Existing educational and social service programs have not been able to reach the young population who may benefit from prevention or treatment services. This difficulty seems to stem from complex origins such as an apparent lack of culturally and linguistically relevant service programs and the communities' culturally deep-rooted denial and resistance to dealing with the issue of teen dating violence and sexuality.

Our own experiences and a review of the literature regarding the experiences of Asian/Pacific young women confirm the overwhelming impression that this group remains in a vulnerable position. The low status they hold in the traditional Asian/Pacific family hierarchy as children and as females, compounded with a culturally based emphasis on maintaining harmony even if it is at the cost of the individual's well-being, continues to discourage these teenagers from asserting their rights and needs. Because of their powerless position, their needs as victims may remain unaddressed.

Young women may suffer from a tremendous sense of guilt about dating since such activities are not viewed as bringing honor to the family. This guilt adds to a sense of responsibility and shame if the young women are victimized in dating situations, resulting in the young women's further withdrawal and isolation from their support systems. Recognizing the vulnerability and isolation of these women, outreach efforts in the area of dating and dating violence are especially important.

Reaching Out

A critical task in reaching out to Asian/Pacific teenagers in an effort to provide education as well as intervention is to offer a sensitive and persistent approach. For example, one approach identifies women who are respected in the Asian/Pacific communities and invites them to speak to teenagers on the issue of dating violence. This requires involving bicultural and, if possible, bilingual women whose own experiences have required working through issues of sexuality, intimacy, femininity and sex-role expectations in a bicultural context; that is, women with whom the teenagers can identify. The respected role these women may have in their community will help ease the shame and guilt often associated with discussing these sensitive, taboo subjects.

Outreach and education can be effectively provided through existing educational or social organizations such as schools and churches, which are well accepted by many Asian/Pacific families.

Selective use of the media can help destigmatize and demystify the subject. The various media play an increasingly significant role in the lives of teenagers, and exposure to the issue of dating violence through the media may create awareness, identification and understanding among teenagers in a nonthreatening way. In communities with a high concentration of Asian/Pacific people, such as Los Angeles, a number of newspapers are published and TV and radio programs are produced in various Asian/Pacific languages. Such media are important in disseminating information to members of Asian/Pacific communities, especially those who are not fluent in English. Information regarding teen dating violence presented through such ethnic media may be accepted as relevant because these sources of information are respected in the community. The ethnic media may help demonstrate that dating violence is a problem of the Asian/Pacific community and confront its being discounted as an issue of only non-Asian cultures.

Because of the intense conflicts about disclosing abusive experiences, Asian/Pacific young women are more likely to reach out to services that allow them to remain anonymous, such as hot lines. Hot lines are accessible and ensure anonymity and confidentiality, which are of tremendous concern for Asian/Pacific young women who decide to disclose their experiences with dating violence. Some youth may prefer to talk to service providers not in their communities to preserve their anonymity. Multilingual publicity of hot line programs through schools and churches may reach isolated young women. Of course, multilingual capability of hot line staff and volunteers further enhances the use of these services.

Intervention

For many Asian/Pacific teenagers, disclosure of dating violence experiences is highly stressful. Disclosing the incidents to family members may provoke punitive and critical reactions because of commonly held values that prohibit dating and premarital sex. The fact that the young women choose to take the risk of disclosure despite these negative consequences indicates the seriousness and desperation of their situations. Disclosing to people outside the family often follows the teenagers' realization that they are having difficulty handling their feelings or advocacy needs without their usual family supports, or it may follow a hostile response from the family to the initial disclosure.

In helping Asian/Pacific teenagers in abusive relationships, the following issues must be considered. Most important is sensitivity to their cultural background and values. Feelings of shame, isolation and vulnerability that are intensified as a result of cultural norms must be understood within the cultural context. It is important to avoid assumptions and generalizations about Asian/Pacific young women; rather, explore these issues with each young woman to help her understand her own experiences. Distinguishing culturally based values and coping behavior from maladaptive, pathological patterns requires a careful exploration of the cultural meaning of behavior and symptoms. If one fails to consider the behavior within a cultural context, the practitioner may define the perceptions and behavior of many Asian/Pacific young women who are healing from physical or sexual abuse as deviant, strange or even pathological. Eastern cultural values that differ from Western values may also be seen as liabilities that must be changed. However, effective intervention involves acknowledging the strengths as well as the weaknesses of these values. Furthermore, practitioners must realize that there can be great differences in value systems and perspectives among Asian/Pacific cultures and must take these differences into account.

Because most people in Asian/Pacific groups, especially recent immigrants, are not familiar with Western psychotherapeutic approaches, a psychoeducational approach is more likely to be effective with Asian/Pacific young women in abusive relationships. This involves taking educator and advocate roles and using a problem-solving approach. Providing information regarding the realities of teen dating violence can be helpful to reduce the isolation and shame and to fill in the gaps in information. The advocate role involves establishing trust to help these clients deal with systems such as law enforcement and schools. In addition, an advocate may assist in dealing with families when faced with the young woman's ambivalence about disclosure and/or possible punitive, unsupportive reactions they may receive after disclosure. Despite the possible negative reactions of family members, involvement of the family can be productive in the Asian/Pacific young woman's healing process if dealt with carefully and sensitively.

Project NATEEN: Building a Bicultural Program

Project NATEEN, a state-funded program of the Division of Adolescent Medicine at Children's Hospital of Los Angeles, California,* serves pregnant and parenting teens seventeen years old and younger. The young women receive case management, support and access to needed resources throughout their pregnancies and beginning parenting years.

Several staff members were interviewed by the editor, Barrie Levy, on March 26, 1990 as a group: Beth Botansky, case manager; Dina Olivas, case manager; Kim Perry, case management coordinator; Susan Rabinovitz, project coordinator.

Levy: Who uses the services of Project NATEEN?

NATEEN: We are working with about 150 pregnant and parenting teens, the majority of whom are Latinas, many of whom have immigrated here from Central America. These teens have given us the opportunity to understand the special issues and vulnerabilities that arise for young women who are new to this country at the time they make use of NATEEN's services.

Levy: Do you see young women who are in abusive relationships?

NATEEN: Like others who work with teens, we see many young women who are in abusive intimate relationships. We have not yet had the opportunity to systematically document characteristics or variability of the abuse, yet we have developed shared im-

---

* Project NATEEN is one of thirty-two Adolescent Family Life Programs funded by the California Department of Health Services, Maternal and Child Health Branch.

196

pressions of the experiences many of these young women face. We do not feel we can fully represent the experiences of young Latinas in general, nor can we describe all of the issues involved. But some of our impressions could be helpful to others who work with adolescents, particularly those who are immigrants from Central America.

Levy: Based on your experiences with the group of young women that you work with, what are your impressions about relationship violence? What patterns have you observed?

NATEEN: We have frequently seen a pattern of restrictive relationships that has been described by other people working with pregnant and parenting teens as well. Some boyfriends may not allow their girlfriends to have friends or contact with others. A boyfriend may restrict her to the activities of child care and maintaining the household, unless she works. If she works, he may be vigilant about her contacts with others and about her time spent before and after work. He may be possessive and controlling. He may enforce the restrictiveness with verbal and/or physical abuse. The restrictiveness of the relationship leads to increased isolation for the teen mother. This pattern sometimes escalates to physical abuse that requires a child abuse or police report and necessitates referrals for shelter. Finding shelter is difficult for these teens because adolescent shelters have no provision for child care and women's shelters usually do not take people under eighteen or twenty.

Levy: What are the stressors that these young women face?

NATEEN: It seems to us that these young women are especially vulnerable to relationship violence. The stressors associated with the experience of being a refugee/immigrant add to the stressors of adolescence, and these circumstances, combined with the stress of adolescent parenthood, make these young women particularly susceptible. Stressors that these young women face include isolation, lack of options regarding work, housing and school and limited opportunities in general. They also include the demands of the adjustment process, fear of deportation if they are here without legal residency status, and prejudice and institutional racism (which the young women in the program talk about experiencing daily). Enormous poverty is often the greatest stressor that these young women face.

We see the symptoms of stress, such as somatic problems and depression. The young women in battering relationships must struggle to cope with the abuse in the context of their limited options and opportunities. In spite of these obstacles, they have successes, they think about the future and they emerge as survivors.

Poverty affects intergenerational relationships as well and impacts on the family's response to the situation. The young woman's family may not be able to protect her from the abusive relationship because of her financial dependence on her boyfriend. If the boyfriend/father is working, he could be contributing to the rent and food for an entire household.

Some of the options for coping that are available to other young women are not available to these young women because they are so affected by the violence, and fear retaliation from their boyfriends. They also have difficulty accessing services because of their fear of using services and because they may not speak English. If they are in this country without documentation, they feel vulnerable and that they lack entitlement to the services available. This may come up in the abusive relationship and be used as a threat by the batterer. Although they may want to protect themselves, they may be afraid to report the abuse because of fear of deportation for themselves and their partners.

Levy: Can you elaborate further on how their experiences as immigrants or refugees affect them?

NATEEN: The young women we see who have come from Central America have often experienced tremendous disruption. Before coming to the United States, their family life may have been disrupted by war, poverty or parents leaving to earn a living or to escape oppression. Several of the young women in the program were brought to this country as adolescents after years of their mothers living here to financially support their children in Central America. They try to make a "new" family, but it is difficult after so many years apart.

The violence of war has a lasting impact. Some of the partners of teens in the program have been soldiers; many of the teens have had relatives killed or have lived in areas devastated by war.

The trauma of immigration itself also has an impact. The process of leaving their home countries and getting to the United States and then the subsequent process of adjustment to a very different environment create tremendous stress. This affects not only Central American young women leaving war-torn countries, but also Mexican-American young women.

Levy: Do the young women you see attend school, and how does this play a part in their relationships?

NATEEN: We have encountered an almost universal desire among these young women to be in school. If they are not in school, school is a goal of theirs. However, going to school is a struggle. Lack of childcare is a major obstacle to school participation: these teens are unable to pay for care, and there are almost no resources for either subsidized care or school site care. The priorities that must be set when families are living in poverty affect them.

Some young women who are in restrictive or abusive relationships experience another obstacle if their boyfriends won't allow them to go to school. Some of them say that their boyfriends want to control them, and do not let them have friends or be around other guys.

Many of the young women are not able to go to school and have limited contact with peers. Many would have gone to school in Mexico and Central America, but some wouldn't have. If they do housework to earn a living—it is one of the few ways teens can earn a living—they may have no way to meet people their own age. They become isolated. Difficulties in finding accessible services may occur, and some struggle because they do not have English-speaking skills. When they become parents, they become more vulnerable, more isolated. As they become more isolated, they may depend more on their partners. These circumstances make them more vulnerable to abuse than most young women. This varies depending on the length of time in this country and the economic needs, the acculturation and education of the family.

Levy: If the young women don't go to school, are they often full-time homemakers or do they work outside the home?

NATEEN: Sometimes these young women have an easier time finding employment than do their male partners. Documentation and gender affect employability as well as the availability of jobs. Because of immigration laws, employers will not hire anyone without proof of legal residency. Usually women can find jobs such as house work, child care and piece work even though they may be in the United States without documentation. Most men want to provide for their families, and the struggle to find work has a profound impact. Men have their own stressors because of lack of documentation, limited education, poverty and discrimination. Many of the girls tell us that their partners constantly struggle to find employment. This sometimes leads to seeking other solutions, often with drugs; involvement with drugs may then increase or trigger violence against their girlfriends. We find that the young men who have been in this country longer (and all the more subject to these stressors) are more likely to use drugs.

The division of labor within the family may follow gender-role definitions according to the traditions of their countries of origin. Whether or not the man or the woman is employed, the woman is often expected to look after and care for him and for the children and the maintenance of the household.

The unique problems with employment for undocumented adolescents and the resulting poverty, combined with the stresses of adolescence and early parenthood, increase the vulnerability of these teens to relationship problems in general, and to violence in particular.

Levy: How do the young women deal with the violence?

NATEEN: Many of the young women feel a sense of resignation, saying, "This is the way life is, this is the way men are." Many women are surprised that in this country it is against the law to hit women. They may feel angry as well as resigned. But because of the sense of resignation, it is difficult for them to talk about their feelings or about their boyfriends. This can lead to depression and a sense of isolation. These young women feel, and often are, dependent on their boyfriends. Their definition of what life will be is based on the reality of what it is.

We find that we have to be careful when we interpret this sense of resignation and try to identify whether what we are seeing is a result of culture, poverty or the denial stage of the cycle of violence. We see that many of these young women make decisions (for example, to stay in the relationship) based on having limited options and based on their poverty.

Levy: How do you help these young women cope with or end their violent relationships?

NATEEN: The practitioner is a vehicle to resources. These young women have a hard time finding out about services, especially if they do not speak English well. The range of services they need is comprehensive. The health care we provide is a way to reach out to teens and to help them access the full range of services they need.

Initially, they may distrust us as well as other institutions. The development of rapport and trust takes time. It may take even longer for these teens because of their fear of deportation. It is common for women with a history of abuse to take a long time to disclose it. They must have sufficient strength and support to be able to talk about it. It is important for us to build a relationship. We must keep asking the questions, not only at the time of intake. We must pay careful attention to the signs of abuse and ask about them without judgment or blaming throughout their participation in the program.

We feel that it is important to have bilingual and bicultural staff. Many young women will not call agencies that offer services to them if they don't know there is someone "Spanish" available who is sensitive to the needs of immigrants. We find that in working with Latina teens we must recognize that the cycle of violence takes years to break. Our expectations must be realistic. They need ongoing support, pacing and acceptance, even when they do not follow through. It can take a long time for the young woman to take action or make a change. They are usually reluctant to go to shelters or take drastic steps. In helping the young woman to clarify her options regarding her relationship, and to decide whether she wants to separate from the father of her children, it is important to be aware that what we are supporting may be contrary to what she has learned and has been brought up to believe. It takes a long time to learn and internalize new ways of behaving.

Levy: How do they learn new ways of seeing their options?

NATEEN: Education is important. They are hungry for skills and information and for ways to feel more effective. As parents, they need to learn from us about nonviolent means to discipline and, with a great deal of opportunity, to internalize new, effective means (and give up old, familiar ones). What we are telling them may be contrary to what they have been brought up with, and the new tools take a long time to learn and internalize. Support groups work well. They can talk to others and are more likely to disclose and talk about the violence. Change takes place in a nurturing, supportive environment in which they can feel less isolated and in which they can learn new strengths.

The stability of the program and the continuity of the services and availability of staff are important. Young women can come, leave and then come back as their lives fluctuate. The movement and changes are slow. We can't just give referrals or expect dramatic changes in a short time. They must have a chance to develop an ongoing relationship and to work at a pace that meets their needs.

Lesbian Teens in Abusive Relationships

Barrie Levy and Kerry Lobel

Uncovering the existence of domestic violence has required confronting sexism, myths and misinformation about the realities of adult women's lives. To recognize that young women and girls encounter physical, sexual and emotional abuse in their dating or primary relationships means further confrontation of misconceptions regarding the realities of adolescence and young adulthood for large numbers of young women.

Similarly, heterosexism, homophobia, the invisibility of the "lesbian existence" (Rich, 1980) and the resulting complicated process of revealing one's lesbian identity to oneself and to others have contributed to myths and misinformation about lesbians (Pharr, 1988).

It is, therefore, not surprising that an exploration of violence in teen and young adult relationships reveals (1) that violence occurs in relationships of young lesbians and (2) that people who work with gay and straight teens consistently do not recognize this. There is a scarcity of information about lesbian teens' experiences with relationship violence. We provide our impressions about the differences between the experiences of young lesbians and those of young heterosexual women. This is only a beginning.

Recognizing the Existence of Lesbian Battering

Since the early 1980s, some activists in the battered women's movement and lesbian communities have recognized that abuse takes place in lesbian as well as heterosexual relationships. The National Coalition Against Domestic Violence (NCADV) and state coalitions have mobilized task forces to address this issue. In 1986, the NCADV Lesbian Task Force compiled stories from battered lesbians and documented organizing efforts in lesbian communities (Lobel, 1986). Since that time, several other publications have further explored the extent of violence in adult lesbian relationships (Minnesota Coalition for Battered Women, 1990; Morrow and Hawxhurst, 1989; Renzetti, 1989). Despite these efforts, the recognition of the existence of lesbian battering has been slow in coming. Even today many gay and lesbian communities, as well as battered women's programs in most communities, have not yet responded to this information by organizing to provide support and services to lesbian survivors of battering or by demanding that batterers be held accountable for their violent and controlling behavior.

Many lesbian communities have denied the existence of lesbian battering. For many, the denial stems from their desire to maintain an image of violence-free feminist and egalitarian relationships. This fear of facing violence in lesbian communities has left survivors of abuse vulnerable, isolated and at risk. It has also left batterers relatively free to deny the reality of their violence and to continue to act in violent and controlling ways. Lesbian communities must establish norms and values opposing power and abuse in lesbian as well as straight relationships. Battered women's services must confront their own homophobia and fears of serving battered lesbians. And just as battered women's services must consider the needs of young battered heterosexual women, they must also expand their services to include battered lesbians who are under twenty years old.

The silence about lesbian battering leaves many women of all ages unaware that there are other battered lesbians besides themselves. While forums have begun to address these issues for adults, there is a scarcity of information and resources available for adolescent lesbians.

Battering in Lesbian Teen Relationships

Like male batterers, lesbians who batter seek to achieve, maintain and demonstrate power over their partners in order to meet their own needs and desires. They desire control over the resources and decisions in family life that power brings and that violence can assure when control is resisted. The same elements of hierarchy, power, ownership, entitlement and control exist in lesbian and nonlesbian relationships. Lesbians batter their partners because violence is often an effective method to gain power and control over intimates (Hart, 1986).

Growing up gay or lesbian is marked by its own special set of dangers and obstacles above and beyond the turmoil of adolescence; these unique circumstances—discussed below—compound the difficulty a young lesbian faces in responding to violence or abuse in her life (Heron, 1983; Hunter and Schaecher, 1987; Slater, 1988; Whitlock, 1989).

Lack of Access to Accurate and Unbiased Information About Homosexuality and Gay Lifestyles

Adolescent lesbians' confusion about what is normal in a lesbian relationship adds to their confusion about emotional, sexual and physical abuse and makes it difficult to name it as a problem. Sometimes this confusion leads to naming the same-sex relationship as the problem, rather than the abuse itself.

After asserting a preference for same-sex partners, despite the stigma attached, a problem in the relationship may stimulate fears that the lifestyle is "wrong" or that there is actually something "wrong" with them individually (as the cruel stereotypes indicate). The denial of the violence may arise from the powerful need for the "choice" to be right.

Young lesbians may never have heard of the existence of same-sex relationships, or they may not recognize their relationship as being the same as what they have learned about same-sex relationships. They may not identify their relationships as being lesbian, or "intimate" the way straight relationships are. This denial is especially likely if the only information they have about lesbian relationships has been stereotyped and prejudiced. Identifying a problem that might arise in an intimate relationship is impossible if the relationship itself is not acknowledged.

Lack of Positive Role Models

Heterosexual teens are often inexperienced and confused about norms in their romantic relationships, too, but lesbian teens do not have the models that heterosexual youths have for relationships. Most lesbian children grow up in heterosexual families, and very few are exposed to lesbian relationships until they seek contact with lesbians as part of their "coming out" process (the process of identifying themselves as lesbians).

Young lesbians may be in relationships before they have had any contact with lesbians who could serve as role models. The lesbians interviewed for this book talked about their confusion about what is "normal." One young couple patterned their relationship after heterosexual relationships, with one taking the feminine ("wife") role and the other taking the masculine ("husband") role. Another couple assumed that lesbians do not have monogamous committed relationships, but instead date and marry men and have affairs with women, as she and her lesbian lover did throughout high school. They could not imagine any other way lesbians are in relationships.

Without role models for lesbian relationships, the control and abuse by one partner of the other may be accepted as "natural" or "normal" to a lesbian relationship.

Fear of Disapproval and Rejection by Family and Friends

It takes a great deal of courage to come out to friends and family. Young lesbians fear real possibilities of rejection as well as physical and emotional abuse. Many are thrown out of their homes or become runaways. Homophobic responses of parents, peers, teachers and others can keep a young lesbian from telling anyone if she is experiencing violence in a relationship. The secrecy of the relationship may make it impossible to reach out for help, and the fear of being seen as socially unacceptable may compound the difficulty of talking about the violence. If responses of others to any aspect of her lifestyle or her lesbian identity are negative, punishing or judgmental, then a young lesbian may not seek help to deal with the violence.

Isolation

If adolescent lesbians are not open about their sexual identity, the secrecy of their relationships adds to their low self-esteem and their vulnerability to isolation and abuse. For example, the bond between partners may become especially intense because they rely so much on one another as the protectors of the secret they share. This bond and protectiveness may keep them together, unable to risk seeking other relationships. It may also make them unable to trust anyone outside the relationship, making it difficult to seek support if a partner becomes abusive. Heterosexual teens often have difficulty trusting adults and seeking support as well, but lesbian teen couples may be as isolated from peers as they are from adults. The secrecy of the relationship also allows the threat of exposure to be used as a weapon to intimidate and maintain control.

Substance abuse, runaway behavior, poor school performance, peer and family conflict, depression and attempted suicide are among the predictable consequences of rejection, isolation and low self-esteem. Suicide is the leading cause of death among gay and lesbian youth. They are three to six times more likely to attempt suicide than are heterosexuals (Gibson, 1986). For lesbians, these attempts are often related to the breakup of relationships (Gibson, 1986).

Reaching Out to Lesbian Teens

Education and outreach that focuses on "dating" and "family violence" may be irrelevant to lesbian teens. They may not assume that such discussions have anything to do with them. Lesbian teens are more likely to relate to clearly defined (and described) patterns of abuse, control, intimidation and emotionally and physically abusive and sexually coercive behavior. We must use explicit definitions and descriptions of these behaviors, not abstract terminology that relies on traditional concepts of female-male relationships. We must be consistently clear that relationship abuse can take place in male-male, female-female and male-female relationships.

For young lesbians to confront the violence that may occur in their relationships, they must be able to be open about their sexual identity and their relationships. The burden for providing this safe space must be on schools, parents, the gay and lesbian community and the network of battered women's and rape crisis services. It is the role of adolescent support networks to facilitate teens' development by providing accurate information and non-judgmental counseling.

Good outreach to young lesbians is a necessary forerunner to providing services and support to lesbian survivors of dating violence. Programs such as Project Ten in Los Angeles and the Hetrick-Martin Institute in New York City rely on a multifaceted approach—education, school safety, and drop-out prevention—and interfacing with the private sector for resources (Whitlock, 1989). Such programs involve sensitizing school staff about gay and lesbian issues, expanding school libraries to include fiction and nonfictional materials related to gay and lesbian youth, removing pejorative materials from the classroom and library and developing a speakers bureau of gays and lesbians. These programs also work toward making the school environment free of harassment and intimidation of sexual minorities and train staff members to respond to victims of harassment. Additionally, they offer rap groups, drop-in counseling, substance abuse programs, peer counseling and lesbian and gay perspectives in discussions of topics such as suicide. Obviously, these perspectives must be included in discussions of teen violence. Importantly, these programs also offer an opportunity for gay and lesbian youth to gather for social experiences, thereby reducing their isolation.

The larger lesbian community also plays an important role in breaking through the isolation of young lesbians. Many communities have support groups for young lesbians. These groups should include materials on physical, emotional and sexual abuse as part of any support group curriculum. The lesbian community must evaluate how accessible its activities are to young women. Those activities that are bar-focused are inaccessible to women under twenty-one. Lesbian adults must explore fears about becoming involved as support systems for young women—fears that have originated with society's views of lesbians as child molesters or recruiters of young women to a lesbian lifestyle.

The role of parents cannot be underscored enough. A young lesbian's access to parental support can make the difference in the prevention of continued abuse. Organizations such as Parents and Friends of Lesbians and Gays offer support and materials for people dealing with their responses to their lesbian or gay friend or family member.

Battered women's and rape crisis centers' outreach programs must evaluate their materials to determine if they are clear about their relevance to young battered lesbians. It is important to use explicit language to explain lesbian battering, to clearly explain services available to young lesbians and to emphasize confidentiality.

Clearly, addressing issues of violence in intimate relationships is complicated for young lesbians. Only through coordinated school, home and community efforts will we be able to break through the silence that perpetuates the violence.

Legal Remedies for Teen Dating Violence

Sheila James Kuehl

There is little doubt that domestic violence is as prevalent in youthful dating relationships as it is in adult relationships. About a third of all females under the age of twenty have either already experienced some kind of violence in dating relationships or will before they are adults. Although the social dynamics of battering found in cases of adult victims may be similar to those found in cases of teenage dating violence, there are a number of differences in the availability and utilization of legal remedies.

Using the Law as a Tool

Since early in the battered women's movement, advocates have used a number of strategies to help the victims of domestic violence. One effective strategy has been to use existing law to help protect battered women and their children, while proposing reform of the law to make it more effective. People working to help victims and their children should not underestimate the value of legal remedies.

Battered women's advocates have taken seriously the potential help the law can give, working to develop and pass legislation to require that battering be treated as a serious crime, to get funding for shelters, to make it possible to obtain restraining orders, to sensitize judges to the relevance of abuse to custody orders, to mandate law enforcement trainings and the training of judges, as well as a panoply of other issues.

The law is a tool to stop the battering. Legislation can empower the victim of domestic violence and let her know she doesn't have to deal with the violence all by herself; at the same time it sends a powerful message to the batterer: The state government knows what you are doing and it not only disapproves but will punish you as well. Once a victim takes that first step to tell someone about the violence and ask for help, she may use the law to aid her in escaping the violence.

However, as you might expect, the law has its limits. The purpose of this article is to explore the ways in which current law may serve teenagers who are victims of violence at the hands of a date or an intimate, as well as the ways in which the law needs to be changed to better serve them.

Overview of Current Laws on Domestic Violence

Laws concerning domestic violence are found in two different sections of state laws: (1) the criminal law, which reflects those actions the legislature of your state has characterized as a crime, for which a person can be prosecuted by a state or local prosecutor, and (2) the civil law, which involves one person suing another to obtain some kind of court order or judgment. In either case, the legislature has to create a law that makes such court actions possible.

Just as there are different kinds of laws available that help victims, there are different courts, in most states, to handle the different kinds of claims: the criminal courts hear criminal matters (the juvenile courts hear criminal matters where a minor is accused) and a variety of state civil courts hear divorces, adoptions and most domestic violence restraining order cases. Sometimes, there is a separate court to hear matters relating to the abuse and neglect of children and to determine whether they should be removed by the county or the state from their parents' custody.

Since it is not possible to profile the different laws of all fifty states in this chapter, a few will be highlighted here.

Obstacles for Minors Who Are Victims of Domestic Violence

In general, whether dealing with criminal or civil legal systems, young women who have been abused in an intimate relationship face several obstacles related to the law and to attitudes in carrying out the law.

In most courts, minors (that is, someone under the age of eighteen) do not have a legal presence. Although minors can usually file a police complaint and testify as a witness in a criminal case, this should be verified with local law enforcement and the local criminal courts or district attorney's office. Minors usually may not file a civil case or ask for restraining orders unless they have a *guardian ad litem* (guardian for the purpose of litigation), who appears with them in the court. The guardian ad litem can be any adult (for example, parent, counselor or advocate) who fills out a form requesting to be appointed guardian and who files the order or case on behalf of the minor. In California, if over fourteen years old, the minor must approve the guardian. If the minor is younger, the guardian is appointed for her.

A guardian ad litem is not necessary if the minor is emancipated, that is, if she has filed an emancipation petition with the court and, fulfilling certain requirements about independent living, has been *legally* declared emancipated from her parents. Some states regard children as emancipated simply because they are living apart from their parents.

The relative informality of the juvenile court procedures can be an obstacle. When a minor is accused of a crime, he is brought into juvenile court (if the victim is a minor, but the accused is not, the case would not be handled in juvenile court). The procedures are usually less formal than in the adult criminal courts. The parents of the accused minor are usually involved, and the juvenile court judge will make more of an attempt to find a way to help the defendant. The court might try to use alternative sentencing, for instance, instead of sending a juvenile to detention. (Minors are not sent to jail.)

The problem such informality creates for the young victim of dating violence is the potential that the judge will not take her abuse seriously, that he or she will see it as youthful indiscretion or "teenage love," or, as reported by some victims, simply tell the young woman to stop dating the abuser. Such an attitude reflects ignorance on the part of judges about the seriousness and prevalence of dating violence, and local *juvenile* courts should be educated, in the same way as local law enforcement is trained, about the real dynamics of relationship violence, no matter how old the victim is.

Many of the laws specifically criminalizing domestic violence or providing for restraining orders are limited to violence against adults. The omission of minors has arisen, in part, because of the serious attention paid to child abuse and to the creation of a separate set of laws about it. But dating violence is not child abuse, as defined in the law, and in all except three states, restraining orders or specific laws criminalizing domestic violence are not available to anyone under eighteen.

In addition, most domestic violence laws do not include dating relationships in the definition of domestic violence. Forty-seven states, in defining the kind of relationship that must exist before such laws can be invoked by a victim, do *not* include a dating, intimate or engagement relationship where the parties have never lived together or never had a child together. Only in Colorado, Pennsylvania and California can minors use both the civil and criminal laws that specifically relate to domestic violence. In other states, people who have simply dated are not covered by domestic violence laws, even if they are adults. Other, more general, laws may be involved, as shown later in this article.

The youth of the victim often presents another kind of problem: The victim is probably not aware that violence against her by her boyfriend is a crime or that she can get a restraining order. She may not even realize that his behavior is not acceptable. Children do not usually believe they have any legal rights at all, and even if they have some idea of their rights, they have no idea how to access them. An advocate with good information about available legal remedies can be an important step in breaking the chain of violence.

Minors' distrust of adults creates another problem. The victim may be ashamed to tell her family and silent with her friends. If adults are willing to help, the victim may be torn between her desire for safety and her desire to protect her abusive boyfriend from adults and, especially, the legal system. As a consequence of not telling adults, she may try to handle a problem that is beyond her resources. Even worse, her family and friends may be unsupportive, telling her that the violence is her fault or that she should just leave the guy alone. Most people unthinkingly reflect these misconceptions about battering, not realizing how tenacious a batterer is about his control of the victim. Such attitudes on the part of the people she trusts the most put an additional burden on the young victim to simply excuse the abuser, and generally, they reflect the underlying sexism of a society that blames the female victim and excuses the male criminal, simply because there is a relationship between the two.

Finally, if a minor does complain to authorities, to her college or high school or to her dorm adviser, for example, there is often a resounding lack of response. Dating violence simply is not taken seriously. Young men are not routinely required to take responsibility for their actions or to suffer consequences. Schools may be unwilling to tackle the problem, and parents may brush off or underestimate it. Young women are thought to lack credibility, whereas, in actuality, teen dating violence is severely underreported.

Following are more detailed discussions of the criminal and civil laws regarding relationship violence and how victims and their advocates can use them to end the violence. Both kinds of laws should be used by victims and their advocates to end violence.

How to Use Existing Criminal Law

Many states have specifically declared that domestic violence is a crime; others have begun to allow people who are in violent domestic situations to use more general criminal laws to take offenders to court. Every state that has a specific criminal statute regarding domestic violence, however, defines the crime of domestic violence in a slightly different way. Generally, the crime of domestic violence is defined as violence against adults. This is done to separate it from crimes involving child abuse. The alleged batterer must be a spouse, or former spouse, of the victim or must live with her or be recently out of the house. If one of these relationships does not exist, the batterer may have committed another, more general crime, but he has not committed the crime of domestic violence.

A person committing behavior described as a crime in your state's criminal code can be arrested. Adults can plead guilty or be tried in a court and sentenced to jail, fined or diverted to counseling. Every action that is a crime if committed by an adult in your state (robbery, rape, murder, battery) is also a crime if committed by a minor. Minors, however, have their cases disposed of in a juvenile court. They are not placed in a jail, but may be placed in juvenile detention or released to their parents and/or put on probation. They may also be given "alternative dispositions" such as being ordered to attend another school or to leave the victim alone.

In California, a juvenile offender will be arraigned in delinquency court. The case is usually continued for two weeks before a trial, and another two weeks go by before there is a disposition. Many juveniles are put on probation.

If victims of domestic violence in a dating relationship report the battering to the police, even if the relationship is not covered by laws criminalizing domestic violence, boyfriends may be charged with other crimes. Every state has its own criminal law, but most have some or all of the following crimes on the books:

• Criminal harassment: subjecting others to physical contact, following them around or phoning them continually if it is done with the *intent* to harass, alarm or annoy them, if it has that *effect*, or if the behavior occurs with *no legitimate purpose*.

• Reckless endangerment: placing another in serious apprehension of bodily injury or death.

• Assault: *intentionally* or *negligently* causing or attempting to cause bodily injury.

• Aggravated assault: intentionally or negligently causing or attempting to cause grave injury, as with a weapon.

Some states may have other crimes that would pertain to dating violence. In addition to specific crimes, victims should be aware that police can arrest someone suspected of criminal behavior if they have "probable cause" to believe that person has committed the crime. Some states specifically allow probable cause arrests in domestic violence. Many, however, require that the officer actually see the behavior in order to arrest. Generally, arrest is discretionary, and local law enforcement should be encouraged to adopt a pro-arrest policy in these cases.

What Can Advocates Do?

Advocates of young victims of relationship violence can help to strengthen the role of criminal law in protecting the victim and prosecuting the perpetrator in several ways:

• Dating relationships need to be included in the definitions section of all domestic violence laws, criminal and civil. Advocates can create and lobby legislation to effect such protection for minors.

• Juvenile court judges may not take violence between dating minors seriously. This can be remedied with judicial education and strong advocacy. Advocates must insist on training for prosecutors, police and juvenile court judges on the real dynamics of dating violence.

• Many prosecutors may threaten to drop a dating violence case if the victim won't testify against her boyfriend in court. Testifying in open court, difficult enough for an adult battered woman, may be even more difficult for a young one. The difficulty is exacerbated by the fact that the juvenile court doesn't have any services to help victims, in contrast to the victim/witness programs to help adult battered women that many district and city attorney's offices now have. The lack of services makes it difficult, too, for prosecutors to understand how family and friends can sometimes pressure a victim to drop a case or to understand that a victim may be threatened by her batterer with further violence if she testifies.

Prosecutors should be encouraged to pursue a prosecution, even if the witness is reluctant, using police and medical evidence and other witnesses. The city attorney's offices in the cities of Los Angeles and San Diego, California, have protocols for doing this. Advocates can press for teenage victims to have the same access to victim/witness services as adult victims.

• Some states have adopted diversion statutes that allow a person charged with domestic battering crimes to go to a counseling program instead of pleading guilty or going to trial. Although this may be a good way to handle some juvenile cases, it is important that advocates demand that programs receiving such referrals have the kind of program that might actually help the young man stop his violence and that there be some accountability with the courts to make sure he has completed the program.

• Other steps advocates can take to help a victim during a criminal prosecution include (*a*) making a safety plan with the victim, (*b*) helping the victim feel stronger about testifying and (*c*) talking to prosecutors about realities of dating violence.

How to Use Existing Civil Law, Family Law and Restraining Orders

Every state now has some kind of Domestic Violence Act. No matter what the act is called in a state, it defines the kinds of relationships and restraining orders covered by civil laws governing

domestic violence. Under these laws, those who have been battered by a family member or certain categories of intimates can
petition a court for a number of different orders restraining the behavior of batterers for a short time (temporary orders) or a longer
time (orders after a hearing, or "permanent" orders, with varying
time lengths). These orders can also arrange for the custody of
children or the division of certain kinds of property. In order to
obtain these orders, a teenage victim or her guardian ad litem
must file a request with the appropriate civil court. In most states,
these orders are heard in the same court where divorces are heard,
but in some states and counties, there may be a separate court-
room just for domestic violence order applications or they may be
heard in a more general, civil court.

Some domestic violence victims may not want to get restraining orders out of fear the batterer will become more angry. Advocates should help the victim understand that almost anything will
make the batterer angry and that the violence will simply escalate
unless some action is taken.

Some victims fear the orders are just pieces of paper and will
not stop the batterer. This is true, as far as it goes. Restraining orders are only as good as the batterer's willingness to comply with
them for fear of legal retribution. For many, that fear serves as an
effective restraint. Additionally, when a victim has already peti-
tioned for and received restraining orders and the police are called
to enforce them, enforcement is generally better than on a first-
time call. After all, a judge has already heard the facts, evaluated
them and believed the witness. Applying for restraining orders
can also help a victim feel a new sense of empowerment.

Domestic Violence Codes

Domestic violence codes usually contain the following:

A definition of abuse. The definition usually includes violence as
well as threats of violence that occurred within a period of time,
such as six months, a year or three years, and usually defines the
violence as physical, not psychological, harm.

*A definition of the relationship that must exist between the batterer and
the victim before a victim can ask for orders under the code.* Domestic violence is *domestic* in that it occurs, so far as the law is concerned,
only between people in certain, defined relationships. As indicated in the section on criminal laws, these relationships are usually spouses or former spouses; people who live together or who

have lived together within the last six months; family members; or, in some states, people who are the biological parents of a child, even if they haven't lived together.

Only Colorado, California and Pennsylvania allow people who have experienced dating violence to apply for domestic violence restraining orders, and they do not limit the orders to adults. In all the other states, a dating relationship is not considered "domestic." The actual wording of the law in Pennsylvania does not specifically include "dating relationships," but defines "domestic" as "family or household members, sexual or intimate partners or persons who share biological parenthood." A Pennsylvania court, faced with a case of teenage dating violence, held that the statute could apply to minors and seemed to suggest that the boyfriend could be considered an "intimate partner," though it never directly addressed the issue (*Diehl v. Drummond*, No. 88-20, 817, Court of Common Pleas of Lycoming County, Pa.). Recent legislation in California added dating and engagement relationships to the civil Domestic Violence Prevention Act.

If a state code limits restraining orders to these definitions and/or limits the orders to adults, victims of dating violence and/or victims who are under the age of eighteen cannot obtain them. If, however, the orders are not specifically limited to adults and the code refers to "intimate" or "sexual" or "dating" or "engagement" relationships, victims of teenage dating violence should be able to get them. (See below for information on civil harassment orders, restraining behavior by people not covered by the domestic violence acts.)

Kinds of orders available. Orders usually include (*a*) "keepaway" orders, ordering the batterer to stay away from the victim, her place of work or her school; (*b*) orders requiring the batterer to leave the family of the victim alone or to stop telephoning; (*c*) orders granting temporary custody if children in common are involved or ordering the batterer to leave the house if he lives with the victim or her family; and (*d*) orders requiring restitution to the victim to cover out-of-pocket expenses incurred by the violence, such as medical treatment or motels.

Duration of the orders. Duration can vary and could be six months, a year or three years. Temporary orders, obtained on an emergency basis by going to the court *ex parte* (without notice to the batterer), usually last one to two weeks; then there must be a hearing before the orders are continued.

Manner of service. Restraining orders must always be served on the person whose behavior is being restrained before they are effective. In states where a party is not allowed by law to serve the papers in her own case, the papers cannot and should not be served by the victim herself. In most states, the police, marshals or deputies provide service of process for a small fee. In states where the victim is allowed to serve the papers herself, she should be accompanied by a law enforcement officer.

Penalties for violation of the orders. Pennsylvania and California, as well as a few other states, have made violations of civil domestic violence restraining orders a crime. Young men who violate the orders may be brought into juvenile court, where they may be sentenced to juvenile detention, ordered to pay a fine or given alternative sentencing like community service or home study or required to attend a school different from the victim's.

Civil Harassment Statutes

Parties who do not qualify for orders under a state's domestic violence act can usually get some kinds of restraining orders under the state's civil harassment law. These laws generally cover violence or annoyance between strangers, neighbors or co-workers. The range of orders is neither as broad nor as clearly defined as the range contained in the domestic violence laws and the application for such orders may be heard in the general civil court instead of in the family court, but these orders should definitely be sought by the teenage victim of dating violence if she does not qualify for domestic violence act orders. Many states have printed forms to apply for orders. If so, the clerk of your local court should be able to provide these forms as well as forms for all other orders.

What Can Advocates Do?

There are several areas in which advocates can help dating violence victims gain access to the courts.

If young victims of dating violence are not included in the categories under a state's domestic violence act, they must, as indicated above, apply for restraining orders under the general civil harassment laws. Sometimes judges who would easily condemn a slap, arm-twisting or kicking between neighbors or co-workers will not take it as seriously between a couple. They may dismiss the action as a manifestation of "teenage love" or assume it was provoked by the victim.

This kind of judicial ignorance can be very dangerous to

young victims of domestic violence. Local advocates must educate the court about the seriousness of such behavior among young couples. Surely if a state has created an entire scheme of laws both criminalizing and restraining violence between adult intimates who are or have been married or who simply live together, then family court judges as well as criminal court judges should be asked to view dating violence with the same degree of seriousness.

Young victims may lack the authority to petition for either civil domestic violence orders or general civil harassment orders in most courts and may be required to have a guardian ad litem petition on their behalf, unless they have been granted emancipated status by a court. Advocates can find out how to assist young victims in obtaining a guardian ad litem so they can proceed in petitioning for the orders.

As indicated above, simply having the orders in hand and filed with the local police station is not always enough to totally ensure that a victim will be safe from her boyfriend. She must also pay attention to her own safety. Sometimes, this is difficult for a young victim to take seriously. The advocate or friend or counselor can contribute to her safety by making a safety plan with her to back up the restraining orders.

A young victim may turn to her school for protection, but authorities at the school may not take her claims seriously or may feel there is nothing they can do. In California, a recent law making it a felony to commit assault against anyone on school campuses may be used to restrain violent dating partners. Training should be provided for administrators and residence hall staff in colleges and universities, as well as for counselors and school personnel at all school levels, so that they are able to recognize dating violence symptoms and the seriousness of the problem and take action on behalf of victims. Action plans for intervention on behalf of a victim identified by school personnel must be developed by each school.

A request for an order keeping the batterer away from the victim's school is a problem, of course, if the batterer attends the same school. The judge may not be willing to order him to change schools. In this case, school authorities should be notified of the existence of the restraining order. If the young man has violated an already existing restraining order, however, it may be easier to convince the judge to remove him to another school or to require home study.

An order removing a batterer from his home is a real problem if he is a juvenile residing with the victim's family. Since someone must always have authority over a juvenile, he is required to be in someone's custody. Excluding him from the residence would require an entire change of custody.

In Pennsylvania, the Pennsylvania Coalition Against Domestic Violence recommends in its handbook (Hart, 1989) that a minor victim of domestic violence and/or her guardian ad litem file a dependency petition, which allows the court to order treatment for the batterer who is a minor and to also order a change of custody if he needs to be separated from the residence of the victim.

As with criminal laws, it is important that advocates lobby state legislators so that dating relationships are included among the intimate relationships that can give rise to orders under state domestic violence laws. In states where the domestic violence laws are limited to adults, advocates may want to lobby legislators to have the minimum age for restraining order applicants lowered to thirteen or fourteen.

Conclusion

This article is, of necessity, set forth in very general terms. Although every state has laws enabling an adult victim of domestic violence to obtain civil restraining orders and some allow her to file a criminal complaint for a specific crime of domestic violence, in most states, teenage victims of dating violence are not included in these laws. However, the law can still be used to help these victims. Victims can file a police complaint for more general crimes as well as file for restraining orders under general civil harassment laws. Advocacy is needed to assist teenage victims in using the legal options available to them and to ensure that existing laws are enforced on their behalf. Legislative change is needed throughout the United States to create legal options now lacking for young victims of relationship violence.

IV

Education and Prevention Projects

The Dating Violence Intervention Project

Carole Sousa

In the fall of 1986 the staff of Transition House, a shelter for battered women and their children, was joined by Emerge, a counseling program working with men who batter, to launch the Dating Violence Intervention Project (DVIP), a prevention education project to reach teenagers.

Counselors at Emerge realized that most of the batterers they saw began their abusive behavior as teens. They also were concerned about the teenage sons of abusive men in the program who had adopted abusive behavior. Advocates at Transition House had been concerned by the increasing numbers of hot line calls from young women being battered by boyfriends. Nurses at the local high school health center had also been asking the shelter to help in serving young women battered by their boyfriends. But perhaps the most troubling cause for concern was that in the prior year, two young women had returned to the shelter as battered wives who had been there years earlier as children when their mothers fled battering relationships.

Studies indicate that dating violence affects at least one in ten teen couples. It is one of the major sources of violence in teen life. Rape by acquaintances accounts for sixty percent of all rapes reported to rape crisis centers, and the majority of victims are between the ages of sixteen and twenty-four. Massachusetts crime statistics indicate that thirty percent of all women homicide victims are killed by a husband or boyfriend. This high percentage also applies to female teen victims ages fifteen to nineteen, indicating that our obligation to prevent woman abuse is as urgent among teenagers as it is among adults. As a result of these statistics and our own experiences and concerns, Transition House and Emerge staff decided to be more aggressive in their outreach and education to teenagers.

To develop a prevention education program, the DVIP staff interviewed teenagers regarding other such programs (such as drug abuse prevention) to find out what approaches worked and what did not. As a result of brainstorming with staff and talking to teenagers, the following project goals were developed:

• To provide prevention education on teen dating violence drawing from the life experiences of teenagers
• To impact the culture of schools by developing a comprehensive curriculum that could be applied throughout a school
• To change student and teacher attitudes so that male or sexist violence against women becomes a recognizable problem and a stigma within the school
• To empower and train teenagers to talk to other teenagers and younger students about dating violence

In the fall of 1987, a thirteen-year-old special needs student was raped by three seventh and eighth grade boys and one high-school-age youth. DVIP staff were called in by the superintendent of Cambridge schools to help with the crisis. With the Boston Area Rape Crisis Center and the support of the Cambridge Women's Commission, they conducted a parents' meeting, a teachers' meeting and classroom discussions with all of the students in the school attended by the victim and perpetrators. DVIP took an active stance in advocating prevention education in schools. Pressure on the school board led to support (verbal, not funding) for prevention education on dating violence and sexual assault. The program began by targeting the high school in its own community.

Changing the Culture of a School

Cambridge Rindge and Latin High School (CRLHS) is located in Cambridge, Massachusetts, and is attended by 2,500 students representing sixty-four nationalities. The school is divided into three divisions, called houses, and five alternative programs. It has a complete teen health center, adolescent parenting programs, a Cooperative Educational program and Student Service

Center, all supervised by over 264 teachers and administrators.

The dating violence prevention programming at CRLHS was initiated in the first year with a Teen Dating Violence Awareness Week, which included workshops and an assembly, in-service training for school personnel and an information table at Parent Night. DVIP staff started recruiting students to be part of a theater troupe, now called the "Can't Be Beat" Theatre Troupe.

The second year saw the addition of peer leadership training for ten students who presented educational programs to eighth grade students. The DVIP also began implementation of a classroom education program for all freshmen in health education classes. Health teachers were trained, and every freshman participated in the three-session teen dating violence prevention program. Funds were received from a state grant to the city for health education.

In the three years since its inception, the DVIP has had an impact on the culture of CRLHS, promoting awareness and intolerance for dating violence. The three-session educational program on teen dating violence mentioned above represents a change in the health education curriculum, and the week of schoolwide awareness activities is now institutionalized as part of the school's yearly activities. The DVIP staff has trained security personnel to intervene appropriately in dating violence situations and has trained peer leaders, who provide classroom education and/or participate as Theatre Troupe members. The Peer Leader Training Program and the Theatre Troupe are also now school-based programs, and students involved receive course credit. The DVIP runs two support groups for female survivors: one for survivors of rape and incest, the other for survivors or current victims of dating violence. The DVIP has become a model as well for dealing with other prevention issues at the school.

Change has also been visible in the attitudes of students. There have been several incidents of students' recognizing abuse and confronting it in the school hallways. Many students wear the "Respect Can't Be Beat" buttons distributed by the project. Peer leaders and Theatre Troupe members have initiated activities without DVIP staff, such as speaking to groups of students and speaking about teen dating violence on a local radio show, and students have done their own fund-raising to support their activities. They identify themselves as advocates for ending teen dating violence. Theatre Troupe members and other students have also established SAVE, Students Against Violence and for Equality at CRLHS.

Teaching Teens About Violence in Relationships

The curriculum developed for prevention education is based on the premise that battering occurs because of the culturally supported belief that men have a right to control their wives and girlfriends.

Due to their inexperience and need to conform, teens are especially susceptible to adhering to the traditionally "appropriate" roles for men and women, including the belief that women should be passive and submissive, whereas men should be dominant and have a right to reinforce their power with violence. This leads teens to feel confused about appropriate behavior regarding sexuality, decision-making and birth control, and contributes to their difficulty in judging what behavior is abusive. For example, when speaking with young women about their first sexual experiences, we have found that often the experience included some form of force or manipulation. Yet they do not identify the experience as "rape." Boys tell us of situations in which they are justified in hitting their girlfriends, most commonly because they think their girlfriends have been flirting. They do not define this as abusive.

However, their inexperience also makes teens particularly open to information about relationships. If effective, we are able to provide teens with insights regarding how to relate to one another that can be applied for a lifetime.

The Prevention Curriculum

The curriculum covers five major questions:

What is abuse? Teens do not understand the term *abuse* or how to identify abuse. In fact, put-downs, threats, possessiveness and physical intimidation are accepted as part of their interactions with one another and, often, with adults as well. Through brainstorming and discussion, a common language is established and the groups come to agreement regarding what abuse and respect look like, setting a standard of mutual respect for themselves. We often add racism as a category of abuse and ask students to give examples of different forms of racism or of ways that racism is abusive.

Who has the power? People with power sometimes use abusive behavior to control the person without power or to maintain power. All teenagers can relate to this experience in their own lives, and the group soon agrees that people feel horrible and angry when they are made to feel powerless. This is effective for boys because it reduces their defensiveness in looking at male-female power issues.

Activities in this unit include having students list different types of relationships. In addition, rich-poor, black-white and straight-gay are examples we use to illustrate power dynamics. Sometimes it is easier for students to grasp the idea of inequality between men and women when they look at these other examples.

What societal messages do we get for how men and women are supposed to act in relationships? How can these messages lead to violence? Students look critically at sources of messages about male-female relationships, such as advertising and songs. They understand that stereotyped assigned role definitions are harmful to both men and women. We begin by asking students to tell us their experiences with stereotyping and how they felt about being stereotyped. We point out that stereotyping based on "race ignorance" is called racism, stereotyping based on class prejudices is called classism and stereotyping based on sex roles is called sexism.

In this unit we also address the pressure to be heterosexual. When looking at advertisements, we point out that none have gay couples, implying that only heterosexuality is acceptable.

What does an abusive relationship look like? Presenters with personal experiences of abuse tell their stories. They demonstrate the subtleties of abuse and control in action. It demystifies the issue and helps students see that it can happen to anyone and that it is possible to end an abusive relationship and survive. As in all of the units, we emphasize that battering crosses all race, class and ethnic lines, and that it takes place in homosexual as well as heterosexual relationships. There is no "typical" batterer or battered woman.

What can we do about preventing abuse? In groups of three or four, students brainstorm ways to make changes that can be implemented in their schools, communities and personal lives. Some of their suggestions become the basis for plans for school activities. The aim is for students to become empowered to change their lives and to influence other teens.

To deal with cultural differences and to assure cultural sensitivity, it is important to show respect for the students and to have a diverse staff. If the available staff members do not reflect the diversity of the students, we ask for help from supportive teachers. We listen to students during discussions, understanding how they see dating violence and valuing their input.

Reaching Adolescent Boys

Talking to adolescent boys about dating violence can be particularly challenging. Although it is important to help boys understand the role of sexism in abuse, we are sensitive to the power that adult women have in their lives, particularly mothers and teachers, and the abuse that teens may be enduring from these sources. It is also true that teenage boys, although highly susceptible to the stereotypical male sex role, do not yet have access to the full institutional, social and cultural power of the adult male. Boys and girls, particularly in the early teen years are also much more equal in size and physical strength. But as the young man grows older and attains adult size and power, the societal support for him to exercise power and control in his relationships with young women increases.

Our approach with young men encourages them to reject stereotypical male roles. When we talk about ways men abuse power, we point out that we are not singling out any individual but that we are talking about a general problem. We say that at some point in his life every male will have to decide whether to use control and abuse over women: He will have to decide whether he will listen to a partner's no or push for what he wants. We often spend a whole session discussing the pressure young men are under to conform to negative male roles. We stimulate discussion by asking questions like the following: "If you are a boy who doesn't like to call out names to girls as they walk by, what do you do in a group of other boys who do?" or "What would you get called if you don't act like them?" or "If you have had a reputation for being tough from second grade on but now as a sophomore in high school, you decide you don't want to "act tough" because this may mean having to do drugs or setting up a girl for rape, what do you do?" or "What is male pride?"

The goal of our work with boys is to help them understand they have a variety of choices when dealing with relationship issues. Using violence is a choice. No one can "provoke" or make someone hit them. We try to build awareness about their choices and which ones lead to abuse. We discuss the legal consequences of choices such as rape or assault. We also discuss the real consequences in relationships that may be opposite to their intentions. For example, a boy who feels he uses abusive, jealous or possessive behavior because he wants his girlfriend to understand how much she means to him, actually pushes her away with this behavior. She may become more distant or become less honest with him in reaction to his accusations. We discuss alternative ways to show someone you care.

"Can't Be Beat" Theatre Troupe

The Theatre Troupe was developed to empower teens to educate and talk to each other about ending teen dating violence. Adolescents struggle with independence and want to solve problems themselves or with peers. Helping them organize their own peer leadership groups against sexism and dating violence meant that we facilitate a structure in which they can educate other teens—to learn about the issue, to talk to each other about their feelings about it, to find a way to convey the information. The Theatre Troupe does this.

Troupe members are trained so that they will think for themselves, be "experts" on the issue and be clear communicators. A two- or three-member adult (male and female) team (theater director and educators) leads the troupe.

The Theatre Troupe develops improvisations during an eight-week (twice a week) educational process. These sixteen rehearsals each include an educational presentation and discussion, a warm-up theater exercise and improvisational work on scenes based on the discussions. At the end of the sixteen rehearsals, eight of the improvisational scenes are selected to form the show, which is eventually performed in school assemblies. The show generally includes scenes on topics such as sexual pressure, jealousy, a friend helping a friend and child abuse. Feedback indicates that the performances stimulate discussion between students and in classes. Frequently, students disclose that they are or have been in violent relationships to program staff following a performance.

Students gain a great deal from their experiences in the troupe and often stay for more than one year. One student said, "I joined the first year to do acting, but being in the Theatre Troupe had an effect on the way I see relationships, so I'm joining this year to learn more about this relationship stuff." The peer leadership groups provide participants with a group identity.

Through the Theatre Troupe, teens can present the information in a way that relates closely to teen life. Teens can be more confrontational with one another than adults can. Peer leaders are an example to other students. The group culture becomes one based upon respect.

The troupe's goal is to produce effective educational theater pieces that capture and hold the attention of the student audience and that communicate important messages about dating violence. The structure and methods by which the troupe does this are consistent with the messages being taught. Respectful treatment of teens means being sensitive to individual differences, to the difficulty that many teens have discussing abuse and to racial and cultural differences.

Conclusion

The DVIP attempts to influence a school community and its response to teen dating violence. Prevention education, comprehensive curricula, teacher training, parent workshops, peer leader and Theatre Troupe programs, support groups for young victims and consciousness raising for young men are all pieces of this approach. Each component may not have as much impact alone, but components properly interfacing with one another can change the culture of the school and impact the school's system, assuring safety for young women. Several outcomes of the program indicate the value of this model to a school system. The development of support groups for young women in abusive relationships and the program's success in advocating for these young women within the school are the result of the improved recognition of dating violence as a problem. The school's response of disciplining students for hitting has conveyed a clear antiviolence message to students. Other educational programs within the school curriculum now include information on sexism and on relationship violence.

The staff of the DVIP feel that preventive education is not an end in itself but a contribution toward ending violence against women. Many social, political and interpersonal changes need to be made in this country to reach this vision.

Support Groups: Empowerment for Young Women Abused in Dating Relationships

Barrie Levy

Support groups can have an empowering effect for young women who are struggling with abusive dating relationships. Teens and young adults in abusive relationships do not tend to reach out to adults for assistance and often become isolated from adults and peers. In confusion, shame and/or fear, they hide the realities of the abuse. Therefore it can be more effective to reach them with a supportive, educational approach rather than a treatment approach. They may be more likely to respond to an approach that views abuse as a social problem rather than a "disease," that offers education and support toward empowerment and that sees "victims" as having strengths and survival skills. Support groups avoid stigmatization of group members. Empowerment comes from the combined power they have as a group and the sense that they can help one another as peers.

The collective disclosure of abuse that takes place in support groups is powerful, cathartic and often the beginning of change (Creighton, 1988). Support groups also allow young women at different stages of violent relationships to help one another. People who work with teens and young adults find that they more easily respond to the supportive confrontation of denial from peers than from adults.

For some ethnic groups, especially young women whose families have immigrated to the United States, mental health institutions and therapy are not relevant or seen as a resource for change. However, education is valued and within the range of their experiences. Support groups, especially those that are easily accessible, for example, in a school setting, may be welcomed in a way that referrals for other kinds of help may not.

The following describes models for support groups conducted in high schools and in counseling or domestic violence centers. Issues that arise for leaders and members of support groups are also discussed.

Support Group Models

The several support group models currently being implemented in programs throughout the United States all have several features in common:

• They use an educational, topic-focused format, often with a planned curriculum.

• They encourage members to contact one another outside of group meetings to provide support when needed.

• They emphasize that the assistance group members can offer to one another is as, if not more, valuable than that provided by professionals.

• They stimulate active, participatory, empowered responses within the group process as well as in dealing with problems of daily life.

• They require confidentiality regarding disclosures and discussions of personal issues during the group to safeguard the emotional and physical safety of members.

• They use education/information and group process to confront denial and minimization of abuse.

• They require that the role of the leader or professional be to facilitate, educate and provide resources, not to analyze, interpret unconscious motivation or encourage members' dependence on the leader.

Most support groups that use a curriculum include basic information about definitions and patterns of emotionally, verbally, sexually and physically abusive relationships; safety issues; resources; and skills such as assertiveness, conflict resolution and identifying and coping with feelings.

Support group models vary according to the setting, the specific formats used, the frequency or time frame of meetings and recruitment strategies.

School-based Support Groups

School-based support groups have been conducted by school counselors, teachers or domestic violence prevention program staff in programs throughout the country. Representative models described here are two domestic violence prevention programs: the Center for Battered Women (Austin, Texas) and Battered Women's Alternatives (Concord, California). They work with young women from junior high or middle school through high school, and from regular school programs as well as continuation schools and pregnant minors' or teen mothers' programs within the schools.

The Center for Battered Women Teen Dating Violence Project conducts four high school groups and one middle school group. The young women in the groups have been or are currently in a dating relationship involving emotional, physical and/or sexual abuse, are daughters of battered women or have a long-term history of abuse in their families of origin. The focus of the groups is on abusive dating relationships, but the young women who have witnessed abuse or been abused as children are included because they are considered to be at high risk for relationship violence in the future.

The Battered Women's Alternatives Teen Program conducts three support groups in three different high schools and two groups in pregnant minors' programs. The young women who participate have self-selected after educational presentations to their classes or have been referred by high school staff.

School-based support groups are conducted by school personnel or rely on at least one contact person on the school staff who is committed to the groups. The contact person may be a school nurse, counselor, vice principal or teacher and functions as a liaison between the young women in the groups, their teachers, the outside organization conducting the groups and the school administration. The contact people also assist with recruitment of group members. Both the Concord and Austin support groups are facilitated by dating violence prevention program staff.

Students are referred by school personnel who know of a student's violent relationship or of the abuse in their family of origin. Other recruitment strategies that have been effective are posters in school hallways, articles in school newspapers, announcements in health and physical education classes and announcements to local agencies and organizations that work with youth and/or domestic violence.

Like other domestic violence programs, the Concord program conducts workshops in classrooms on domestic violence and dating violence, and potential group members seek to join the groups or are referred by teachers as a result. The Austin program found that clients of their agency-based services for battered women referred their daughters to the support groups. They were surprised to discover how many of the group participants were self-referred or came at the urging of or with their friends.

An important issue regarding recruitment concerns how the groups are described or named so that stigma is reduced and so that young women will decide that the group is relevant for them. So often, teens do not define themselves as battered or abused and so would not respond to a group that is publicized as being for battered teens or about violent relationships. The Concord program recruits students for women's empowerment, women's leadership, or skills for violence-free relationships groups or workshops. The groups generally meet weekly, although the Concord program also offers an intensive weekend retreat. The weekly groups meet after school, during a lunch recess, in last period or during rotating school periods so that students do not repeatedly miss the same class. The after-school or last period groups are able to meet longer—one to one and a half hours. Otherwise group sessions are generally the length of a class period (about fifty minutes). The number of sessions offered by various programs varies from four to fifteen or as many as can be scheduled so that the group meets throughout the school year. The schools generally require parental permission, which most report has not been a problem to obtain. The Concord program works with school staff to acquaint parents with the program.

The groups generally have a format for each meeting that includes checking in, introductions of new members, a topic-focused "lesson" and discussion and time for group process, that is, focusing on current issues for individual members or for the group.

The Austin program uses a four-phase curriculum. During the first phase, group members learn how to define their experiences and name the abuse. They learn about the cycle of violence and the power and control dynamics of battering relationships. During the second phase, the members talk about their personal experiences, with the aim of confronting their beliefs about the abuse and affirming their rights to respect and safety. During the third phase, leaders introduce information regarding new skills, such as recognizing controlling behavior, setting limits (assertiveness) and handling conflicts. The fourth phase involves evaluating the effectiveness of the support group using feedback from group members and school staff.

The Concord program uses a similar curriculum for its eight-week groups: (1) introductions and sharing of personal histories; (2) "Growing up female" (sex-role socialization); (3) sexuality and relationships; (4) violence against women and assertiveness exercises; (5) sharing personal experiences of violence; (6) understanding power; (7) resources for help; and (8) relationships among women (support).

Counseling Center-based Support Groups

One model for a counseling center's support group program is that of the South Shore Women's Center (SSWC) Violence Prevention Project in Plymouth, Massachusetts, a multiservice agency for battered women and their children.

The Center's first dating violence support group was an outgrowth of its school-based dating violence prevention program. The referrals to the first group came from the community (awareness had been created through newspaper articles), school and counseling center staff, parents and court advocates. Subsequent referrals have come primarily from classroom presentations in schools and from parents.

The SSWC groups for teens use an educational therapy model. The goals are stopping abuse, living without abuse, increasing social interaction skills and developing a belief that abuse is not deserved. The emphasis of the groups is on peer support as well as the affirmation that, although the group participants may feel isolated in an abusive relationship, they are not alone in their experience.

The SSWC educational therapy model starts with individual counseling sessions to "prepare the teen client for group work." After six weeks of sessions, a decision is made regarding the young woman's referral to the group. Neither individual nor group counseling is time-limited, but group members are required to make a six-week commitment to individual counseling and a six-month commitment to the group. Individual counseling ends when members join the group but is available to them at any time if they experience a crisis.

Unlike with the school-based models described above, young women can join the SSWC groups at any time. The format for each session includes checking in, sharing personal experiences and an educational discussion initiated by group leaders. Although repetition of educational components could be a problem with ongoing admittance, leaders have found that it allows longer standing group members to help newer members to deal with certain issues. This becomes the basis for the development of a support system among the group members and enhances the self-esteem of the "older" group members.

The group sessions are held at the counseling center, which is centrally located near several schools. The program had considered conducting support groups at schools, but schools were not willing to cover liability or otherwise take risks that may have been involved. The center now considers it advantageous to conduct the groups "off campus." The geographic area served includes several towns, and with limited staff hours available, scheduling ongoing groups in several schools was impossible. The center is also considered a confidential and neutral place by the group participants. Transportation can be a problem and is worked out with each individual. Parental permission is required for participation.

Issues for Support Group Leaders

Several issues have been discussed by support group facilitators in evaluating their effectiveness. Participation of young women in support groups to deal with dating violence was affected by confidentiality concerns, the multiplicity of their problems and their advocacy needs, their reluctance to identify dating violence as a serious problem and their dilemmas regarding communication with parents and school personnel.

Confidentiality. Young women express reluctance to participate or to talk openly about their experiences in their dating relationships because of their fear that their boyfriends or other friends and classmates will find out both that they have experienced violence and that they have talked to others about it. Their abusive partners often attend the same school or live nearby and have the same social network as they do, and these may overlap with those of other group members as well. This is an especially pressing issue for members of school-based support groups. The groups have strict confidentiality rules, restricting members from discussing anything that is said by any group member with anyone outside the group except that which directly concerns themselves. They are also restricted from telling others who is in the group.

Multiplicity of problems. Dealing with relationship violence often requires a variety of intervention strategies, and violence is often only one of a number of problems affecting a group member. For example, young women may have problems with health, alcohol or drug abuse, school failure and absenteeism, previous suicide attempts, pregnancy, family conflicts or financial resources. In confronting the violence in a relationship, they may need assistance from school administrators, the criminal justice system, the social services system or employers. The Austin group facilitators (Holland and Hodges) observed that most of the young women who dropped out of their support group program had multiple problems and expressed dissatisfaction with the narrowness of the focus of the group. Support group leaders generally acknowledge the importance of providing advocacy services and resource referrals to group participants. The SSWC program (Edwards) noted that safety issues must generally be dealt with by interacting with schools and courts. Teen dating violence prevention programs that offer support groups often work with schools in general, in addition to working with them on behalf of group members. They educate administrators and assist schools in setting procedures and policies regarding student safety and responsiveness to relationship violence. Schools vary in their responsiveness to this issue.

Reluctance to identify dating violence as serious. Since support groups are often offered as workshops or as support groups for dealing with general issues, such as families or relationships in general, participants may not identify themselves as victims of dating violence at the time of their entry into the group. Group leaders have found that participants tend to minimize or deny the relationship abuse at least until they have been in the group for a while and have developed trust of leaders and other members. They also gradually name the behavior taking place in their relationships as abusive as the educational process progresses. Often group members are more open to discussing abuse in their families of origin before they disclose and label their intimate relationships as abusive. The Austin program suggests that the sequence of topics covered in the educational component to the groups start with family violence rather than dating violence.

Communication with parents and schools. Group leaders face a dilemma in dealing with parents. Parental consent is generally required for groups for young women under eighteen, and parents have only rarely withheld consent. However, group participants may not wish to have parents included in their problem-solving and coping strategies, regardless of whether or not group leaders feel this would be helpful. If a young woman's safety is at stake, group leaders may face difficult decisions regarding confidentiality and a process of working within the group to support the young woman to make decisions regarding disclosure and communication with parents. In cases where parents are not supportive or where communication with parents leads to more abuse, young women need help to seek support elsewhere. Similar dilemmas arise regarding the group leaders' role in mediating between group members and school personnel.

Conclusion

Support groups are important resources for teens who are in or are at risk for battering dating relationships. They are based on principles of empowerment that are inherent in self-help and peer support. Support groups are especially effective with teens because of the importance of peers during this stage of development. The creative development of support group models that reach young women through schools, domestic violence programs and counseling and health centers is an important strategy for confronting teen dating violence.

Contributors to this article included: Allan Creighton, Battered Women's Alternatives, Concord, California; Heidi Hodges and Lisa Holland, Center for Battered Women, Austin, Texas; and Susan Edwards, South Shore Women's Center, Plymouth, Massachusetts.

Addictive Love and Abuse: A Course for Teenage Women

Ginny NiCarthy

For at least ten years, I had been distressed about the lack of information and services to teens abused by boyfriends and husbands. So when Ann Muenchow, teacher-counselor at an alternative school for pregnant teens, asked me to co-teach a class on battering, I welcomed the challenge.*

Ann and I decided to call the course "Addictive Love and Abuse" on the hunch that it would attract students' interest without sounding too threatening. We wanted to focus on the close relationship between battering, emotional abuse and addictive love. We hoped to appeal to students who were already suffering from those situations as well as those who could be helped to avoid them.†

Nurturing, Romantic and Addictive Love

Love has been described in many ways, but for purposes of this discussion, it is useful to distinguish among nurturing, romantic and addictive love relationships. Conceptions about these types of love informed our work and added to our discussions during the course, although they were not presented formally to the students.

---

* Medina Children's Services and New Beginnings Shelter for Battered Women, both in Seattle, were sponsors of this course.

† This is a revised version of the course description published in *The Second Mile: Contemporary Approaches in Counseling Young Women* (1983), edited by S. Davidson. Available from New Directions for Young Women, 626 1/2 36th Ave., Seattle, WA 98122.

Nurturing Love

Nurturing love incorporates a wish that the loved person will grow and flourish, developing her or his fullest potential. This implies that each partner encourages the other's pleasure in additional close friendships as well as satisfactions in independent activities. A partner is even capable of accepting the other's wishes if he or she wants to reduce the degree of intimacy between them. If the relationship ends before one partner is ready, he or she will experience grief, but not self-destructive devastation.

Romantic Love

In romantic love, everything about the relationship or the loved one is filtered through a screen that makes it seem perfect. Songs, stories, films and advertising insist that there is one person in the universe who is just right for each of us and that we'll know this person is *the one* the instant we set eyes on him or her. When we think we have found that person, unattractive or threatening traits are simply not recognized. Others are redefined or reevaluated so that they seem like positive characteristics. "Selfish," "stubborn" or "thoughtless" become "independent," "determined" or "poetically absent-minded." "Possessive" becomes "devoted."

This process is enhanced by the lovers' determination to put only the best foot forward. It is exacerbated when immediate sexual involvement confounds sex with love and, even more, when resistance to even brief separations is interpreted as proof of true love. Sooner or later disillusionment is sure to follow.

In most cases, the desire for extreme "togetherness" and suspension of critical faculties gradually diminish on the part of one or both partners. The type of relationship that develops over time may depend upon how the couple handles the period that follows this "honeymoon" state. At this point, the relationship can evolve into a nurturing or an addictive one. At best it develops into deeper, more complex, mutual appreciation—perhaps with romantic interludes. It includes recognition and acceptance of each other's limitations.

Addictive Love

Addictive love is a learned habit, not a disease. It is a habit handed down from one generation to another. Women, even more than men, have been socialized in Western societies to believe they cannot have a full life without one special partner. (Until very recent times, that partner has been assumed to be a person of the opposite sex.) Economic and domestic roles are designed to make women financially dependent on men. Women have been defined as the emotional sex, the ones who nurture intimacy and "need" romantic partners. Men are assumed to manage quite well without the love of an intimate partner. Thus women get the idea they are lucky to have a man who will *let* them love him. They believe men do not really need them. As women grow older, some realize how little these beliefs resemble reality. But teens are especially susceptible to dichotomous views of male and female roles. Even among many adult women, dependency on men is seen as both natural and practical, and economic and emotional dependency have become confounded.

Numerous societal forces come together to encourage women in a dependent love (addiction) long before they are of an age to commit to a man. Much has changed in the past thirty years, but assumptions about "true love" die hard. In this society it is still "normal," even admirable, for a woman to give up many things for the sake of her man (or her children and other family members). In fact, a woman who places her career or other interests ahead of her intimate relationships is considered selfish or overly ambitious. (Although small changes have begun, men are admired for sacrificing everything to their work in order to support their families—to be "responsible breadwinners.")

A couple is in for serious trouble if one or both believe they cannot survive without the other, whether because they fear loss of love or of security. The desire to be together every minute develops into a need or demand for the partner to be continually available. Addiction implies an urge far beyond desire. The refrain in the addicted person's mind becomes a variation on "I'll die if he doesn't call me," "I can't live without her," "She's everything to me." The words of popular songs provide numerous examples of those sentiments, although in everyday conversation they may be expressed in less histrionic language, especially by people in midlife and by men.

When men become addicted, they are often adept at hiding it from their partners—and even from themselves. Because dependence does not fit with a "manly" image, addicted men are less likely than women to admit to being "hooked." A man may claim he does not need his woman, yet insist she has no right to "ne-glect" him; he may say she is uncaring, unfeminine and selfish; he may frequently threaten to leave her. His demands are expressed in terms of control and criticism rather than admission of his need.

The way the man presents his demands may lead the woman to believe the problem lies not in his dependence, but in her defi-ciencies as a caring woman. If she accepts his criticisms as valid and believes his assertions that he does not need her, she becomes insecure about the relationship. She narrows the focus of her life to concentrate on pleasing him. By this time, she has few plea-sures in life except him, which—along with her fear he will leave her—contributes to an exaggerated idea of how necessary he is to her life.

Signs of addictive love include the following:

• A conviction that the loved person is needed for survival.

• Diminishing numbers of happy, stimulating, interesting or satisfying experiences with the partner, compared with the time spent in recriminations, apologies, promises, anger, guilt and fear of displeasing.

• A reduction in feelings of self-worth and self-control on the part of the addicted person.

• An increasingly contingent way of life; that is, all plans hinge on the partner's availability.

• A reduced capacity to enjoy the time away from the partner; a sense of marking time until he or she is available.

• Frequently breaking promises to limit dependency on the partner: "I won't call him," "I won't insist she account for her time since I last saw her," "I won't wait for the phone to ring."

• A feeling of never being able to get enough of the loved one.

• Increasing efforts to control the partner.

Addiction and Abuse

It is not the addiction that differentiates women who are abused from others. Dependency does not *cause* abuse, and many women addicted to their partners are not abused. Likewise, many abused women are not addicted. (They are afraid to leave for a variety of reasons, not the least of which is terror that the men will follow through on threats to injure or kill them.) But women who *are* addicted to violent partners are especially vulnerable, and doubly at risk because their emotional dependency is an added barrier to escape.

An abusive man takes advantage of an addicted woman's perceived need for him and uses force to control her. The woman's addiction tempts her to ignore or excuse his abusiveness. She fears that any objection she makes will result in abandonment. She equates abandonment with being totally alone in the world, a situation she will do almost anything to avoid. Her failure to resist or leave is perceived by her partner as permission to continue and even escalate his abusive control. Then, whenever he feels an urge to release tension or wants to blame someone else for his inadequacies or the conditions of his life, he uses the addicted woman as a handy target without fear of reprisals.

Paradoxically, the more the man abuses her, the more the woman is likely to think she deserves it. The more she "deserves" it, the less likely it seems that anyone else could care for her. If this man who insists he *loves* her treats her this way, surely, no one else would want her. All these psychological roads lead back to terror of being left and being totally alone.

If the man is also addicted, he may be willing to do anything he can think of to stave off the threat of losing his loved one. He may use techniques that keep women cowed and afraid to assert their own needs. Many men rely on these techniques to gain women's loyalty, and they confuse compliance with loyalty or devotion.

Addiction is not the cause of the abuse. However, as can be seen even from the brief description above, male and female socialization to traditional roles increases tendencies for addicted men to abuse women and for addicted women to be abused by male lovers. Men's presumed independence and dominance and women's supposed passivity and submisssiveness play into individual vulnerability to both addiction and abuse.

The Course: Setting, Participants and Goals

The "Addictive Love and Abuse" classes were offered under the auspices of a social service agency that provides courses for high-school-age women who are pregnant or already parents. The classes took place at two alternative schools, one mostly attended by black students in the South End of Seattle, Washington, and one mostly attended by white students in the North End of the city.

The South End group consisted of young women who were either parents or pregnant. It included one Chicana, one white woman and eighteen black women. The North End group was composed of white women and two black women who attended once and another black woman who attended twice. Although this group was also sponsored by the teen pregnancy program, only two participants were actually in that program. The others were from the general population of the alternative school.

Our classes were elective and had the attraction of no grades or tests. However, they had to compete with classes that would help students graduate, a goal most students were eager to attain as quickly as possible. Students were recruited by Ann, who was a teacher and counselor in both schools, and by a nurse at one of the schools. A number of students were referred to us by their school counselors, who knew the students had been abused by intimate partners.

Our goals were that the young women would:

• Become aware of the pervasiveness of violence and abuse in intimate relationships
• Recognize signs of addictive love in intimate relationships
• Recognize emotional, sexual and physical abuse
• Understand the relationship of addictive love to abuse
• Understand the roles of power and sex roles in abuse
• Know their rights, including the right not to be abused
• Learn about alternatives to emotional abuse, including negotiation, assertiveness and separation
• Learn about helpful resources for battered women, including the police, prosecutors and shelters

Although it was not a formal goal, we also wanted to provide an accepting atmosphere for anyone who chose to talk about her own experiences with battering or abuse or addiction to a man. We had reason to expect that all participants would be heterosexual, but were also open to hearing from any young women addicted to or abused by a woman partner.

The course material that follows has been reorganized somewhat for clarity and ease of presentation. For example, we did not always use the exercises in the sequence presented here. However, we tried them all, plus quite a few others, with varying degrees of success.

Exercises and Students' Responses

In the following pages, I state the objective(s) for each session, discuss the exercises we used to reach the objective(s) and describe the outcome in one or both groups. We are uncertain about the reasons that some exercises had different results in the two groups. Among the important variables between the two groups were ethnicity and the impact of pregnancy or parenting. Readers should take such factors into account in offering similar courses, modifying each exercise as seems appropriate to the composition of the group, the setting and the response leaders elicit as they adapt the model to their individual styles.

Exercise 1: Bragging

Objective: Set a tone of informality, acceptance, openness and curiosity.

Guidelines: Leader says, "Please tell us your name and something you did in the past week that you feel proud of or good about. You can brag about something you did for yourself or for another person. Most of us have felt abused by someone—a boyfriend, parent or teacher—at some time or other, even if we haven't thought of ourselves as an abused woman. Sometimes we just feel as though someone is taking advantage of us or exercising too much power over us. When you feel that way, it's a good idea to treat yourself particularly well. One way to do that is to give yourself credit for the things you're doing that seem to be right or useful. Making a habit of appreciating yourself is also a good way to keep yourself in a frame of mind that will help you avoid abusive relationships."

The bragging exercise should be used to introduce *each meeting* of the group.

Reactions of the South End and North End Groups: Most group members were reluctant to "brag." Even after gentle prodding, only a few responded the first time the exercise was introduced. We continued to open each session with the exercise, and after three or four meetings, nearly everyone participated. Once started, group members looked forward to the exchange of "brags."

Exercise 2: Defining Addictive Love

Objective: Convey an understanding of the term *addictive love.*

Guidelines: Leader says, "I'm wondering whether you've heard the phrase *addictive love* and what it means to you. You probably know something about drug and alcohol addiction. Perhaps you can imagine what it's like for a person in love to feel that she *has to have* a particular man or she'll fall apart. What is that like?" List students' responses on newsprint and save them for discussion of the relationship between addictive love, abuse and battering.

South End Group: Students were enthusiastic about discussing addictive love and responded to our questions by saying, "Oh, you mean 'sprung'!" In this group, we did not arrive at our anticipated list of the characteristics of being "sprung." The first two traits to be mentioned, jealousy and possessiveness—along with many accompanying complaints about men—were the springboard for such a lively discussion that we focused on these subjects for the rest of the period.

   The most common refrain was, "They expect you to be there for them, but they go out with other women." We discussed various ways to deal with men who cheat. Some suggestions were to act sweet and ignore it; to get mad and show it; and to keep score quietly until a later time, when you can let them have it if they get mad at you for something. No consensus was reached. The group also discussed the question of whether jealousy indicated true caring or not. Participants arrived at a tentative conclusion that it does not.

North End Group: Students gave these responses to our questions of how addicted lovers act and feel:

Can't stand being away from him	Boring
With the person for a long time	Dependent
Hard to break ties	

   A group member asked, "Why do people think they have to stay in those kinds of relationships?" We turned the question back to the group and listed these responses:

Low self-esteem	Feel worthless
Special times hard to give up	Live in the past
Deserve bad treatment	First boyfriend

Can't get away   Hard to let go
Feel sorry for him   Hope for change
Need to rescue him

We commented that most reasons given for staying were negative and asked whether anything positive might keep someone in an addictive relationship. Group members identified closeness and sex as important. They also noted that it is acceptable to have sex with a first boyfriend, but if a young woman breaks up with him and becomes sexually involved with a second boyfriend, her reputation will be spoiled. We then talked about the unfairness of this double standard. Other comments about the difficulty of giving up a first boyfriend were "He becomes your best friend"; "You lose self-consciousness when you have a boyfriend"; "You feel complete." The class discussed how "stuck" a young woman feels if she gets pregnant: how it adds to her feeling of helplessness and to her fears of separating from the man.

Exercise 3: Continuums of Abuse: Physical, Emotional, Sexual

Objective: Raise the awareness of kinds and degrees of abuse.

Guidelines: Leader says, "What are some of the ways that men abuse women physically? Emotionally? Sexually? How do women abuse men?" List answers to each question on newsprint, discussing them in as much depth as seems appropriate and interesting for your group. Arrange the responses on a continuum for each type of abuse, from less to more damaging. Explain that since opinions of the relative damage of each item may vary, the order of the continuum is, to some extent, arbitrary. Ask students whether you have placed some items toward the wrong end of the continuum. Point out that there is a tendency for abuse to escalate when the victimized partner seems to accept or cannot stop it in the early stages. Therefore, it is important to notice and stop the seemingly mild abuse when it is first observed. Point out that battering crosses all class and race and lifestyle lines, that it happens to millions of women each year and that pregnant women are especially at risk for miscarriages from assaults by violent men.

South End Group: We asked what kinds of abuse anyone had experienced at any time in their lives, but the students would not give us direct answers. One or two students, in side comments to friends, hinted at having had such experiences. We asked for clarification of those comments, so that we could use them to make generalizations about the problem, but the students quickly retreated into silence.

In order to discuss our continuum without intruding into group members' privacy, we tried a more general question: "What are some of the ways that men physically abuse women?" They readily responded, but to our surprise, they simultaneously answered a question we had not asked: "How do women physically abuse men?" We listed both sets of responses:

What Men Do to Women	*What Women Do to Men*
Scratch	Scratch
Slap	Slap
Pull hair	Bite
Bend fingers	Pull Hair
Sock in arm	Punch
Twist arm	Hit with shoe, broom, pan
Punch face, eyes	Hit with can opener
Kick in stomach when	Cut with knife
pregnant	Hit with iron
Choke	
Beat up	
Dump out of car	

Some of these items are common forms of abuse one sees or hears about from newspaper accounts and on television. But some, like bending fingers back, men scratching women and women attacking with can openers and hot irons, have the ring of personal experience or observation. Our general question had allowed group members to begin to speak about the violence in their lives without feeling that they were under personal scrutiny.

We made a short list of responses to the questions during this session and returned to them later, adding to each category at the next two meetings. The first day we dealt with physical abuse, the list supplied by group members included only the first eight items on the "what men do" side. We expressed our surprise at the fact that the women's violence seemed more dangerous than the men's. Class members explained that women had to defend themselves against the superior muscle power of men by using instruments like knives and hot irons. When we returned to the question, there were few changes on the "what women do" side;

however, the list of violent acts by men against women became longer, and the items more dangerous. For the most part, the students thought men and women abuse each other emotionally in similar ways, except for the insulting names each sex typically calls the other.

Emotional Abuse of Men and Women by Each Other

Yelling
Public humiliation
Telling other people about private affairs
Blaming the partner for own faults
Labeling "crazy," "mess," "stupid," "dumb," "bed-hopper"
Not caring about the other's feelings
Stealing money or coercing the partner into giving it up
Sex-specific name calling

The group discussed the implication, in many of the negative labels for women used in name-calling, that being highly sexual is unacceptable for a woman, whereas terms that describe men as sexual (for example, *stud*) are complimentary. The group agreed that there should not be different standards for males and females.

"How do women abuse men sexually?" was the only one of the three questions asked in this exercise that did not immediately elicit a response about women's abuse of men as well. We asked, "Why is it that women don't sexually abuse men?" The group replied, "Oh, but they do!"

Sexual Abuse of Women by Men	*Sexual Abuse of Men by Women*
Call sexual names	Bite his lip
Act jealous	Pinch/scratch butt
Act indifferent	Bite neck
Threaten to get a new woman	Spit in face
	Kick butt
Accuse of being with other men	Pull penis
	Kick penis
Call other women in front of you	Burn with cigarette
	Kick/squeeze balls
Always wants to "do it"; mad when you don't	Bite penis
Biting, pinching titty	
Slaps, pinches to get his way	

Makes woman walk home
  nude
Wants sex after hitting you
Forces sex
Rape
Rape with bottles, etc.
Kills

North End Group: In response to our questions on ways that men physically, emotionally and sexually abuse women, North End students mentioned items similar to those of the South End group. But they did not offer comments about women's physical and emotional abuse of men until we specifically asked about it. They did not percieve women as sexually abusive to men, even when we brought it up.

Exercise 4: Emotional Abuse and Brainwashing

Objective: Elicit information about emotional abuse of students by boyfriends and give information about its dangerous impact.

Guidelines: Leader says, "We're going to list some types of emotional abuse, and we'd like you to give examples of ways that men emotionally abuse women under each of these categories." On newsprint, write these headings with space for filling in examples under each:

- Enforces isolation of the partner
- Insists on attention being focused on his own comfort and convenience and away from the desires of the woman
- Makes degrading, humiliating comments about the woman or degrading, humiliating demands
- Causes exhaustion or feelings of helplessness, incompetence or dependency
- Threatens
- Demonstrates power or superiority over the woman
- Enforces trivial demands
- Grants occasional rewards or favors

As each heading is listed (you may want to shorten them), allow for a short discussion for clarification of meaning. Depending on their sophistication, some students may have difficulty understanding the concepts quickly, although once they do, they are likely to respond with their own examples.

After students have listed some examples under each heading, explain that the major categories are adapted from a list of methods used in brainwashing prisoners of war. Help students understand that even in prisons, walls are not enough to control prisoners. Psychological control is the most effective, whether used by jailers or lovers. The methods are similar in each situation, and they say something about the person who uses them, rather than about the one who is subjected to the brainwashing.

South End Group: This exercise was not presented.

North End Group: Student discussion yielded these examples under the categories we had listed:

Enforces isolation. "Comes on" sexually to your friends, so they stop wanting to be with you. Imagines you're going to pick up somebody everywhere you go. Refuses to take you out. Wants to be with you, always. Questions your other relationships.

Insists the woman's attention be focused on him. Punishes you for lack of attention or imagined rejection, so you're continually worried, even obsessed, about being even a minute late when meeting him, about being seen talking to other guys or girls, about looking the way he likes you to look. You ask permission for everything and soon begin to tell lies about minor things to protect yourself from his punishment.

Makes degrading, humiliating comments or demands. Insists on kinds of sex you don't want. Tells you he's having sex with someone else; flirts with other women when you're right there.

Causes exhaustion, feelings of incompetence, dependency. Presses for information about your activities. Tells you, he'll take care of you.

Threatens. Says he's going to break up with you. Says he'll kill himself. Threatens to expose your secrets to your friends, parents.

Demonstrates power or superiority over the woman. Makes decisions for you. Assumes he knows what's best for you and what you want. Says or implies that he's smart and you're stupid.

Enforces trivial demands. Makes you do his wash, get his coffee, dress the way he wants, wear (or not wear) makeup.

Grants occasional rewards or favors. Buys gifts. Takes you to movies or dinner. Gives loving support—especially after he's been mean.

We discussed the tendency of women who are treated in these

ways to think that something is wrong with them. We pointed out the importance of overcoming this reaction, of realizing that "If I feel humiliated, threatened, isolated, it is *because* someone is humiliating, threatening, isolating me."

Exercise 5: Rights List

Objective: Raise awareness of individual rights.

Guidelines: Ask students to state the rights they believe they are entitled to as students, parents, children or in other appropriate categories. Discuss them as you list them on newsprint.

South End Group: Students told us they have the right to the following:

Have a home	Good health
Speak out	Go to school
See friends	Fail in school
Talk on the phone	Keep our children
Go out	Use birth control
Not be discriminated against	Have an abortion
on the basis of race	Have enough money to
Not be a slave to anyone	survive
	See family members

As part of a couple, or specifically in relation to men, they claimed the right to:

Be open and honest with each other
Express feelings without punishment
Spend time together
Refuse sex when it isn't wanted
Have a good sex life, the way you want it

North End Group: They arrived at a rights list that was similar to the South End group's list.

Exercise 6: Negotiation and Assertiveness

Objectives: (1) Help students recognize the difference between choosing to give up rights and having them taken away; (2) practice negotiating for rights when a partner does not recognize them.

Guidelines: Discuss situations in which one might choose to give up one's rights as part of a compromise or because at a particular moment it is not of great importance to exercise them, and the difference between giving them up and having them taken away. Include brainstorming of the various reasons why it is sometimes difficult to exercise rights (fear of angering a partner or of losing him) and what a woman can do if her man steps over boundaries, infringing on her rights.

Choose for discussion the problem that seems most common for members of your group. Without attempting to reach agreement on which ideas are best, ask students for suggestions of what to do and say when a man refuses to recognize a woman's rights. Encourage students to develop their individual standards and styles of negotiations.

Move from the discussion to role playing. Demonstrate an assertive reponse to a boyfriend's attempt to abrogate his partner's rights. Enlist the help of a student to play the boyfriend, and play the young woman assertively standing her ground. Then repeat the role play with the variation that the young woman holds her point, but offers some amount of compromise. Emphasize that compromise is very good and useful in relationships, when it is *willingly* given, but that it becomes submissiveness if it is coerced or forced. The person in the young woman's role should not offer to compromise unless she really wants to, and she will be more confident of that decision if she decides what she is willing to give *before* the discussion with her boyfriend. During the role play, she can ask for time to think about it by herself before agreeing to anything. If she does that in a real situation, it will help her to be certain she has not been manipulated or frightened into giving in, only to regret later that she gave up an important right.

Leader says, "We are going to demonstrate how you can talk to someone who may be treating you badly, without being hostile yourself and without giving in. I'm going to play a young woman being mistreated by my boyfriend, and I'll try to say how I feel, what I want and what I'm willing to do, with respect for him and for myself, and without giving up my principles. He may decide to go along with the idea or not. I will stick to what I know is right for me and not stoop to manipulation and disrespect, as he might, because I know I will feel better about myself if I do." Ask a student to play the boyfriend and to try to do everything they can think of to intimidate you or make you feel guilty or scared of losing him.

At the end of the role play, do a self-evaluation of the things you said you would try to do and ask the "boyfriend" to say how "he" felt in the role. Open the discussion to comments from other class members.

South End Group. This exercise was not presented.

North End Group. The discussion that followed the role play indicated that students could hardly imagine risking losing the relationship, even though they thought the boyfriend was not worth holding on to. When we asked two students (rather than the leaders) to do a role play, we had difficulty getting volunteers. Two reluctant volunteers felt uncomfortable and had difficulty thinking of what to say. We asked other students to feed them lines. With this approach, almost everyone participated in some way and all had the opportunity to imagine what they might say, and how they would say it, in a similar situation.

Exercise 7: Film and Discussion

Objectives: (1) Create empathy for women in abusive situations; (2) show how shelters and safe homes can help abused women; (3) explain legal options.

Guidelines: Show a film of your choice on battering. Try to use a film no more than thirty minutes long. You may vary this exercise by suggesting students watch a drama about battering currently on television. Some useful questions after the film are: "What do you think she should have done at... point?" "How do you think she felt?" "What would you do if... ?" However, films often have an emotional impact, and you will need at least twenty minutes for students to express their reactions, discuss them and recover from what might be disturbing feelings. They may take the opportunity to respond more to their own situations than to your questions, which is all to the good.

South End Group. We showed a film about a woman who is beaten by her husband, some of the effects on their child and the ways in which the law operates to help the woman. Comments during the film were mostly to the effect that "I'd kill him."

After the film, Maria talked about the father of her child, whom she had to marry because it is "the Mexican way." Maria described at length her troubles with her husband, his physical abuse of her and the difficulties of getting a divorce. The phrase "the Mexican way" was threaded throughout as an explanation for battering. We pointed out that battering is not the "way" of Mexicans any more than of whites or blacks, that it cuts across all class and race lines and seems to happen to all kinds of people.

Cheryl talked about a recent fight she had been in with the best friend of her baby's father. The friend is gay, and Cheryl believed he was after her man. When she attacked him, the police came, but decided that the incident was "petty." They did not arrest her. Telling the story to the class, Cheryl laughed and bragged a bit. "He won't mess with me. He knows how crazy I am. I would kill him."

The film, followed by these stories, created a mood of excitement. The talk suggested that the class saw killing a violent, troublesome man as a sensible and effective way of dealing with him. Students observed that the deed can be done when the man is asleep and that the woman will probably "get off on self-defense." During this session and later ones, the class discussed ways of preventing anger from reaching the point at which there is danger of a lethal act. They thought about the moral, legal, emotional and social consequences of killing a loved one.

North End Group: After the film, the group sat in tearful silence. Finally, Susie broke the silence, sounding angry, frustrated, almost desperate. "Don't they ever fight back?" she blurted out. Marion spoke up soberly. "I did. I broke his nose." There was another silence. One of the leaders asked if she would like to talk about it. Marion became tearful but she was glad to talk about socking her violent boyfriend. It made him stop hitting her long enough for her to escape. She thinks it was the right thing to do, as was calling the police, although she expressed some sadness about his having gone to jail for assaulting her. We discussed legal options and resources available to victims of battering.

Exercise 8: Addictive Love, Abuse and Battering

Objective: Recapitulate major points about the relationships between addictive love, abuse and battering.

Guidelines: Put up newsprint sheets on addictive love and emotional abuse from the sessions on continuum of abuse and brainwashing. The leader says, "What do you see as the connection between addictive love, emotional abuse and battering? How might one lead to the other? What are some of the things that might cause emotional abuse to escalate into battering?"

South and North End Groups: Both groups understood the connections quite well, and were concerned about how to stay out of potentially damaging relationships.

Exercise 9: Identifying Addictive Love

Objective: Help students recognize early signs of addictive love.

Guidelines: Ask students what some of the first signs of addictive love might be. List them on newsprint. Ask for suggestions on what to do when one notices those signs. Write suggestions next to each of the early signs. After you have listed students' suggestions, add any of the following options that have not been brought up:

• You can end the relationship.

• If you *act* as if you're not addicted by continuing to see other friends, engaging in sports, doing well in school, there is a chance you can stop the addiction.

• Ask yourself what is missing in your life that makes you feel that you "have to have" this man. Search for other ways to meet these needs.

Present possibilities for nonaddictive and nonabusive relationships by using "Questions to Ask Yourself About a New Man" from *Getting Free* (NiCarthy, 1986).

South and North End Groups: We presented this exercise in pieces during other exercises and therefore cannot report on students responses to this exercise as a discrete unit.

Conclusion

Students felt that the sessions had been beneficial and regretted their ending. We told them: "In a way, the ending of this group is a beginning. Some of you will see each other from time to time, and you will have a kind of common language from this group. You can continue using the insights learned in the group, and its common language, among yourselves and with other women in the future."

The Minnesota School Curriculum Project: A Statewide Domestic Violence Prevention Project in Secondary Schools

Linda E. Jones

The recognition of the problem of domestic violence, including dating violence among adolescents (Henton, Cate, Koval, Lloyd and Christopher, 1983; Jones, 1987; O'Keefe, Brockopp and Chew, 1986; Roscoe and Callahan, 1985), has led to prevention education efforts directed toward young people, with the goal of decreasing the occurrence of violence in both current and future relationships. Adolescent violence prevention programs have utilized different approaches and methods in efforts to reach similar goals. This article discusses one model. Specifically, it explains the rationale and goals for a statewide violence prevention project carried out in Minnesota secondary schools, describes the curriculum materials used and the implementation plan, and presents findings from the evaluation of the project.

Background, Goals and Rationale of the Project

Recognizing the need for a comprehensive, statewide plan to contribute to the prevention of domestic violence and to address the issue of adolescent dating violence, the Minnesota Coalition for Battered Women (MCBW), the membership organization of the state's programs for battered women, received a two-year grant from the Bush Foundation which provided the majority of the funding to develop a secondary school violence prevention curriculum (including audiovisual materials), to train teachers in the use of the curriculum in the context of various standard courses and to evaluate its results.

The project's overall goal was to provide young people with information about the problem of domestic violence, to examine why this abuse occurs and to teach skills that reduce the likelihood they will be abused or abuse their partners. The first phase of the violence prevention curriculum project was directed toward junior and senior high schools, with preschools and elementary schools targeted in the second phase of the project.

In addition to being a statewide effort rather than a community or individual school's, the approach chosen for this prevention project differed from others in that it was designed to train teachers to incorporate violence prevention information into their regular courses. Other known violence prevention programs for adolescents were designed to have this information provided primarily by personnel from community agencies or programs working in the area of woman abuse. There were several rationales for choosing the teacher-training approach:

• Training teachers to address domestic violence in their classrooms was seen as having the potential to be a long-term, system-altering effort, increasing the likelihood that the material would be used on an ongoing basis.

• The approach placed fewer demands on local woman abuse programs and agencies to provide prevention education and training for the students. Instead, trainers and speakers from local programs were linked with the teachers participating in the training and were asked to update teachers periodically and to discuss their services with students each year, as one segment of the curriculum.

• Connections between school teachers and other school personnel and local agencies and programs would be strengthened as the teachers learned about local services and became acquainted with the people connected with these services when they presented their part of the curriculum.

• The approach would be efficient: Teachers throughout the state would be trained in groups, so the prevention curriculum would reach many students in a relatively short period of time. In addition, teachers would be effective at implementing the curriculum because they already have skills in communicating with students.

The Secondary Prevention Curriculum

At about the same time the Minnesota School Curriculum Project was conceptualized, the Southern California Coalition on Battered Women published *Skills for Violence-Free Relationships*, a curriculum for students thirteen to eighteen years of age to be used in educational settings "for the primary prevention of abuse of women in intimate relationships" (B. Levy, 1984). After judging it to be of high quality, the Minnesota School Curriculum Project decided to base its efforts in secondary schools on this curriculum.

Goals of this curriculum for young people include the ability (1) to define important terms such as *abuse, domestic violence,* and *battered woman;* (2) to know facts to dispel myths about battered women; (3) to know why battering occurs; and (4) to have skills and knowledge that will reduce the likelihood that young people will be abused or abuse their partners. These broad goals and more specific, related objectives are accomplished through the use of several types of activities, including brainstorming, exercises, guided discussions, role-playing and storytelling.

To adapt this curriculum for use in Minnesota, some additional information on battering and some new exercises were included, as well as information about state domestic violence statistics and legal issues, available resources, audiovisual materials and local services. A section on dating violence was also added for senior high students.

Early in the project, the lack of good, age-appropriate audiovisual materials about dating violence was identified as a concern. A slide show on teenage dating violence, developed by a shelter program in Minnesota, was used the first year. Responding to some concerns about the slide show—including the lack of racial diversity portrayed—and realizing that videotape is a much more convenient format for classroom use, the production of a video about teenage dating violence was undertaken. The Greater Minneapolis Chapter of the National Council of Jewish Women raised the funds and coordinated the production of the video with the consultation of the School Curriculum Project.

The completed video, *The Power to Choose,* consists of an introductory sequence and four dramatic scenes designed to help teens explore issues of power and violence in adolescent dating relationships. A guide to assist teachers in facilitating classroom discussion was prepared by the curriculum project coordinator.

School Curriculum Project Implementation

A coordinator, with many years of experience in the battered women's movement as well as secondary school teaching experience, was hired to develop, implement and oversee the School Curriculum Project. An advisory council, including educators, children's advocates and prevention specialists provided valuable assistance in the early planning during the project's first year.

With the endorsement of the Minnesota Board of Education and its encouragement of local school districts to participate, information about the project was mailed to all school districts in the state. Following the initial pilot training of school personnel and advocates, the curriculum was tested in twelve schools by the end of the project's first year.

Contacts were made with all local woman abuse programs around the state asking that they provide a liaison to the project for their local school districts. Twelve local programs contracted to provide a formal liaison and received funding from the project for twenty-five hours to carry out the requested functions. Typically, a children's advocate or community education staff member assumed this role, which included assisting with the recruitment and training of teachers in the local area, presenting a segment of the curriculum in the classrooms about where to go for help and providing ongoing support and information to teachers and students after the curriculum was taught. This arrangement also ensured that a quick response would be available to students experiencing violence who might request help after presentation of the curriculum.

During the next two school years, the all-day trainings were conducted by the project coordinator and local woman abuse agency liaisons in twenty-nine locations throughout Minnesota. Four hundred teachers and other school personnel from 210 schools in 146 districts were trained in the use of the curriculum. During these two years, the curriculum reached approximately twenty thousand secondary students. The grant provided the training and the curriculum materials free of charge to the districts that provided substitute teachers so that teachers could attend the training. The following school year, more of the coordinator's attention was directed toward the development and implementation of a preschool and elementary school violence prevention curriculum; recruitment and training of secondary teachers was continued by the local liaisons. A follow-up survey was sent to all school personnel trained in the use of the curriculum to determine if it had been incorporated in their courses on a permanent basis. Of the seventy-two percent responding to the follow-up questionnaire, eighty-six percent reported that the material had been or soon would be included in their classes.

The project's success in getting the materials incorporated into the schools was largely due to the ability to provide both the materials and the training for the teachers. Many teachers reported that if they had received the materials without the training, they would have felt unqualified to present them. In addition, the curriculum and the trainings were flexible so that they could be adapted to fit the needs of a school or a district. Teachers also were encouraged to make decisions about the use of the curriculum relative to their particular classroom. In most cases, the curriculum was incorporated into classes on health, family life or social studies.

While the approach used had many strengths and was viewed as highly successful overall, there were some concerns. Individual school districts have the authority to determine the curriculum used in their district, and this led to a variety of approaches and outcomes among districts, or even among schools in the same district. For example, some districts mandated the use of the curriculum, some left it to the discretion of individual teachers, some would not allow the teachers time to attend the training and some did not respond at all. Second, some teachers expressed concern about available time to incorporate new materials into existing courses. The establishment of statewide requirements that violence prevention curriculum be included at all grade levels would help resolve these concerns.

Some concerns were also expressed that uninterested or hostile teachers, or even teachers who are batterers, might be involved in presenting the materials, which they might distort. Ultimately, there is not a lot of control over how teachers use any materials in their classroom, but it is hoped that the completeness of the School Curriculum Project materials will minimize the potential for major distortions. Others questioned the ability of teachers to keep the materials current. Assistance with this was a specific task of the liaison from the local program, although their ability to do this might vary from time to time. These concerns about teachers presenting the curriculum could be alleviated by the model of prevention education in which personnel of local woman abuse programs present the material in schools. However, a major trade-off to this approach is that many fewer students are reached than was the case with the model developed by the School Curriculum Project.

Evaluation of the Project

Part of the foundation's grant to the project was for an evaluation of the curriculum. Of course, it would be extremely difficult and costly to attempt to determine the long-term effects of a prevention curriculum on the students who had been exposed to the material: For one thing, the relationships among changes in knowledge and attitudes, and the effects on later behavior, pertaining to an issue such as domestic violence are unresolved. On the other hand, if the curriculum is not at least achieving its short-term goal of increasing the basic knowledge level and possibly changing some attitudes of students that suggest a tolerance or acceptance of domestic violence, it will certainly not contribute to the prevention of woman abuse.

During the first full school year in which the project was implemented, the 225 teachers who attended the training sessions were asked if they would be willing to participate in an evaluation of the curriculum; almost all said they would. This population was then stratified by grade level (junior high or senior high) and by location of the school (rural, suburban, urban). Teachers were then randomly selected within each of the six subgroups, and their students constituted the sample.

Those who participated in the evaluation agreed to teach only specified portions of the curriculum for a specified number of days so that all the students being evaluated would receive the same contents. The junior and senior high students in the evaluation were exposed to the same parts of the curriculum for five days; however, the senior high students spent one additional day on dating violence. Finally, participating teachers had to locate a comparable group of students in their school (or a nearby school) to serve as a matched control group for the evaluation. This method of constructing a matched control group was successful in that the control groups for both the senior and junior high samples were comparable to the experimental groups on a variety of demographic characteristics.

The quasi-experimental design of the evaluation utilized a pre-test and a post-test, which were administered to the experimental and matched control groups. The pre- and post-tests consisted of eighteen true-false items that assessed students' knowledge about domestic violence, five items that assessed attitudes and three open-ended questions to determine their knowledge of available resources for help in addressing problems of abuse.

Approximately 560 junior high students, almost evenly divided between the experimental and control groups, participated in the evaluation. Among these students, the mean number of items answered correctly by the experimental and the control groups on the true-false knowledge questions were almost identical on the pre-test. However, on the post-test, following exposure to the curriculum, the experimental group increased its mean correct score slightly over three points (to 12.5) while the mean of the control group improved only nine-tenths of one point (to 10.6), possibly indicating some testing effect. The difference in the post-test scores of the two groups was statistically significant (p.001). This difference in the mean knowledge scores of the experimental and control groups was maintained when controlling for gender and for urban, suburban or rural location.

The five attitude items paralleled prevalent societal attitudes, primarily concerning sex roles, which relate to the perceived acceptability of violence in male-female relationships (for example, it is never okay to slap the person you are in a relationship with; it's no one else's business if a husband hits his wife; in serious relationships between men and women, men should be the leaders and decision-makers). The responses to the attitude items were collapsed into three categories: agree, not sure, disagree. The responses of the junior high experimental and control groups to the same questions were very similar on the pre-test, and there was very little change in the experimental group on the post-test, indicating that, over all, the curriculum had done little to affect attitudes toward domestic violence.

However, on the post-test, there were large and statistically significant differences on four of the five items in the frequencies of the responses of the male and female students who had been exposed to the curriculum, with the attitudes of the female students always being the more desirable. For example, on the item stating that, in serious relationships, men should be the leaders and decision-makers, only fifty-eight percent of the boys, compared to ninety-four percent of the girls, disagreed. About one-quarter of the boys were not sure, and seventeen percent agreed with the statement. A relatively high degree of uncertainty was obvious among the boys, compared to the girls, on all five items.

About six hundred senior high students were presented with the same knowledge items as the junior high students, and the outcomes of the evaluation were similar. The experimental group (N = 382), actually scored one point lower on the pre-test than the control group, but improved its mean correct score about three points, while the control group improved slightly less than one point between pre-test and post-test. The difference between the mean scores of the experimental and control groups at the time of the post-test was statistically significant (p.01). As with the junior high students, controlling for gender and for urban, rural or suburban location did not alter these findings.

On the attitude items, the patterns of the responses of the senior high students were again similar to those of the junior high students. For each item, a substantially higher percentage of the girls, compared to boys, responded in the desired direction. On four of the five items, the differences were statistically significant (p.002). On each item, more boys than girls were "not sure" of their positions indicating ambivalence in the boys' attitudes.

Both the junior and senior high experimental group students became somewhat more knowledgeable about general agencies— such as a mental health center or a hospital—to turn to if dealing with abuse in a relationship. However, there was a smaller improvement in the ability of the experimental group to name specific, local services that could assist in situations of abuse.

At the time of the post-test, the senior high students also responded to a survey about their experience with and perceptions of violence in dating relationships. Overall, among the 473 senior high students who said they had dated, twenty-six percent reported at least one experience with dating violence, which was defined to include the behaviors specified on the Conflict Tactics Scale (Straus, 1979). However, this percentage differed by gender, with thirty-four percent of the girls, compared with only fifteen percent of the boys, reporting experience with dating violence. When asked who they would or did talk to about an incident of dating violence, the most typical responses were friends, followed by "no one." Fathers and teachers were mentioned least frequently. When asked what they perceived as the meaning of a violent incident, the girls most often reported that their partner was angry and/or confused; the next most frequent response was that the violence was a way to exert control of the relationship. Boys most typically thought that violence meant their partner was confused or that it was a way to express love. Few boys perceived the violent behavior of a partner as a means of exerting control. Additional findings from this survey are reported in Jones (1987).

In summary, there is evidence that the primary goal of increasing the knowledge of students in the area of domestic violence was achieved on both the junior and senior high levels. However, it does not appear that the attitudes of the students concerning issues related to domestic violence changed substantially after being exposed to the curriculum. Given the knowledge-building focus of the curriculum presented to those participating in the evaluation and the relatively short period of time in which it was presented, the lack of changes in attitudes is not surprising. The evaluation did indicate that the attitudes of boys compared to those of girls were quite different. To the extent that undesirable responses on these attitude items undergird or support a tolerance for violence in male-female relationships and indicate a stance supporting traditional sex-role behavior for men and women, these responses among the boys may be cause for concern. On the other hand, the attitudes of the girls, in general, are more encouraging. The results also indicate a fair amount of ambivalence in the attitudes of the boys, which probably indicates some degree of uncertainty in their opinions at this point.

A Model Secondary School Date Rape Prevention Program

Marybeth Roden

The article that follows describes a model secondary school sexual assault awareness and prevention program. Although the program includes information about sexual abuse and stranger rape, special emphasis is placed on date rape. The model was developed by the Rape Treatment Center (RTC) of Santa Monica Hospital Medical Center, Santa Monica, California.

Why Focus on Sexual Assault in the Secondary Schools?

A critical need for sexual assault awareness and prevention programs for adolescents exists because although adolescents account for less than ten percent of the population, they are the targets of an estimated twenty to fifty percent of all reported rapes. A survey of studies reveals that a range of forty-five to seventy-eight percent of adolescents who are raped are assaulted by someone they know (Katz and Mazur, 1979), which establishes that acquaintance or "date" rape is of special significance for this population. In one study, sixty-seven percent of adolescent and college-age women reporting rape were raped in dating situations (Ageton, 1983). Approximately fifty percent of all offenders are under twenty-five years old (FBI, 1989).

Misinformation about sexual assault is rampant among adolescents. Their ideas about rape tend to be naive and stereotypical, with most adolescents believing that rapists are usually strangers in dark alleys, wielding weapons and physically injuring their victims. Recent research suggests that teenagers are relatively accepting of forced sex in certain dating situations (Aizenman and Kelley, 1988; Goodchilds and Zellman, 1984; Miller, 1988). These attitudes can result in adolescent victims of date rape not recognizing that they have been victimized. Such victims are unlikely to seek needed medical and psychological services. Adolescent males, as well, may not recognize aggressive sexual acts for what they are, capitulating instead to peer group expectations and sexual stereotypes about what constitutes "manly" behavior.

Ineffective communication, lack of assertiveness, peer pressure and sex-role stereotypes contribute to many date rapes involving adolescents.

Ineffective Communication

Failure to respond assertively to unwanted sexual overtures and to clearly state sexual preferences and limits may render young women more vulnerable to assault. In such situations, some young women may wish to refuse sexual activity, but to do so in a way that does not hurt their partners' feelings. They may say no, for example, but giggle and avert their eyes at the same time. Some young men may perceive such behavior as a "mixed message," indicative of ambivalence, and force themselves on an unwilling victim instead of asking for clarification.

Peer Pressure

Young men often feel pressured by members of their peer group to be sexually active. Some young men may feel that in order to be accepted by their peers, they must "prove" themselves sexually by seducing their girlfriends or dating partners. In response to such pressure, some men may use force. Peers may also pressure both young men and women into participating in activities, such as heavy drinking, which place them at greater risk of either committing or being victimized by sexual assault.

Sex-role Stereotypes

Acting in accordance with stereotypes about what constitutes "appropriate" male and female behavior may increase vulnerability to date rape. Young men who believe the stereotype that a "real man doesn't take no for an answer" or that "all women say no, but really mean yes" may ignore their partners' refusals of sexual activity and force themselves on unwilling victims. Young women who believe that women should be compliant and accommodating may have difficulty asserting themselves in situations where they feel threatened.

Secondary school prevention programs can help adolescents recognize those factors that place them at risk for sexual assault and provide them with skills to communicate more effectively and to resist peer pressure and the influence of sex-role stereotypes.

More than any other crime, rape enjoins its victims to silence. This is especially true among adolescent date rape victims. Their tendency not to report or discuss date rape usually compounds the severity of the trauma that follows. Date rape is a particularly devastating form of the crime because post-rape trauma is often exacerbated by heightened feelings of shame and guilt. The victim may mistakenly feel that she is somehow to blame for the assault since she consented to be with the assailant by accepting a date or agreeing to some sexual contact such as kissing. The adolescent victim who violates a parental curfew or drinks heavily and is then raped may mistakenly assume reponsibility for the assault. The date rape victim also often experiences heightened feelings of betrayal because the assailant is someone she knew and initially trusted.

The victim's ability to trust others may be more seriously impaired than if she had been raped by a stranger, complicating recovery and the ability to utilize support systems. The victim may feel that if someone she knew and trusted could assault her, she cannot ever trust others or her own ability to assess people and situations again. Secondary school prevention programs can reduce the likelihood that a young woman's trauma from date rape will be exacerbated by silence.

Program Goals

The primary goal of the program is to provide students, parents and teachers with information about the incidence and nature of sexual assault, adolescents' vulnerability to the crime and ways in which adolescents can protect themselves against victimization. The program aims to teach students skills such as effective communication and assertiveness, as well as ways of confronting stereotyped sex-role expectations.

Equally important is the prevention of revictimization and further trauma for students who have already been sexually assaulted by raising awareness regarding the impact of rape on victims, providing information about resources and providing an opportunity for students who have been assaulted to receive individualized attention from a trained professional through the program's crisis intervention component.

Program Format

The RTC has provided prevention programming to public and private high schools throughout Los Angeles County for eight years and has reached more than one hundred thousand students. From 1985 through 1990, the RTC program was funded by landmark California legislation requiring that all children in California public school systems receive child abuse prevention education four times throughout their school experience, kindergarten through secondary school. The program includes classroom prevention education presentations and crisis intervention counseling for students as well as training seminars for school personnel and parents. The program is presented by instructors employed by the RTC. Participating schools are located in semi-rural, suburban and inner-city areas, with students representing a wide socioeconomic and ethnic diversity.

Student workshops are presented in ninth- and tenth-grade health classes. Health classes are required for all students, ensuring that the largest possible number of students participate in the program.

The RTC program is three classroom sessions, or approximately three hours in length, and is presented during three consecutive days. This time frame permits a fuller exploration of relevant issues and fosters a stronger rapport between instructor and students than would be possible in a one-session format. The program is presented, with few exceptions, in coeducational classes.

Crisis intervention counseling is provided through the program's "Individual Time" component. Program instructors are available to meet with students individually at specified times in a location on campus that ensures privacy. Students are advised of these times and locations during the classroom sessions.

The availability of crisis intervention counseling is critical. The program may precipitate a crisis for student victims who, until participation in the program, have managed to suppress feelings associated with their victimization. For some, the knowledge gained through the program may enable them, for the first time, to correctly identify current or past sexual assault experiences. Immediate resources are needed by such students. Since it is difficult for many adolescents to use community resources without support and guidance, simply providing them with information about ways to access off-campus community resources is insufficient. Providing on-site crisis intervention by trained professionals can also help alleviate school personnel's anxiety about being left to handle student disclosure crises after the prevention specialists have left the school.

The Program Curriculum

The main topics covered during each day of the program are as follows:

Day One

Definitions and Incidence

The instructor provides information about the definitions and prevalence of the various forms of sexual abuse to which adolescents are most vulnerable, including incest, molestation, and stranger, acquaintance and date rape. Although the RTC program focuses primarily on rape, information about other forms of sexual abuse such as incest and molestation is also provided. Such information is included since discussing issues of coercive sexual activity may raise concerns not only for students who have experienced rape, but also for students who have been victims of incest or molestation. These students need clarification about the nature of these crimes committed against them and available resources.

In defining the various forms of sexual abuse, the instructor emphasizes that force or some type of coercion is always involved, that such activity occurs without the consent of the victim and that sexual abuse is *never* the fault of the victim.

Sensitization to the Impact of Rape on Victims

Many adolescents react to the subject of rape by denying their own vulnerability to sexual assault. Misconceptions and attitudes that blame the victim reinforce this denial. ("If a rape happens because the victim has done something 'stupid' or risky, and I never behave in a similar fashion, then it can't happen to me.") The expression of victim-blaming attitudes in the classroom not only interferes with the students' ability to recognize their vulnerability and the importance of acquiring prevention skills, but also can be extremely distressing to victims in the classroom. For this reason, the RTC program places a major emphasis on sensitizing students to the nature of victimization trauma through class discussion and exercises.

Sensitization exercise. One of the first classroom exercises presented to the students is a discussion of "nontouching" forms of sexual abuse, such as exhibitionism, voyeurism, obscene phone calls and verbal sexual harassment. Students are asked if they have ever seen a "flasher" or received an obscene phone call. They are usually comfortable discussing such incidents. The instructor then asks them to describe their feelings about having been made to participate, however briefly, in such unwanted sexual activity. Students can easily identify feelings such as fear, anger, disgust, betrayal and shame and, equally important, they can recognize how such incidents occurred without their consent. In addition, since students find it easier to discuss nontouching forms of sexual abuse, the exercise introduces the topic in a less threatening or frightening manner than beginning the discussion with more intimidating subjects such as incest, molestation and rape.

Discussion of rapist's motivation. When asked why rapists rape, students often respond that offenders rape because of sexual frustration. This reflects a common misconception of rape as a sexually motivated crime. Such a misconception can lead to misunderstandings about the victim's culpability for "provocative" behavior, that victims somehow "ask for" or "deserve" to be raped. Accurate information that rapists rape to achieve a sense of power and control and/or to express rage and anger is presented in order to help students recognize that rape is a crime of violence and not sexually motivated. This enhances sympathy for the victim.

Videotaped interview. A videotaped interview with a woman discussing her assault by a stranger is shown. Students are asked to focus not on the details of her experience, but on her description of her feelings about the rape. Since adolescents tend to be more critical of victims of date rape, listening to an account of a stranger rape more readily elicits empathy for the victim.

Day Two

Impact of Rape

At the beginning of the second hour of the program, students are guided in a discussion of the videotape shown on the previous day. This not only facilitates student sensitization to victims, but also provides a bridge to a discussion of date rape. Students often express more anxiety about and interest in stranger rape and its prevention than about date rape, the form of the crime to which they are more vulnerable. The instructor allows the class to fully discuss the feelings expressed by the victim of stranger rape and then points out that although victims of date rape are assaulted under very different circumstances they experience the same feelings. The instructor can then more easily lead the students into a discussion of the incidence and causes of date rape.

Prevalence and Causes of Date Rape

Students are informed about the incidence of acquaintance and date rape in their age group and provided with information about how peer pressure, sex-role stereotypes and ineffective communication contribute to date rapes.

Importance of Reporting the Crime and Obtaining Help

Students are given information about what to do immediately following a sexual assault, including brief information about how to report the crime and obtain medical treatment. Students are encouraged to obtain counseling and advocacy assistance, and they are given concrete information about how to obtain such help. "Referral cards" containing the names and phone numbers of local rape crisis centers and other appropriate counseling resources are distributed.

Date Rape Film

A short film dramatizing the aftermath of an adolescent woman's disclosure of sexual assault to a high school counselor is shown. The film is designed to trigger a discussion among students about some of the factors contributing to date rape. These include peer pressure, sex-role stereotypes, ineffective communication, and alcohol.

Peer pressure. Male students are encouraged to look critically at peer pressure and how they respond to it. They are invited to consider how pressure to "score" may cause them to ignore their own values and limits and how such pressure may create the expectation that in order to fit in with his friends, a young man must be sexually active. In response to such pressure, a young man may ignore his own sexual preferences and limits and engage in sexual activity merely to gain peer acceptance and not because he, himself, wishes to do so. Students are informed that if a man uses force in a sexual situation in response to peer pressure, he is guilty of rape. Students are also informed about the risks of gang or group rape, as a potential victim or as a potential rapist. Male students are warned to assess situations for themselves and never become involved in a situation where a woman might be victimized. The instructor emphasizes the positive potential of peer pressure and encourages the males in the class to intervene in social situations where they suspect that a young woman is at risk of being victimized by other young men.

Sex role stereotypes. Male and female students are invited to examine common expectations regarding what constitutes "appropriate" behavior on the part of men and women in dating situations. Some of the questions used to elicit such discussions include:

• "If a girl goes to a guy's house when she knows no one else will be there, does that mean that she is willing to have sex?"
• "If a girl dresses in a sexy way, what message is she trying to give out?"
• "If a girl goes to a party and gets drunk, does that mean she's looking for sex?"
• "Do all guys want sex all the time?"

Typically, young men and women respond differently to these questions. Many young men, for example, claim that provocative clothing indicates a young woman's willingness to engage in sexual activity. The young women in the class often respond that women dress in order to be fashionable and to fit in with their friends, not to signal an interest in sex. Through discussion, students are sensitized to the fact that behavior in social situations is frequently interpreted differently by men and women and that it is important to discuss assumptions in dating situations. The instructor also emphasizes that misunderstandings that arise in such situations are never justification for the use of force to have sex.

Male students are informed that belief in male sex-role stereo-types, such as "a real man never takes no for an answer," can put men at risk of perpetrating sexual assault. Both male and female students are informed that everyone has the right to refuse sexual contact at any time, regardless of the circumstances and in spite of any prior sexual intimacy.

Ineffective communication. Emphasis is placed on the need for clear communication in dating situations. Women are encouraged to state their intentions and limits verbally and directly. They are advised to avoid sending "mixed messages" and to be sure that their verbal and nonverbal messages are consistent. Male students are told that they must obtain consent from their partners in sexual situations. They are provided with suggestions for handling situations in which they feel they are receiving "mixed messages." Both male and female students are warned against assuming that their partners will automatically understand their wishes, expectations and limits. These must be communicated clearly.

The role of alcohol in date rapes. Students are informed that drinking may place them at greater risk of victimization or of committing sexual assault. Young men are told that being drunk does not diminish responsibility and that, if they commit a rape while under the influence of alcohol, they may still be charged with sexual assault. Young women are advised that drinking may make it more difficult for them to recognize when they are at risk, to communicate their limits clearly or take action if they are in an assault situation. The instructor is careful to emphasize that, although it is advisable to avoid excessive drinking, a victim who is drunk at the time she is assaulted is in no way responsible for the rape.

Day Three

The third and last hour of the curriculum is devoted to the development of practical prevention skills. The greater part of the hour is devoted to date rape prevention skills.

Rape Prevention

A brief review of personal safety strategies to help minimize the risk of stranger assault is provided. Students are asked to imagine themselves in common situations that may pose some risk and invited to think about how they would handle such situations.

Examples include being home alone when a stranger knocks on the door to deliver an unexpected package; being followed while walking on the street; and receiving a phone call from a stranger requesting personal information. The class and instructor discuss various suggestions for responding to such situations effectively.

Role Play Exercise

A role play exercise provides students with an opportunity to practice assertive communication and effective listening skills. Student volunteers are given common dating scenarios to role play. The volunteers, instructor and other class members then discuss the interchange. Scenarios include the following:

• A student refusing a telephone request for a date from another student
• One partner of a couple on a date trying to verbally persuade the other to have sex
• A young man responding to a buddy who is bragging about being ready to "score" on a date he has planned for the evening

Since the role plays are of situations relatively low in threat, they provide an opportunity for the instructor to close the program on an "upbeat," playful note, while still reinforcing the program's messages regarding the importance of clear communication and effective dialogue in dating situations.

Effective Implementation

The program is designed so that the instructors are effective in responding to the needs of high school students when implementing this curriculum.

Adequate Class Discussion

Information about the role of peer pressure, sex-role stereotypes, ineffective communication and alcohol in date rape situations is best imparted through class discussion. It is far more effective for students to talk to one another rather than for the adult instructor to tell them this information—for example, for male students to hear from the females in the class that being drunk or going to a guy's house when no one else is present does not indicate a willingness to have sex. The purpose of such discussion is to encourage open dialogue between male and female students concerning their attitudes and expectations in dating situations. In addition to raising student awareness of how their behavior may be interpreted or misinterpreted by members of the opposite sex, such discussions also serve to model the type of dialogue necessary in dating situations.

Responding to Student Comments

The instructor's role is to encourage and facilitate discussion, to correct victim-blaming statements and to reinforce basic concepts when necessary. It is important for the instructor to foster an atmosphere in which students feel free to discuss these sensitive issues candidly. The instructor avoids evaluating student responses or statements as "wrong" or "right." If a student expresses an opinion that appears to condone violent behavior (for example, "I think girls who dress provocatively are saying to guys, 'I'm available,' and you can't blame a guy if he gets a little carried away."), the instructor asks the rest of the class what they think about the remarks rather than hastening to "correct" the statement. After full discussion of the point, however, the instructor emphasizes that the use of force is never acceptable.

Male Students

The need for prevention information is as critical for male as for female students. Adolescent males are also vulnerable to sexual victimization. In addition, they may be affected by the rape of a family member, friend or acquaintance and therefore need information about how to be sensitive and supportive. Most important, male students need information about the causes of date rape and the dynamics of situations in which they or members of their peer group may potentially commit rape.

The instructors remain sensitive to the reactions of male students. Some male participants may feel that information about sexual assaults is important only for women. Others may feel defensive, as if the discussion is suggesting that *all* men are potential rapists and as if the instructor is "making girls afraid of guys." To address these feelings, the instructor emphasizes that most men would not use force to have sex with an unwilling victim. The instructor validates the young men's feelings of frustration and confusion in dating situations where they feel they are receiving mixed messages, but emphasizes that, although these feelings may be real and understandable, the use of force is *never* acceptable.

The instructor points out that although most rapes are committed against women, men can also be the victims of sexual assault.

Conclusion

Date rape is a problem for men and women, and this coeducational approach that openly confronts myths and misunderstandings about date rape effectively involves young men and young women in addressing the problem.

Dealing with Dating Violence in Schools

Carolyn Powell

School personnel such as teachers, counselors and administrators can play an important part in intervening with and preventing dating violence. Jordan High School, where I am Drop-Out Prevention Adviser, is located in the community of Watts in Los Angeles, California. Sixty-eight percent of the school's 1,850 students are Hispanic, and thirty-one percent are black. Sixteen percent of the students have limited proficiency in English. Seventy-five percent of the families receive public assistance. At Jordan, we respond to the problem of dating violence in several ways. We do not have a program that is specifically geared toward dealing with violence in dating relationships, but the problem becomes apparent in the classroom and in other special programs. Perceptive teachers have responded to the nonverbal (for example, withdrawn behavior) and physical (bruises and so forth) signs of problems and have identified violent dating situations. As part of special school programs, I lead groups for pregnant and parenting teens and groups for students in our drop-out prevention program, and I consult with deans and the probation officer who leads a group for students on probation. When relationship patterns are discussed in the groups I lead, group members often indicate that they are having a problem with a violent relationship. They may not say it directly, for example, "My boyfriend is hitting me," but changes in their demeanor or statements about an "argument" lead us to explore it.

Dealing With Dating Violence in Groups

When we discuss dating violence in any of the groups we offer at Jordan High School, we encourage group members to talk to one another. They respond more to one another than to adult facilitators. When a girl in the group is talking about violence in her relationship, we encourage the group members to talk with her by asking questions such as the following: "How controlling is this?" or "What are your experiences of getting out of violent situations?" Some of the girls are stronger, more independent and self-caring and more likely to counter the others in the group if their responses are victim-blaming. We try to have the girls who are stronger support the girls who are less secure. They are good models.

Students are less aware of what *verbal* violence is, that certain things *said* constitute violence. We emphasize that verbal attacks can escalate into physical violence and that violence is more threatening to deal with once it becomes physical. We talk with girls about how to evaluate their relationships, encouraging them to ask themselves what they want in their relationships and to expect to be treated with respect. We have formerly battered women speak in the groups about how they handled the violence and how they got away.

When we talk about relationships in general, for example with siblings or parents, we talk about jealousy, about attitudes and about resolving conflicts. We also discuss violence in the community. We consistently relate these subjects to dating violence and emphasize how these problems are related to one another. For example, several group members have lost family or friends to domestic violence or other kinds of violence. In reaction, some of the boys have become violent with their girlfriends, and some of the girls have become more intensely involved with their boyfriends. An example of the impact of community violence is the group influence evident in the abusive behavior of the boys in front of their friends or gangs (although they may not treat their girlfriends badly when they are alone).

Dealing With Dating Violence on Campus

Sometimes we initiate discussions with students about dating violence on the basis of behavior observed by staff or information received from other students. We see evidence of violence in the way boys talk to girls on campus. School staff stop them, talk to them and confront their belief that it is okay or "manly" to talk to girls this way or that the girls expect it. Staff talk with the girls by themselves and sometimes find out that girls tolerate sexual attention or their boyfriends touching or hugging them on campus when they do not want to participate. They appreciate help in being more assertive about rejecting sexual attentions they do not want.

It takes a continuous effort. We know that some students stop their abusive behavior only when we see them. But it is important to keep confronting them. We know that for at least some of the students the way they are behaving presents a conflict for them. They may be behaving the way they feel they are expected to by their friends, but they may not be comfortable with it. Adults can give students options with acceptable justifications that can be used with their friends. Students begin to confront one another (for example, "Ms. P's going to tell you... " or "Hey, man, you don't have to... " or "Girl, I wouldn't let... "). We try to stimulate positive peer pressure. This works best when students have respect for the adults involved and believe that the adults respect them.

Staff work together in dealing with this. For example, a teacher called me to help when he took a boy out of class for making abusive remarks to a girl. The teacher did not want the boy to be suspended, but he did not want to ignore the behavior. I was able to talk to the boy about considering how his girlfriend felt, and I met with the couple and helped them find a way to resolve their conflict. Not all situations work out this easily. Boys often do not think of the impact of their behavior on the girls, nor do they consider their behavior abusive. Teachers and counselors working together try to stimulate their empathy and help them see how conflicts escalate. We try to teach them what to do so disagreements do not escalate.

Some teachers take the responsibility to deal with dating violence when it surfaces in their classrooms and incorporate related discussions in their lesson planning. These discussions (in coeducational classes) include self-esteem, male-female roles, their role expectations for themselves and their partners, conflict resolution, empathy, respect for others and how to say "stop." Teachers can use more training to facilitate this type of discussion. It is not adequately built into the school curriculum, although learning to have healthy relationships is one of the major developmental tasks of adolescence. But it can be included as part of a discussion on behavior expectations in the classroom or related to the academic curriculum (for example, in government class, a discussion of sexual harassment, or in economics, a discussion of images of women in advertising). At the very least, teachers tell students to stop the behavior and/or send them to the dean's office for disciplinary action. When handled this way, students at least find out that this behavior is not acceptable, but they do not learn alternative behaviors. Teachers also refer students to the school counselors for counseling.

The School Environment

The students' connection with the school helps so much. If the girls are successful in school or are in other positive groups of friends, then they question the violence in their dating relationship. But if the relationship is the only one they have or they are not having success in some other area of their life, the pressure to keep a boyfriend is greater. When they have success in school and make plans for the future, they feel they have choices: If their boyfriend does not want them to go to school or to be in an extracurricular activity, for example, then they have to make decisions between what *they* want and his control. If the school atmosphere encourages the girls in their goals and pursuits, they can talk about looking for a boyfriend that encourages them as well. The girls can find support at school to pull out of the abusive relationship, to deal with the "withdrawal pains."

Peer counselors and school staff at Jordan High School have recently been participating in conflict resolution training. Peer counselors are now receiving referrals from the deans. This is a promising resource for students who are looking for peer support in dealing with a violent relationship.

There are certain teachers and staff to whom students gravitate. Clerical, security and custodial staff relate to students as well. The sensitive adults in the environment who notice change or to whom the student attaches are excellent resources. This is especially true of staff who live in the community. They listen when students talk to them and make referrals within the school.

The linkages between the school, the students and their parents are important in dealing with dating violence. We see a positive response from students when the school counselors can enhance communication between the student and his or her parents. Parents and the school working together can help a girl handle her safety if she is afraid of being assaulted by her boyfriend or former boyfriend. Parental support makes a difference for a girl going through the pain of separating from an abusive boyfriend. Working to improve the communication and relationship between a boy and his parent(s) can have an impact on his use of violence and control.

Dealing with dating violence is most effective in an open atmosphere where people talk to one another—students, staff and parents. It depends on the willingness of staff to say to one another, "What do you think?" All school counseling disciplines and administrators have a role as supports to other staff in dealing with dating violence. The school environment should encourage the asking of questions, the expression of concern and an *active* stance in relation to students and abusive behavior.

References

Adams, C. & J. F., Loreen-Martin, J. (1984). *No is not Enough: Helping Teenagers Avoid Sexual Assault*. San Luis Obispo, CA: Impact Publishers.

Ageton, S. S. (1983). *Sexual Assault Among Adolescents*. Lexington, MA: Heath.

Aizenman, M. and Kelley, G. (1988). The incidence of violence and acquaintance rape in dating relationships among college men and women. *Journal of College Student Development*, 305–311.

Alexander, S. (1979). *Anyone's Daughter*. New York: Viking Press.

———(1985). *Nut-cracker, Money, Madness, Murder: A Family Album*. New York: Dell.

Allen, C. and Straus, M. A. (1980). Resources, power and husband-wife violence. In M. A. Straus and G. T. Hotaling (Eds.), *The Social Causes of Husband-Wife Violence* (pp. 188–208). Minneapolis, MN: University of Minnesota Press.

American College of Obstetricians and Gynecologists (1988). *The Abused Woman*. Washington, DC: Author.

———(1989). *The Battered Woman*. Washington, DC: Author.

American Psychiatric Association (1980). *Diagnostic and Statistical Manual, Third Edition*. Washington, DC: Author.

Arias, I. and Johnson, P. (1989). Evaluations of physical aggression among intimate dyads. *Journal of Interpersonal Violence, 4* (3), 298–307.

Arias, I., Samios, M. and O'Leary, K. D. (1987). Prevalence and correlates of physical aggression during courtship. *Journal of Interpersonal Violence, 2* (1), 82–90.

Atkins, S. (1977). *Child Satan, Child of God*. Plainfield, NY: Logos International.

Barry, K. (1979). *Female Sexual Slavery*. New York: Avon.

Bem, S. L. (1974). The measurement of psychological androgyny. *Journal of Consulting and Clinical Psychology, 42* (2), 155–162.

Benedict, H., (1987). *Safe, Strong, and Streetwise: Sexual Safety at Home, on the Street, on Dates, on the Job, at Parties, and More*. Boston: Little, Brown and Company.

Bernard, J. L., Bernard, S. L. and Bernard, M. L. (1985). Courtship violence and sex-typing. *Family Relations, 34*, 573–576.

Bernard, M. L. and Bernard, J. L. (1983). Violent intimacy: The family as a model for love relationships. *Family Relations, 32*, 283–286.

Berne, E. (1964). *Games People Play.* New York: Grove Press.

Bettelheim, B. (1943). Individual and mass behavior in extreme situations. *Journal of Abnormal and Social Psychology, 38*, 417–452.

Billingham, R. E. (1987). Courtship violence: The patterns of conflict resolution strategies across seven levels of economic commitment. *Family Relations, 36*, 283–289.

Billingham, R. E. and Sack, A. R. (1987). Conflict resolution tactics and the level of emotional commitment among unmarrieds. *Human Relations, 40*, 59–74.

Bogal-Allbritten, R. and Allbritten, W. L. (1985). The hidden victims: Courtship violence among college students. *Journal of College Student Personnel, 19*, 201–204.

Bouvier, L. F. and Gardner, R. W. (1986). Immigration to the U.S.: Unfinished story. *Population Bulletin, 41*, November.

Briere, J. and Malamuth, N.A. (1983). Predicting self-reported likelihood of sexually abusive behavior: Attitudinal versus sexual explanations. *Journal of Research in Personality, 17*, 315–323.

Breslin, F. C., Riggs, D. S., O'Leary, K. D. and Arias, I. (1990). Family precursors: Expected and anticipated consequences of dating aggression. *Journal of Interpersonal Violence, 5* (2), 247–258.

Brodbelt, S. (1983). College dating and violence. *College Student Journal, 17*, 273–277.

Browne, A. and Finkelhor, D. (1986). Impact of child sexual abuse: A review of the research. *Psychological Bulletin, 99* (1), 66–77.

Bugliosi, V. and Gentry, C. (1974). *Helter Skelter: The True Story of the Manson Murders.* New York: W. W. Norton.

Bullock, L. and McFarlane, J. (1988). A program to prevent battering of pregnant students. *Response, 11* (1), 18–19.

———— (1989). The birthweight-battering connection. *American*

Journal of Nursing, 89 (9).

Bullock, L., Maloney, L. and McFarlane, J. (1990). Battering among pregnant teenagers: A unique role for the school nurse. *School Nurse, 6* (1), 10–12.

Burke, P. J., Stets, J. E. and Pirog-Good, M. A. (1989). Gender identity, self-esteem, and physical and sexual abuse in dating relationships. In M. A. Pirog-Good and J. E. Stets (Eds.), *Violence in Dating Relationships: Emerging Social Issues* (pp. 72–93). New York: Praeger Publishers.

Burtle, V. (1985). Therapeutic anger in women. In L. B. Rosewater and L. E. A. Walker (Eds.), *Handbook of Feminist Therapy: Women's Issues in Psychotherapy* (pp. 71–79). New York: Springer.

Campbell, J. (1986). Nursing assessment for risk of homocide with battered women. *Advances in Nursing Science, 8* (4), 36–51.

Campbell, J. C. (1987). A nursing study of two explanatory models of women's responses to battering. *Dissertation Abstracts International, 47,* 3704-B (available from University Microfilm No. 86–21.192).

Carlson, B. (1987). Dating violence: A research review and comparison with spouse abuse. *Social Casework: The Journal of Contemporary Social Work, 68* (1), 16–23.

Cate, R. M., Henton, J. M., Koval, J., Christopher, F. S. and Lloyd, S. (1982). Premarital abuse: A social psychological perspective. *Journal of Family Issues, 3,* 79–91.

Centers for Disease Control (1988). CDC Surveillance Summaries, February 1988. *MMWR, 37* (no. SS-1), 1–4.

——— (1989). Education about adult domestic violence in U.S. and Canadian medical schools, 1987–88. Editors Note. *MMWR, 37* (2), 19–21.

Chan, C. (1988). Asian-American women: Psychological responses to sexual exploitation and cultural stereotypes. In L. Fulani (Ed.), *The Psychopathology of Everyday Racism and Sexism.* New York: Harrington Park Press.

Chow, E. N. L. (1985). The acculturation experience of Asian American women. In A. Sargent (Ed.), *Beyond Sex Roles,* St. Paul, MN: West Publishing.

Coleman, J. (1985). *At Mother's Request.* New York: Pocket Books.

Comins, C. A. (1984). *Courtship violence: A recent study and its implications for future research.* Paper presented at the Second National Conference on Family Violence Research, University of New Hampshire, Durham, NH, August, 1984.

Committee on Trauma Research, Commission on Life Sciences, National Research Council and the National Academy of Sciences (1985). *Injury in America: A Continuing Public Health Problem.* Washington, DC: National Academy Press.

Courtois, C. (1988). *Healing the Incest Wound.* New York: W. W. Norton.

Creighton, Allan (1988). *Teens Need Teens: A Workbook and Education Curriculum for High School Students on Dating and Domestic Violence Prevention.* Battered Women's Alternatives, P.O. Box 6406, Concord, CA 94524.

Crowne, D. and Marlowe, D. (1964). *The Approval Motive.* New York: John Wiley.

Dating Violence Intervention Project (1988). *Three Session Curriculum on Teen Dating Violence Prevention and Peer Leader Training Manual.* Dating Violence Intervention Project, P.O. Box 530, Harvard Square Sta., Cambridge, MA 92238.

Deal, J. E. and Wampler, K. S. (1986). Dating violence: The primacy of previous experiences. *Journal of Social and Personal Relationships, 3* (4), 457–471.

Keseredy, W. S. (1988). Women abuse in dating relationships: The relevance of social support theory. *Journal of Family Violence, 3* (1), 1–14.

Maris, A. (1987). The efficacy of a spouse abuse model in accounting for courtship violence. *Journal of Family Issues, 8* (3), 291–305.

Dobash, R. E. and Dobash, R. (1978). Wives: The 'appropriate' victims of marital violence. *Victimology, 2* (3–4), 426–442.

———— (1979). *Violence Against Wives.* New York: Free Press.

———— (1989). *Domestic violence and the economic dependence of women.* The Role of Women in the American Economy Lecture Series, University of Cincinnati, Ohio, November 6, 1989.

Dutton, D. G. (1986). Wife assaulter's explanations for assault: The neutralization of self-punishment. *Canadian Journal of Behavioral Science, 18* (4), 381–390.

Dutton, D. G. and Painter, S.L. (1981). Traumatic bonding: The development of emotional attachments in battered women and other relationships of intermittent abuse. *Victimology, 6,* 139–155.

Ehrlich, S. (1989). *Lisa, Hedda, and Joel: The Steinberg Murder Case.* New York: St. Martin's Press.

Eisner, F. (1980). *The Survivor.* New York: William Morrow.

Ellis, A. (1962). *Reason and Emotion in Psychotherapy.* Secaucus, NJ: Lyle Stuart.

Erikson, E. H. (1950). *Childhood and Society.* New York: W. W. Norton.

Everstine, D. S. and Everstine, L. (1989). *Sexual Trauma in Children and Adolescents: Dynamics and Treatment.* New York: Brunner/Mazel.

Fagan, J., Stewart, D. and Hansen, K. (1983). Violent men or violent husbands? Background factors and situational correlates. In D. Finkelhor, R. Gelles, G. Hotaling and M. Straus (Eds.), *The Dark Side of Families.* Newbury Park, CA: Sage Publishers.

Fairbank, J. A., Gross, R. and Keane, T.M. (1983). Treatment of Posttraumatic Stress Disorder. *Behavior Modification, 7* (4), 557–567.

Federal Bureau of Investigation (U.S.) (1989). *Uniform Crime Reports.* Washington, DC: Author.

Finkelhor, D. (1983). Common features of family abuse. In D. Finkelhor, R. J. Gelles, G. T. Hotaling and M.A. Straus (Eds.), *The Dark Side of Families* (pp. 17–28). Newbury Park, CA: Sage Publishers.

———— (1988). The trauma of child abuse: Two models. In G. Wyatt and G.J. Powell (Eds.), *Lasting Effects of Child Abuse.* Newbury Park, CA: Sage Publishers.

Fisher, G. J. (1986). College student attitudes toward forcible date rape: I. Cognitive predictors. *Archives of Sexual Behavior, 15* (6), 457–467.

Flynn, C.P. (1990). Sex roles and women's responses to courtship violence. *Journal of Family Violence, 5* (1), 83–94.

Foy, D. W., Resnick, H. S., Carroll, E. M. and Osato, S.S. (1990). *Handbook of Comparative Treatments for Adult Disorders.* New York: John Wiley.

Frank, E., Anderson, B., Stewart, B. D., Dancu, C., Hughes, C. and West, D. (1988). Efficacy of cognitive behavior therapy and systematic desensitization in the treatment of rape trauma. *Behavior Therapy, 19,* 403–420.

Gamache, D. and Weiner, J. P. (1988). *"The Power to Choose": A Video-based Curriculum on Power and Violence in Teenage Relationships (Teacher's Guide).* Agency for Institutional Technologies, Box A, Bloomington, IN, 47402.

Gardner, R. W., Robey, B. and Smith, P. G. (1985). Asian Americans: Growth, change, and diversity. *Population Bulletin, 40,* October.

Gelles, R. (1975). Violence and pregnancy: A note on the extent of the problem and needed services. *Family Coordinator, 24* (1), 81–86.

Gelles, R. J. and Straus, M.A. (1988). *Intimate Violence.* New York: Simon and Schuster.

Gibson, P. (1986). Gay male and lesbian youth suicide. *Report of the Secretary's Task Force on Youth Suicide,* U.S. Department of Health and Human Services, National Institute of Mental Health.

Gilligan, C. (1982). *In a Different Voice: Psychological Theory and Women's Development.* Cambridge: Harvard University Press.

Goodchilds, J. D. and Zellman, G. L. (1984). Sexual signalling and sexual aggression in adolescent relationships. In N. Malamuth and E. Donnerstein (Eds.), *Pornography and Sexual Aggression.* Orlando, FL: Academic Press.

Gould, K. (1988). Asian and Pacific Islanders: Myth and reality. *Social Work, 33* (2).

Graham, D. L. R. (1987). *Loving to Survive: Men and Women as Hostages.* Unpublished manuscript.

Graham, D. L. R., Foliano, J., Latimer, D. and Rawlings, E. I. (1990). *Stockholm Syndrome and Violence in Dating Relationships.* Unpublished manuscript.

Graham, D. L. R. and Rawlings, E. I. (1987). Psychological mechanisms, psychodynamics, and indicators. In D. L. R. Graham (Ed.), *Loving to Survive: Men and Women as Hostages.* Unpublished manuscript.

Graham, D. L. R., Rawlings, E. I. and Rimini, N. (1988). Survivors of terror: Battered women, hostages and the Stockholm Syndrome. In K. Yllo and M. Bograd (Eds.), *Feminist Perspectives on Wife Abuse* (pp. 217–233). Newbury Park, CA: Sage Publishers.

Gwartney-Gibbs, P. A., Stockard, J. and Brohmer, S. (1987). Learning courtship violence: The influence of parents, peers, and personal experiences. *Family Relations, 36,* 276–282.

Hacker, F. J. (1976). *Crusaders, Criminals, Crazies: Terror and Terrorism in our Time.* New York: Bantam.

Hart, B. (1986). Lesbian battering: An examination. In K. Lobel (Ed.), *Naming the Violence* (pp. 173–189). Seattle: Seal Press.

———— (1989). *Domestic Violence Protection Orders: Handbook for District Court, Administrators, Prothonotaries, and Special Court Administrators.* Harrisburg, PA: Pennsylvania Coalition Against Domestic Violence.

Helton, A., McFarlane, J., and Anderson, E. (1987). Battered and pregnant: A prevalence study. *American Journal of Public Health, 77* (10), 1337–1339.

Henton, J., Cate, R., Koval, J., Lloyd, S., and Christopher, S. (1983). Romance and violence in dating relationships. *Journal of Family Issues, 4,* 467–482.

Heron, A. (1983). *One Teenager in Ten: Testimony by Gay and Lesbian Youth.* New York: Warner Books.

Hilberman, E. (1976). *The Rape Victim.* New York: Basic Books.

Hilberman, E. and Munson, K. (1978). Sixty battered women. *Victimology, 2* (3–4), 460–470.

Hill, E. (1985). *The Family Secret: A Personal Account of Incest.* Santa Barbara, CA: Capra Press.

Hillard, P. J. (1985). Physical abuse in pregnancy. *Obstetrics and Gynecology, 66,* 185–190.

Hofferth, S. and Hayes, S. (Eds.) (1987). *Risking the Future: Adolescent Sexuality, Pregnancy and Childbearing.* Washington, DC: National Academy Press.

Hotaling, G. T. and Sugarman, D. B. (1986). An analysis of risk markers in husband to wife violence: The current state of knowledge. *Violence and Victims, 1* (2), 101–124.

Hughes, D., Johnson, K., Rosenbaum, S., Butler, E. and Simmons, J. (1988). *The Health of America's Children: Maternal and*

Child Health Data Book. Washington, DC: Children's Defense Fund.

Hughes, D., Johnson, K., Rosenbaum, S. and Liu, J. (1989). *The Health of America's Children: Maternal and Child Health Data Book.* Washington, DC: Children's Defense Fund.

Hunter, E. (1956). *Brainwashing.* New York: Pyramid Books.

Hunter, J. and Schaecher, R. (1987). Stresses on lesbian and gay adolescents in schools. *Social Work in Education,* Spring, 180–190.

Hurston, Z. N. (1978). How it Feels to Be Colored Me. In *I Love Myself When I Am Laughing.* Old Westbury: The Feminist Press, p. 153.

Janoff-Bulman, R. (1985). The aftermath of victimization: Rebuilding shattered assumptions. In C. R. Figley (Ed.), *Trauma and Its Wake.* New York: Brunner/ Mazel.

Jones, L. E. (1987). Minnesota Coalition for Battered Women School Curriculum Project Evaluation Report. St. Paul, MN: Minnesota Coalition for Battered Women (available from the author).

Kanin, E. J. (1957). Male aggression in dating-courtship relations. *Journal of Sociology, 63,* 197–204.

———— (1967). Reference groups and sex conduct norm violations. *Sociological Quarterly, 8,* 495–504.

———— (1985). Date rapists: Differential sexual socialization and relative deprivation. *Archives of Sexual Behavior, 14* (3), 219–231.

Kanin, E. J. and Parcell, S. R. (1977). Sexual aggression: A second look at the offended female. *Archives of Sexual Behavior, 6,* 67–76.

Kanuha, V. (1987). Sexual assault in Southeast Asian communities: Issues in intervention. *Response, 10* (3).

Katz, S. and Mazur, M. A. (1979). *Understanding the Rape Victim: A Synthesis of Research Findings.* New York: John Wiley.

Kenrick, D. T. and Cialdini, R. B. (1977). Romantic attraction: Misattribution versus reinforcement and explanations. *Journal of Personality and Social Psychology, 35* (6), 381–391.

Kessner, E. (1988). Sweetheart murders: When teen boyfriends turn into killers. *Redbook,* March, 130–189.

Kilpatrick, D. G., Saunders, B. E., Veronen, L. J., Best, C. L. and Von, J. M. (1987). Criminal victimization: Lifetime prevalence, reporting to police, and psychological impact. *Crime and Delinquency, 33,* 479–489.

Koss, M. P. (1987). *Outrageous acts and everyday seductions: Sexual aggression and victimization among college students.* Paper presented at Romance, Rape and Relationships: A Conference on Teen Sexual Exploitation, Seattle, WA.

Koss, M. P. and Leonard, K. E. (1984). Sexually aggressive men. In N. A. Malamuth and E. Donnerstein (Eds.), *Pornography and Sexual Aggression.* Orlando, FL: Academic Press.

Koss, M. P., Gidycz, C. A. and Wisniewski, N. (1987). The scope of rape: Incidence and prevalence of sexual aggression and victimization in a national sample of higher education students. *Journal of Consulting and Clinical Psychology, 55* (2), 167–170.

Kuleshnyk, I. (1984). The Stockholm Syndrome: Toward an understanding. *Social Action and the Law, 10* (2), 37–42.

Lane, K. E. and Gwartney-Gibbs, P. A. (1985). Violence in the context of dating and sex. *Journal of Family Issues, 6* (1), 45–59.

Laner, M. R. (1983). Courtship abuse and aggression: Contextual aspects. *Sociological Spectrum, 3,* 69–83.

———— (1989). Competition and combativeness in courtship: Reports from men. *Journal of Family Violence, 4* (1), 47–62.

Laner, M. R. and Thompson, J. (1982). Abuse and aggression in courting couples. *Deviant Behavior, 3,* 229–244.

Lang, D. (1974). A reporter at large: The bank drama. *The New Yorker,* Nov. 25, 56–126.

Le, N. (1982). The Asian perspective on rape. *Proceedings from Conference on Rape and Women of Color,* sponsored by Edgewater Uptown Community Mental Health Center, Rape Victim Assistance Program, June 1982.

Lerner, G. (1986). *The Creation of Patriarchy.* New York: Oxford University Press.

Levis, D. J. (1980). Implementing techniques of implosive therapy. In A. Goldstein and E. Foa (Eds.), *Handbook of Behavorial Interventions.* New York: John Wiley.

Levy, B. (1984). *Skills for Violence-Free Relationships.* Southern California Coalition for Battered Women, P.O. Box 5036, Santa Monica, CA 90405.

Levy, P. (1984). Courtship often a violent time. Minneapolis Tribune.

Li-Repac, D. and Fong, L. (1986). Cultural considerations in the treatment of Asian sexual assault victims. In *Hospital Protocol,* Office of Criminal Justice Planning, Sacramento, CA.

Lobel, K. (1986). *Naming the Violence: Speaking Out About Lesbian Battering.* Seattle: Seal Press.

Lundberg-Love, P. and Geffner, R. (1989). Date rape: Prevalence, risk factors and a proposed model. In M. A. Pirog-Good and J. E. Stets (Eds.), *Violence in Dating Relationships: Emerging Social Issues* (pp. 169–184). New York: Praeger Publishers.

Lyons, J. A. (1987). Posttraumatic Stress Disorder in children and adolescents: A review of the literature. *Developmental and Behavorial Pediatrics, 8,* 349–356.

Mahoney, E.R., Shively, M. and Traw, M. (1985). Sexual coercion and assault: Male macho and female chance. *Sexual Coercion and Assault, 1* (1), 2–7.

Makepeace, J. M. (1981). Courtship violence among college students. *Family Relations, 30,* 97–102.

——— (1983). Life events, stress and courtship violence. *Family Relations, 32,* 101–109.

——— (1986). Gender differences in courtship violence victimization. *Family Relations, 35,* 383–388.

——— (1987). Social factors and victim-offender differences in courtship violence. *Family Relations, 36,* 87–991.

——— (1988). The severity of courtship violence injuries and individual precautionary measures. In G. T. Hotaling, D. Finkelhor, J. T. Kirkpatrick and M. A. Straus (Eds.), *Family Abuse and Its Consequences: New Directions in Research* (pp. 297–311). Newbury Park, CA: Sage Publishers.

——— (1989). Dating, living together, and courtship violence. In M. A. Pirog-Good and J. E. Stets (Eds.), *Violence in Dating Relationships: Emerging Social Issues* (pp. 95–107). New York: Praeger Publishers.

Malamuth, N. M. (1981). Rape proclivity among males. *Journal of*

Social Issues, 37 (4), 138–157.

——— (1984). Aggression against women. In N.A. Malamuth and E. Donnerstein (Eds.), *Pornography and Sexual Aggression.* Orlando, FL: Academic Press.

Marshall, L. L. (1987). *Gender differences in the prediction of courtship abuse from family of origin violence, anxiety proneness and recent positive and negative stress.* Paper presented at the Third National Conference on Family Violence Research, University of New Hampshire, Durham, NH, July, 1987.

Marshall, L. L. and Rose, P. (1987). Gender, stress and violence in adult relationships of a sample of college students. *Journal of Social and Personal Relationships, 4,* 299–316.

——— (1988). Family of origin and courtship violence. *Journal of Counseling and Development, 66* (9), 414–418.

Marshall, W. L. (1985). The effects of variable exposure in flooding therapy. *Behavior Therapy, 8,* 349–356.

Martin, D. (1976). *Battered Wives.* San Francisco: Glide.

Matthews, W. J. (1984). Violence in college couples. *College Student Journal, 18,* 150–158.

McFarlane, J. (1989). Battering in pregnancy: The tip of the iceberg. *Women and Health, 15* (3), 69–84.

McFarlane, J., Anderson, E. and Helton, A. (1987). Response to battering during pregnancy: An educational program. *Response, 10* (2), 25–26.

McGuire, C. and Norton, C. J. (1988). *Perfect Victim.* New York: Arbor House/William Morrow.

Kinney, K. (1986a). Measures of verbal, physical, and sexual dating violence by gender. *Free Inquiry into Creative Sociology, 14* (1), 55–60.

——— (1986b). Perceptions of courtship violence: Gender difference and involvement. *Free Inquiry into Creative Sociology, 14* (1), 61–66.

Mercy, J. and O'Carroll, P. (1988). New directions in violence prediction: The public health arena. *Violence and Victims, 3* (4), 285–301.

Miller, B. (1988). Date rape: Time for a new look at prevention. *Journal of College Student Development, 29,* 553–555.

Miller, B. and Marshall, J. (1987). Coercive sex on the university campus. *Journal of College Student Personnel, 28* (1), 38–47.

Mills, J. (1979). *Six Years with God: Life Inside Reverend Jim Jones' Peoples Temple.* New York: A and W Publishers.

Minnesota Coalition for Battered Women (1990). *Confronting Lesbian Battering: A Manual for the Battered Women's Movement.* M.C.B.W., 570 Asbury Street, #201, St. Paul, MN 55104.

Morrow, S. L. and Hawxhurst, D. M. (1989). Lesbian partner abuse: Implications for therapists. *Journal of Counseling and Development, 68,* 58–62.

Muehlenhard, C. L. (1988). Misinterpreted dating behaviors and the risk of date rape. *Journal of Social and Clinical Psychology, 6* (1), 20–37.

Murphy, J. E. (1988). Date abuse and forced intercourse among college students. In G. T. Hotaling, D. Finkelhor, J. T. Kirkpatrick and M. A. Straus (Eds.), *Family Abuse and Its Consequences: New Directions in Research* (pp. 285–296). Newbury Park, CA: Sage Publishers.

National Center for Health Statistics (1988). *Health, United States 1987.* DHHS Pub. No. (PHS)88–1232. Public Health Service. Washington, DC: Government Printing Office.

National Institute of Mental Health, Center for Prevention and Control of Rape, Conference on Issues Pertaining to Sexual Assault: Special Populations, Oakland, CA, 1977.

NiCarthy, G. (1986). *Getting Free: You Can End Abuse and Take Back Your Life.* Seattle, WA: Seal Press.

Norton, E. H. (1985). Restoring the Traditional Black Family. *New York Times Magazine,* June 2, 1985.

Ochberg, F. M. (1982). A case study: Gerard Vaders. In F. M. Ochberg and D. A. Soskis (Eds.), *Victims of Terrorism* (pp. 9–35). Boulder, CO: Westview Press.

O'Keefe, N., Brockopp, K. and Chew, E. (1986). Teen dating violence. *Social Work, 31,* 465–468.

Olday, D. and Wesley, B. (1983). *Premarital courtship violence: A summary report.* Unpublished paper, Moorhead State University, Moorhead, MN.

Osmond, M. and Martin, P. (1975). Sex and sexism: A comparison of male and female sex-role attitudes. *Journal of Marriage and the Family, 37,* 744–758.

Pence, E. (1987). *In Our Best Interest.* Duluth, MN: Minnesota Program Development, Inc.

Pharr, S. (1988). *Homophobia: A Weapon of Sexism.* Inverness, CA: Chardon Press.

Pirog-Good, M. A. and Stets, J. E. (1989). The help-seeking behavior of physically and sexually abused college students. In M. A. Pirog-Good and J. E. Stets (Eds.), *Violence in Dating Relationships: Emerging Social Issues* (pp. 108–125). New York: Praeger Publishers.

Plass, M. S. and Gessner, J. C. (1983). Violence in courtship relations: A Southern example. *Free Inquiry in Creative Sociology, 11,* 198–202.

Puig, A. (1984). Predomestic strife: A growing college counseling concern. *Journal of College Student Personnel, 25,* 268–269.

R.A.P.P. (Relationship Abuse Prevention Project) (1986). Curriculum for secondary students. Developed and available from Marin Abused Women's Services, 1717 5th Ave., San Rafael, CA, 94901.

Remer, R. and Witten, B. J. (1988). Conceptions of rape. *Violence and Victims, 3* (3), 217–232.

Renzetti, C. (1989). Building a second closet: Third party responses to victims of lesbian partner abuse. *Family Relations, 38,* 157–163.

Rich, A. (1980). Compulsory heterosexuality and lesbian existence. *Signs, 5* (4), 631–660.

Rickett, A. and Rickett, A. (1973). *Prisoners of Liberation: Four Years in a Chinese Communist Prison.* Garden City, NY: Anchor Press.

Riggs, D. S., O'Leary, K. D. and Breslin, F. C. (1990). Multiple correlates of physical aggression in dating couples. *Journal of Interpersonal Violence, 5* (1), 61–73.

Roscoe, B. and Benaske, N. (1985). Courtship violence experienced by abused wives: Similarities in patterns of abuse. *Family Relations, 34,* 419–424.

Roscoe, B. and Callahan, J. E. (1985). Adolescents' self-report of violence in families and dating relations. *Adolescence, 20,* 545–553.

Roscoe, B. and Kelsey, T. (1986). Dating violence among high school students. *Psychology, 23* (1), 53–59.

Rosenberg, M. (1965). *Society and the Adolescent Self-image.* Princeton, NJ: Princeton University Press.

Rouse, L. P., Breen, R. and Howell, M. (1988). Abuse in intimate relationships: A comparison of married and dating college students. *Journal of Interpersonal Violence, 3* (4), 414–429.

Russell, D. E. H. (1986). *The Secret Trauma.* New York: Basic Books.

Sack, A. R., Keller, J. F. and Howard, R. D. (1982). Conflict tactics and violence in dating situations. *International Journal of the Sociology of the Family, 12,* 89–100.

Saigh, P. A. (1987). In vitro flooding of an adolescent's Post traumatic Stress Disorder. *Journal of Clinical Child Psychology, 16* (2), 147–150.

Schechter, S. (1982). *Women and Male Violence: The Visions and Struggles of the Battered Women's Movement.* Boston: South End Press.

Schein, E. H., with Schneier, I. and Barker, C. H. (1961). *Coercive Persuasion: A Socio-psychological Analysis of the "Brainwashing" of American Civilian Prisoners by the Chinese Communists.* New York: W.W. Norton.

Sigelman, C. K., Berry, C. J. and Wiles, K. A. (1984). Violence in college students' dating relationships. *Journal of Applied Social Psychology, 14* (6), 530–548.

Slater, B. (1988). Essential issues in working with lesbian and gay male youths. *Professional Psychology: Research and Practice, 19* (2), 226–235.

Smith, A. and Stewart, A. (1983). Approaches to studying racism and sexism in Black women's lives. *Journal of Social Issues, 39* (3), 1–16.

Smith, B. (1983). *Home Girls.* New York: Kitchen Table Press, pp. xxxiv–xxxv.

Solomon, R. L. (1980). The Opponent-Process Theory of acquired motivation: The costs of pleasure and the benefits of pain. *American Psychologist, 35* (8), 691–712.

Spence, J. T. and Helmreich, R. L. (1972). The attitude toward women scale: An objective instrument to measure attitudes towards the rights and roles of women in contemporary society.

JSAS, Cataog of Selected Documents in Psychology, 2 (66), 1–51.

Spence, J. T., Helmreich, R. L. and Stapp, J. (1975). Ratings of self and peers on sex role attributes and their relation to self-esteem and conceptions of masculinity and femininity. *Journal of Personality and Social Psychology, 32,* 29–39.

Stacey, W. and Schupe, A. (1983). *The Family Secret.* Boston: Beacon Press.

Steketee, M. S. S. and Foa, E. B. (1987). Rape victims: Post-Traumatic Stress reponses and their treatment. *Journal of Anxiety Disorders, 1,* 69–86.

Stets, J. E. and Pirog-Good, M. A. (1987a). *Control and dating violence.* Unpublished manuscript, Family Research Laboratory, University of New Hampshire, Durham, NH.

———— (1987b). Violence in dating relationships. *Social Psychology Quarterly, 50* (3), 237–246.

———— (1989). Patterns of physical and sexual abuse for men and women in dating relationships: A descriptive analysis. *Journal of Family Violence, 4* (1), 63–76.

Stets, J. E. and Straus, M. A. (1989). The marriage license as a hitting license: A comparison of assaults in dating, cohabiting, and married couples. *Journal of Family Violence, 4* (2), 161–180.

Straus, M. A. (1979). Measuring intrafamily conflict and violence: The conflict tactics scale. *Journal of Marriage and the Family, 41,* 75–88.

Straus, M., Gelles, R. J. and Steinmetz, S. K. (1980). *Behind Closed Doors: Violence in the American Family.* New York: Anchor Books.

Straus, M. B., Schechter, S., Grace, P. and Michalek, J. (1987). *Advocacy for battered women with abused children in a pediatric hospital.* Paper presented at the Third National Conference on Family Violence Research, University of New Hampshire, Durham, NH, July 6–9,1987. (Available from AWAKE Project, Family Development Study, Children's Hospital, 300 Longwood Ave., Boston, MA, 02115.)

Sugarman, D. B. and Hotaling, G. T. (1989). Dating violence: Prevalence, context, and risk markers. In M. A. Pirog-Good and J. E. Stets (Eds.), *Violence in Dating Relationships: Emerging Social Issues* (pp. 3–32). New York: Praeger Publishers.

Surgeon General's Workshop on Violence and Public Health (1986).

Washington, DC: U.S. Department of Health and Human Services, Public Health Service.

Symonds, M. (1975). Victims of violence: Psychological effects and after-effects. *American Journal of Psychoanalysis, 35,* 19–26.

Tam, M. (1983). *Counseling and Asian victims.* Paper presented at the Asian Sexual Assault Awareness Conference, San Francisco, CA, June 22, 1983.

Tedeschi, J. T., Smith, R. and Brown, R. (1974). A reinterpretation of research on aggression. *Psychological Bulletin, 81,* 540–562.

Thompson, W. E. (1986). Courtship violence. Toward a conceptual understanding. *Youth and Society, 18* (2), 162–176.

Tontodonato, P. and Crew, B. K. (1988). *The role of alcohol use and sex typing in dating violence: Some preliminary findings.* Paper presented at the American Society of Criminology meetings, Chicago, IL.

Walker, A. (1970). *The Third Life of Grange Copeland.* New York: Harcourt Brace Jovanovich.

Walker, L. (1979). *The Battered Woman.* New York: Harper and Row.

——— (1984). *The Battered Woman Sydrome.* New York: Springer Publishing.

Warshaw, R. (1988). *I Never Called it Rape: The MS. Report on Recognizing, Fighting and Surviving Date and Acquaintance Rape.* New York: Harper and Row.

Waterman, C.K., Dawson, L.J. and Bologna, M.J. (1989). Sexual coercion in gay male and lesbian relationships: Predictors and implications for support services. *Journal of Sex Research, 26* (1), 118–124.

White, E. (1985). *Chain Chain Change: For Black Women Dealing with Physical and Emotional Abuse.* Seattle: Seal Press.

Whitlock, K. (1989). *Bridges of Respect: Creating Support for Lesbian and Gay Youth.* Philadelphia: American Friends Service Committee.

Yee, M. S. and Layton, T. N. (1981). *In My Father's House: The Story of the Layton Family and the Reverend Jim Jones.* New York: Berkley Books.

Yllo, K. and Straus, M. A. (1981). Interpersonal violence among married and cohabiting couples. *Family Relations, 30,* 339–347.

Yllo, K. and Bograd, M. (1988). *Feminist Perspectives on Wife Abuse.* Newbury Park, CA: Sage Publishers.

Zambrano, M. (1985). *Mejor Sola Que Mal Acompañada: For the Latina in an Abusive Relationship.* Seattle: Seal Press.

Resources

Educational Curricula

Creighton, Allan. *Teens Need Teens: A Workbook and Education Curriculum for High School Students on Dating and Domestic Violence Prevention.* Teen Program, Battered Women's Alternatives, P.O. Box 6406, Concord, CA 94524, 1988.

Gamache, Denise. *Minnesota Teacher's Guide to the Prevention Curriculum: Skills for Violence-Free Relationships.* Minnesota Coalition for Battered Women, Physician's Plaza Building, Suite 201, 570 Asbury Street, St. Paul, MN 55104, 1988.

Gubrud, Jan. *When Love Really Hurts: Teenage Dating Violence Curriculum.* Network Against Teenage Violence, Family Crisis Shelter, P.O. Box 1893, Williston, ND 58802-1893, 1987.

Levy, Barrie. *Skills for Violence-Free Relationships: Curriculum for Young People Ages 13–18.* Southern California Coalition on Battered Women, P.O. Box 5036, Santa Monica, CA 90405, 1984.

Lewis, Debra J. *Dating Violence: A Discussion Guide on Violence in Young People's Relationships.* Battered Women's Support Services, #203-1847 W. Broadway, Vancouver, B.C. V6J 1Y6, Canada, 1987.

Rogers, Anne B. *STOP: School Targeting Operation for the Prevention of Interpersonal Violence.* Council on Battered Women, P.O. Box 54737, Atlanta, GA 30308, 1987.

Sousa, Carole, Lundy Bancroft and Ted German. *Preventing Teen Dating Violence: A Three-Session Curriculum for Teaching Adolescents.* Dating Violence Intervention Project, P.O. Box 530, Harvard Square Station, Cambridge, MA 02238, 1989.

Manuals

Braham, Regina. *Breaking Patterns: A Program on Teenage Dating Violence.* Jersey Battered Women's Services, P.O. Box 363, Morris Plains, NJ 07950, 1989.

Relationship Assault Prevention Project (RAPP). Manual on how to establish an in-school domestic violence prevention education program. Includes: 1–3 day curricula; student and teacher evaluation forms; a sample resource card; a sample packet on gaining access to a school. Marin Abused Women's Services, 1717 Fifth Avenue, San Rafael, CA 94901, 1986.

Films and Videos

Pregnant Teen. Twenty-minute video for health care practitioners addressing battering and teen pregnancy. Also: "Is Someone Hurting You?" and "Are You in a Safe Relationship?" pamphlets for distribution to teen and adult women. Prevention of Battering During Pregnancy, Texas Woman's University, 1130 M.D. Anderson Blvd., Houston, TX 77030.

The Power to Choose. Nineteen-minute video dramatizing dating violence in four scenes followed by questions to stimulate discussion. 1988. Also: Denise Gamache and J. Pamela Weiner, "A Teacher's Guide to *The Power to Choose:* An Instructional Program on the Use of Power and Violence in Teenage Dating Relationships." Agency for Instructional Technology, Box A, Bloomington, IN 47402.

When Love Hurts. Seventeen-minute video dramatizing physical, sexual and emotional abuse among dating couples. Marin Abused Women's Services, 1717 Fifth Avenue, San Rafael, CA 94901.

Contributors' Notes

Margaret Anderson is a writer and political activist who skulks about in business clothes (a disguise) between eight and five. Domestic violence is the issue closest to her heart—because it happened to her, and because she knows that escape is possible. She is grateful to her lover and her therapist for an empowering, inspiring recovery process.

Py Bateman is Executive Director of Alternatives to Fear. She has developed and produced date rape prevention programs for adolescents and has authored educational booklets, including *Macho, Is That What I Really Want?* for teenage boys, as well as others for teen girls and for parents. She developed a videotape and manual for schools, *Teen Sex: Drawing the Line.*

Doris Boyington is the Director of the Pasadena Y.W.C.A. Child Abuse Prevention Program in Southern California, and previously served as Assistant Director of the Y.W.C.A. Rape Hotline. For thirteen years she has trained Rape Crisis Workers to assist Asian Pacific survivors of sexual and physical assault. Her mother was born in Japan and her father was born in Alabama.

Regina Braham, A.C.S.W., is Community Education Coordinator for Jersey Battered Women's Services, in Morris Plains, New Jersey. She is coauthor of *Hospital Training on Domestic Violence, Hospital Protocol on Domestic Violence* and *Breaking Patterns: A Teenage Dating Violence Program.*

Cathleen E. Chadwick, M.P.H., is Project Coordinator, Maternal and Child Health Leadership Skills Training Institute at the Graduate School of Public Health, San Diego State University in California. She was previously Children's Services Coordinator and Assistant Director of the Y.W.C.A. Battered Women's Services. She was President of the San Diego Community Child Abuse Coordinating Council and the Southern California Coalition for Battered Women.

Vicki Crompton is founder and President of Scott County PACT (Protecting All Children Together), a volunteer organization in Iowa which lobbies for child protection laws. She is on the board of the Iowa Organization of Victim Assistance and the Iowa Crime Victims Assistance Board. She has spoken about teen dating violence throughout the country on television and in schools.

304

Elizabeth has been working in the area of lesbian battering for the last several years and recently completed her doctoral dissertation on violence in lesbian relationships. She is currently a practicing psychotherapist in Southern California, where she happily resides with her life-partner.

Johanna Gallers, Ph.D., is founder and Director of the Valley Trauma Center, a crisis and counseling center for survivors of sexual crimes that is part of the Department of Educational Psychology and Counseling at California State University, Northridge, where she is a part-time faculty member. She maintains a private practice and consults with agencies and television programs.

Denise Gamache's fourteen years of experience in the battered women's movement include shelter advocacy and coordination of domestic assault intervention projects within the criminal justice system. Recently, as coordinator of a statewide school curriculum project, she coauthored *My Family and Me: Violence Free,* an elementary school curriculum. She is currently Program Director at WHISPER in St. Paul, Minnesota.

Dee L. R. Graham, Ph.D., is an Associate Professor in the Department of Psychology and a member of the Women's Studies faculty at the University of Cincinnati, Cincinnati, Ohio. She received both her M.A. and Ph.D. from George Peabody College for Teachers.

Kenneth M. Greene, M.A., facilitates expressive arts therapy groups with adolescent male sex offenders for the Escondido Youth Encounter, San Diego, California. He has worked in the field of domestic violence as Art Therapist at Haven House, a shelter for battered women in Pasadena, California, as counselor and coordinator of Daughters and Sons United in Los Angeles and San Diego, and as consultant to Parents United International.

Gerald T. Hotaling, Ph.D., is an Associate Professor of Criminology at the University of Lowell and is a Research Associate Professor in the Family Research Laboratory of the University of New Hampshire. His work in family violence has spanned a number of areas, including marital violence, dating violence, sexual child abuse, and missing and abducted children.

Jan K. Jenson is Resource Coordinator for the Center Against Sexual and Domestic Abuse in Superior, Wisconsin. She holds a

Master's Degree in psychology from the University of Wisconsin-Superior and is a formerly battered woman.

Linda E. Jones, Ph.D. is Assistant Professor, School of Social Work and is affiliated with the Women's Studies Department, the Center for Advanced Feminist Studies and the Hubert H. Humphrey Institute of Public Affairs at the University of Minnesota in Minneapolis.

Sheila James Kuehl is a Managing Attorney of the Southern California Women's Law Center. She was Associate Professor at the Loyola Law School. She is a member of the California Judicial Council's Gender Bias Advisory Committee, and the chair of its Domestic Violence Subcommittee. She was President of the Women' Lawyers Association of Los Angeles and a Trustee of the Los Angeles County Bar Association.

Kathy J. Lawrence is a graduate student in clinical psychology at the Fuller Theological Seminary in Pasadena, California. She has been employed at two different colleges where she conducted individual and group therapy for survivors of sexual abuse. Her principal clinical and research interests focus on adult survivors of childhood abuse.

Kerry Lobel is an organizer in the South. She works at the Women's Project in Little Rock, Arkansas, an organization committed to the elimination of sexism, homophobia and racism. She edited *Naming the Violence: Speaking Out Against Lesbian Battering* and served for three years as the Chair of the National Coalition Against Domestic Violence.

Lucille was born in Arkansas and moved to Los Angeles as a child. She has lived and worked in the same neighborhood since elementary school. Since 1978, she has been working in the drug abuse treatment field. She has been married twice and has two daughters.

Debbie Mattson lives in rural Maine with her two children, Sam and Abe. She currently works as the Children's Services Coordinator for WomanKind, a domestic violence project.

Judith McFarlane, R.N., Dr. P.H., is Professor, College of Nursing, Texas Woman's University—Houston Center. She is Director of the National Preceptorship on the Prevention of Battering During Pregnancy, and Principal Investigator of the study, Intentional Injury During Pregnancy, funded by the Centers for Disease Control.

Meybel is nineteen years old and a student at Business Industry School in Los Angeles. She has a three-year-old son. She is in training to be a bricklayer. Meybel was born in El Salvador, and moved to Los Angeles when she was twelve.

Ginny NiCarthy, M.S.W., is the author of *Getting Free: You Can End Abuse and Take Back Your Life; You Can Be Free: An Easy to Read Handbook for Abused Women; The Ones Who Got Away: Women Who Left Abused Partners;* and *Talking it Out: A Guide to Groups for Abused Women.* She has been active in the battered women's movement for fifteen years and is a therapist and writer in Seattle.

Asha L. Parekh, M.S.W. has worked with victims of child abuse and their families in South Central Los Angeles. She also worked with victims of domestic violence and sexual assault at a women's shelter for Asian/Pacific victims in Los Angeles. She served as a coordinator of the shelter's Sexual Assault Program.

Carolyn Powell, M.S.W., is Student Attendance and Adjustment Counselor and Drop Out Prevention Advisor at Jordan High School in Los Angeles. She has twenty years' experience in the public school system. She has served as a member of the Board of Governors of Coastal Community Mental Health Center and as a member of the Los Angeles County Department of Mental Health Regional Community Liaison Committee, Coastal Region.

Laura Prato, A.C.S.W., is a consultant to Jersey Battered Women's Services in Morris Plains, New Jersey. From 1982–1986, she was Coordinator of Children's Services at JBWS. She is the author of two orientation books for children who are shelter residents and coauthor of a manual on teenage dating violence.

Edna I. Rawlings, Ph.D., is a Professor of Psychology and clinical psychologist in the Psychological Services Center at the University of Cincinnati. She is a faculty member of the Women's Studies Department. She is co-author of *Psychotherapy for Women: Treatment Toward Equality.* She is a feminist therapist who specializes in treating clients with abusive histories.

Marybeth Roden is the Assistant Director of the Rape Treatment Center of Santa Monica Hospital. She wrote the Center's adolescent curriculum and administers the Center's date rape prevention program. She co-produced "Linda," an adolescent date rape prevention film, and co-wrote "How it Happens: Understanding Sexual Abuse and Date Rape."

Carole Sousa is Outreach Coordinator for Transition House shelter for battered women and their children and cofounder of the Dating Violence Intervention Project in Cambridge, Massachusetts. She lives with her eleven-year-old daughter and their two cats. She is a formerly battered woman.

Salina Stone works at Sojourner Shelter for Battered Women in Minnesota. She does speaking in schools on the topics of domestic and dating violence. She is involved in women's spirituality, where she has found her peace.

David B. Sugarman, Ph.D. is an Associate Professor of Psychology at Rhode Island College and is a Post-doctoral Research Associate in the Family Research Laboratory of the University of New Hampshire. His research in family violence has focused on risk factors associated with marital and dating violence.

Evelyn C. White is the author of *Chain Chain Change: For Black Women Dealing With Physical and Emotional Abuse* and editor of *The Black Women's Health Book: Speaking for Ourselves.* Her writing has appeared in numerous publications including the *San Francisco Chronicle* and *Essence* and *Smithsonian* magazines.

Mieko Yoshihama, M.S.W. is Coordinator of the Asian/Pacific Outreach Project of the Didi Hirsch Community Mental Health Center in Los Angeles. She is a doctoral student in the School of Social Welfare at U.C.L.A. She has worked extensively with Asian/Pacific victims of domestic violence, child abuse and sexual assault in both agency and school settings.

Bonnie Zimmer is a white feminist social worker who spent two years working with pregnant and parenting teens in Massachusetts. She now works in a community mental health center and a private practice where she specializes in helping women heal from the consequences of physical, emotional and sexual abuse.

Index

309

appropriate 78, 107, 267–68
vulnerability to abuse 4–7, 74, 85–86, 149, 185–90, 192–93, 197–98, 268–69
Therapy, with young women in abusive relationships
cognitive behavior therapy 128
cognitive distortions, reframing in terms of Stockholm Syndrome 127–28
countertransference behaviors 128–29
creating safe therapeutic environment 126
crisis intervention counseling 270–71
diagnosing PTSD 174–75
discriminating between different ego states 130
educational therapy model 236–37
flooding, as treatment for PTSD 175–76
group therapy (*see* Support groups)
helping clients understand their experiences 126–28
lessening conditions that produce Stockholm Syndrome 130–33
psychoeducational approach 195
repairing psychological damage 134–35
sensitivity to cultural backgrounds and values 194–95
validating love-terror polarities 129
victim-blaming during 165–66, 168, 171
Threats. *See* Abuse, coercion and threats
Trust
building, with abused teen mothers 168–71
disruption of, in raped teen 173–74, 269
obstacles to victims' 212–13

Victims of abuse
anger and grief of 133–34
blaming of, for abuse 77, 165–66, 168, 171, 173–74, 189, 212, 271–72
bonding to abusers, as survival strategy 119–21

friends' reactions to 80, 160–61, 206
gender patterns 8, 73–74, 105–6
help-seeking behavior 107–8
and hostages, parallel predicaments 119–24
legal options for escape (*see* Legal remedies, for victims of violence)
minimizing or denying abuse 80, 131, 133, 149, 170, 186–87, 200, 205, 238–39
psychological trauma of 172–74, 269
range of violent experiences 75
responses to abuse 107–8, 121–24, 174–75, 189–90, 193, 200
self-esteem of 75, 111, 115, 174
testifying in court 215
therapy issues with (*see* Therapy, with young women in abusive relationships)
unborn infants as 138–39
victim/witness services 215
violence in families of origin of 112–13, 133
Violence. *See also* Abuse; Dating violence
and conflicts about sexual behavior 78
considered justifiable by teens 3, 95, 98
cultural norms that support 71–72, 116–17
in family of origin, risk marker for dating violence 112–13
in lesbian communities, recognizing 203–4, 207–8
measuring 101
as perceived proof of love 77–78, 107, 117, 149–50
positive attitudes toward 115, 116–17
positive consequences of, for abuser 72
during pregnancy (*see* Teen pregnancy)
prevention projects (*see* Prevention/ intervention projects)
and substance abuse 9–10

About the Editor

Barrie Levy, M.S.W., is the author of *Skills for Violence-Free Relationships: Curriculum for Young People Ages 13-18,* and has been active in the movement against domestic violence for many years. She resides in Los Angeles, California, where she works as a therapist and consultant.

Other New Leaf Titles from Seal Press

GETTING FREE: *You Can End Abuse and Take Back Your Life* by Ginny NiCarthy, 0-931188-37-7 $12.95

YOU CAN BE FREE: *An Easy-to-Read Handbook for Abused Women* by Ginny NiCarthy, 0-931188-68-7 $6.95

THE ONES WHO GOT AWAY: *Women Who Left Abusive Partners* by Ginny NiCarthy, 0-931188-24-5 $11.95

TALKING IT OUT: *A Guide to Groups for Abused Women* by Ginny NiCarthy, 0-931188-24-5 $12.95

THE OBSIDIAN MIRROR: *An Adult Healing from Incest* by Louise M. Wisechild, 0-931188-63-6 $10.95

CALLED TO ACCOUNT: *The Story of One Family's Struggle to Say No To Abuse* by M'Liss Switzer 0-931188-55-5 $8.95

CHAIN CHAIN CHANGE: *For Black Women Dealing with Physical and Emotional Abuse* by Evelyn C. White 0-931188-25-3 $5.95

MEJOR SOLA QUE MAL ACCOMPAÑADA: *For the Latina in an Abusive Relationship/Para la Mujer Golpeada* by Myrna Zambrano 0-931188-26-1 $9.95

NAMING THE VIOLENCE: *Speaking Out About Lesbian Battering* edited by Kerry Lobel, 0-931188-42-3 $10.95

MOMMY & DADDY ARE FIGHTING: *A Book for Children About Family Violence* by Susan Paris, illustrated by Gail Labinski, 0-931188-33-4 $7.95

Now on Audiocassette:
GETTING FREE: *Are You Abused? (And What to Do About It)* narrated by Ginny NiCarthy (based on her book, *Getting Free*) 60 minutes 0-931188-84-9 $9.95

SEAL PRESS, founded in 1976 to publish women writers, has many other titles in stock; fiction, self-help books, anthologies and translations. Any of the books above may be ordered from us at 3131 Western Ave., Suite 410, Seattle, WA 98121 (include $2.00 for the first book and .50 for each additional book). Write to us for a free catalog or if you would like to be on our mailing list.